THE NEW AMERICAN MIDDLE AGES

THE NEW AMERICAN MIDDLE AGES

Why Modern Times are Like Medieval Times

GINI GRAHAM SCOTT, PHD

Waterside Productions

Printed in the United States of America

First Printing, 2021

ISBN-13: 978-1-951805-31-9 print edition
ISBN-13: 978-1-951805-32-6 ebook edition

Waterside Productions
2055 Oxford Ave
Cardiff, CA 92007
www.waterside.com

TABLE OF CONTENTS

PREFACE

In July 2013, I published a *Huffington Post* article, "The New Middle Ages," which later led to a book of the same name in 2015. It described how the growing disparity between rich and poor and the decline of the middle class was creating conditions which paralleled medieval society, with its kings, nobility, servants, peasants, and powerful clergy giving its blessings, much like the megachurches and the media honors celebrities today. I spoke to many once successful professional and businesspeople like myself who were now struggling, while the media celebrated wealthy celebrity families like the Kardashians and Trumps, who had become a kind of modern royalty. At the same time, there were growing protests from groups such as Occupy Oakland and Causa Justa, speaking for the 99%, who were angry about inequality and people losing their homes.

Now we are on an even more dangerous course due to the growing income disparity that has triggered revolts in the past, leading to the same kind of police and military crack downs we are experiencing today. But now the situation is even worse, as the world is rocked by a pandemic, collapsing economy, and new protests throughout the United States and in many cities around the world. In the U.S., a series of protests were triggered by the killing of George Floyd in Minnesota at the hands of four police officers. But while this killing was the match that lit the fuse, the underlying causes run deep due to continued racism and inequality. Now the protest has been joined by individuals who are impoverished by the loss of jobs and a growing pandemic that has been most deadly for the lower classes, since they are crowded together and are forced to work at low paying service and factory jobs to feed their families. Even more recently, the election has triggered massive protests, attempts to suppress votes and intimidate voters, and attacks against protests, though the win of Joe Biden and Kamala Harris may lead to more peaceful days ahead and the hope for a new American Renaissance.

Thus, because of the timeliness of this topic, I have published a new edition of the book, called *The New American Middle Ages.* It draws on books and articles dealing with medieval history and the state of modern American society to illustrate the parallels between these two time periods. It also notes some key differences, although the emphasis is on how the two periods are similar and why this growing inequality is creating a dangerous tinderbox in America as well as other societies, much like the disparity of wealth in medieval times contributed to extensive turmoil and occasional peasant revolts.

FOREWORD

Today, as the rich get richer and the poor get poorer, we seem to be approaching a new Middle Ages in America, as inequality increasingly spreads through the land. It is as if the superrich are the new royalty and the top 1% – or perhaps more accurately the top 10% of this 1% – are living in mansions, like the castles of kings in the medieval kingdoms that eventually became melded into the countries of Europe and the U.K. Meanwhile, the media wields the power of the medieval church, placing its blessing on those with wealth and celebrity, who are protected by their retinue of publicists, handlers, lawyers, chauffeurs, and servants. This entourage is much like the landed nobility and courtiers who were part of the king's court. Together, the royals and the high-ranking individuals who surrounded them formed a protected and privileged enclave far removed from the large class of peasants who worked their land and paid their taxes. At the same time, the royals and nobles were served by lowly servants who cleaned their houses, cooked for them, drove their carriages, and waited on them hand and foot to support their grand style.

I thought of this comparison after a friend emailed a link to a YouTube video – *Wealth Inequality in America*, at the same time that I was watching several TV series set in the Middle Ages. One was *Monarchy* about the kings and queens in England, starting in 400 AD with the warring feudal lords who were united into a kingdom under Alfred in 871. Another was *Borgia*, about the growing power and wealth of the papacy under Rodrigo Borgia, who became Pope Alexander VI, in the late 1400s. And the third was *World Without*

End, about the struggles of the peasants in England in the 1300s, during the reign of King Edward V.

The *Wealth Inequality in America* video makes a frightening case that the middle class is being undermined and the poor are becoming poorer than ever. The video also shows how a growing number of professional and businesspeople are out of jobs, have failing businesses, are losing their homes to default or foreclosure, and are filing for bankruptcy or plan to do so in the near future. And today, after over eleven months of lockdown and 40 million Americans applying for unemployment, the situation is ever more dire.

For example, ten years ago, the top 20% had about 85% of the wealth and next 20% about 10%, leaving about 5% for the remaining 60% of Americans. And the top 1% had nearly 40% of the wealth, while the bottom 80% has only 7% of the wealth.[1]

Much of this increase occurred since the 1970s and 80s, so that ten years ago, the richest 1% earned 24% of the income whereas in 1976, that number was only 9%. Moreover, the top 1% owned half the country's stocks, bonds and mutual funds, while the bottom 50% owned only .5% of them.[2] A CEO mades 380 times the income of average employee, so the average employee had to work about a month to earn what CEO made in 1 hour.[3]

Now the numbers are becoming even worse. For example, according to a 2020 report on inequality, the top 20% of households earn on the average about 16 times more than households in the bottom 20%. A member of the top 10% makes more than 39 times as much as the average earner in the bottom 90%, and the average member of the richest 1% earns about 188 times more than an average earner in the bottom 90%.[4] So the poorest Americans are barely getting by, the middle class is barely distinguishable from the poor, and the top 10% are much better off, especially the top 1% with 40% of the wealth.

The Pew Research Center has similarly reported that upper-income households have had more rapid growth in income in recent decades, while the share of the nation's income going to middle – and lower-income households has been falling. As a result, the U.S. middle class, once was the majority class in America, has been shrinking.[5] On the other hand, the greatest income growth has been experienced by the top 5% of families since the 1980s, averaging an increase of about 2-3%, except for the decade including the Great Recession.[6] The result was that the 5% of all households — those with incomes of at least about $250,000 in 2018 increased their share to 23% that year, compared to 16% in 1968.

This uneven growth in income has also meant that over the past 50 years, the top 20% of U.S. households have gained a larger share of the country's total income, according to another Pew Research Center article. It went to 23% in 2108 from 16% in 1968. And now income inequality is highest in the U.S. for all G7 nations based on data from the Organization for Economic Cooperation and Development, which used the Gini coefficient, where the numbers range from 0 for perfect equality to 1 for complete inequality. As of 2017, the U.S. coefficient was .4 compared to .326 in France to .392 in the UK.[7]

This situation is much like what existed in the Middle Ages, with today's poor underclass much in the position of the peasants, and the superrich like the nobility. For example, look at the huge McMansions of the celebrities, wealthy CEOs, and Internet millionaires. These homes are often high on bluffs and surrounded by gates, while bodyguards, security guards, and an entourage providing various services surround them, much like the retainers, servants, and knights protected the medieval kings, queens, or other high ranking nobles. Likewise, the marriages of celebrities and the wealthy with one another, celebrated through features in the celebrity press about their glamorous marriages, are much like the marriages of the royals of different countries, with families seeking to cement alliances through these matrimonial ties. Then as now, the wealthy families had access to the finest education, travel, and clothes, while private jets are a modern-day equivalent to the fine carriages and horses of old.

The modern day superwealthy also find plenty of loopholes to preserve their wealth, such as tax shelters in the Caymans and other no-tax islands, while the middle and lower income classes, much like medieval peasants, are required to pay more and more, such as the extra taxes the English peasants had to pay to finance the Hundred Years War from 1337 to 1453. And now there are debates about cutting much of the social safety net, including cuts in health-care and social security.

As for the media, they play the role of the medieval church in the way they support and celebrate the doings of the superrich in the growing number of celebrity and style publications, such as *In Touch, Star,* and the *Globe.* And to make one more comparison, the reality shows where competitors seek to be the last one stand-ing are like the jousts of knights, especially in shows like *American Ninja Warrior,* where the competitors face extremely difficult and even dangerous challenges. Though players they wear safety har-nesses and a team of medics stand by to take care of any physical or emotional challenges that might arise, there could be long-term damages, much like thousands boxers and NFL players commonly experience a mental decline as they grow older due to their inju-ries. But such risks would seem to be the price the players pay for a shot at a little fame and glory, much like the knights gained the kings and queens accolades for winning a tourney, though in each one, they risked injury or an early death.

The one major downside for the wealthy superrich of medieval times is that they were continually subject to plotting by the other superrich seeking to overthrow them, along with repeated peasant revolts against their mistreatment. In turn, some of the modern day protests, like the Better Lives Matter protests have parallels with the peasant protests that deposed many kings and nobles and with some social revolutions like the French Revolution that led to a shift to a fairer society for a time, before the rise of a new wealthy class once again.

Could a revolution happen today? It could be one of the out-comes of the spread of the new Middle Ages. Or might there be another outcome through efforts to create a more equal society before the growing inequality becomes even worse?

The New American Middle Ages explores these parallels between medieval and modern times, with a focus on America, although these patterns are replicated elsewhere because the superwealthy are part of a global community, which includes the multinational corporations, global entertainment industries, and Internet media

INTRODUCTION

Today we are facing frightening times. The headlines in the daily newspapers and on the Internet proclaim this. Each day brings news of more bombings by terrorists all over the world – in the Middle East, China, Pakistan, India, and in the UK. In the USA fear of terrorists, such as the Boston bombers, or the latest disgruntled employee, spouse, or vengeful student, ready to kill other workers, students, family members, or friends dot the news. There are the stories about devious hackers breaking into computers and stealing millions of private identities to be used in scams worldwide, and rings of underworld criminals involved in drugs, prostitution, sex slave trafficking, and other crimes, who are involved in global networks, and from time to time, they engage in kidnapping and murder for hire. Additionally, illegal immigration grows, and wars between rebels and rulers or between states for territory have led to the largest migrations of uprooted citizens, now homeless, to refugee camps or to other countries to try for a new start. Also, there are the trials for corruption after one ruler is deposed, and another takes over through a military coup, as in Egypt. Plus there are massive protests against rulers all over the world including Belarus, Hong Kong, Syria, Guatemala, and many countries in Africa.

Meanwhile, the general population seems caught up in the latest scandals, conflicts, and lavish events of the super-rich and very famous, which may serve as a distraction from the major social and economic upheavals going on today, creating a society that has many parallels with the Middle Ages, characterized by a great class divide. In fact, at the time, this inequality was given a sanction by theologians and followers of the Christian faith, who saw this vast division of classes as part of the natural order of things, which helped to freeze the existing hierarchy in place, so that sons and daughters would follow in the class roles of their parents as part of the great chain of being that was sanctified by God. Today this growing inequality gap has similarly made it increasingly difficult for most individuals to climb up the ladder, since the middle class has been shrinking, although the image of possibilities has been kept alive by the notable exceptions with a special talent that has propelled them into the economic stratosphere to join the modern day royalty – such as the fast track to riches by huge names in entertainment like Ariana Grande and Taylor Swift, sports figures like Lebron James and Kevin Durant, and new tech titans such as Elon Musk of Tesla and Jack Dorsey of Twitter.

But these tales of the doings of today's rich and royalty that dominate the popular news and entertainment mask the transformations in the social structure and economic and political universe that are creating a growing class of impoverished. These landless families and individuals are much like the medieval peasants who faced increasing economic hardship when times got tough due to increasing taxes and conscripted labor to help support a wealthy upper class given to more and more lavish living, as well as participation in wars to gain more territory or protect their current boundaries from invaders.

It is a marked transformation noted by some academics today, who also use the term the "New Middle Ages" to refer to what is happening, leading to the undermining of the central authority as new organizations akin to feudal lords spring up, such as the gangs of criminals and terrorists and the ethnic groups that are striving to carve out their own territories with links to other movements worldwide. In fact, this undermining of states by these nascent and growing organizations has become so pervasive, reflected in the growing chaos around the world today, that a new "Dark Ages" could be possible.

The following chapters describe these parallels with the Middle Ages in society today, though here I want to briefly sketch out these major themes and highlight the defining characteristics of life in medieval times to provide a backdrop for these comparisons.

From Modern Times to the New Middle Ages

Even the U.S. Government is comparing the upheavals that are transforming modern society to the New Middle Ages. In fact, a report by Dr. Phil Williams of the Strategic Studies Institute describes over a decade ago the decline of the state as already leading to the New Middle Ages and threatening a further deterioration of society into the New Dark Age — a descent which already seems to be happening in 2020 as the pandemic, wars, and protests spreads all over the world.

According to Williams this comparison to the Middle Ages is apt, in that now the state has become "only one of many actors, and the forces of disorder loom large." It is a time when "global politics are now characterized by fragmented political authority, overlapping jurisdictions, no-go zones, identity politics, and contested property rights."[8] And now if the U.S. and other national states don't act, the forces of global disorder and chaos could lead today's world into a New Dark Age.

As Williams describes, the nation states had reached their pinnacle of power in the 20th century and now are in a period of "absolute decline." Increasingly, modern states are unable to "manage political, social, and economic problems that are increasingly interconnected, intractable, and volatile."[9] The result is a growing dissolution of the nation state that has led to a political and economic structure akin to the Middle Ages, as described in a doctoral thesis in 2001[10] by Gregory O' Hayon at the University of Pittsburg and in articles by and Jorg Friedrichs[11] and Philip Cerny[12] in 2001 and 1998 respectively, but still very relevant for describing conditions today.

According to Cerny's analysis, which these other writers have built on, global politics has come to be characterized by several related and reinforcing conditions, which give it a neo-medieval quality. These include the following characteristics:

(1) There are competing institutions with overlapping jurisdictions, between states and other actors, which include
organizations such as criminal syndicates, and networks of
terrorists.

(2) The increasingly fluid territorial boundaries within and
between states, reflected in the movement of peoples from
place to place.

(3) The inequality and marginalization of various groups, especially in many African and Latin American countries. These
marginalized individuals and groups make up a large majority of the population and their deprivation exists in marked
contrast with the ostentatiously displayed wealth of the political and business elites.

(4) The multiple or fragmented loyalties and identities, which
has led to growing conflicts between ethnic groups. Most
prominently, there is the rise of militant Islamic groups and
white supremacist groups which are prone to violence.

(5) The unofficial property rights and conventions, such as those
between slum dwellers who live within an informal economy
outside of state control.

(6) The spread of no go areas in regions of the world which are
not subject to the state's rule of law, but instead are governed
by groups which "act as surrogates for the state."

(7) A growing gap between the mix of growth and deprivation
in the "dynamic and technologically innovative north" and
the countries in the south that are falling behind or falling
apart, in which people live like they did in the 14th century,
suffering from "civil war, plague, (and) ignorance.[13]"

As Williams writes, the modern era is something of a para-
dox in that increasingly political conditions and the dispersion of
authority resemble the Middle Ages, despite the increasing growth
of the forces of "modernity, technology, and globalization." Yet, as
disorder spreads, the danger is that the New Middle Ages will lead
to a New Dark Ages, a time when there is spreading chaos and an

undermining of state power creating an inability to control this. He points to numerous examples of this dissent into chaos, reminiscent of the political and social upheavals in medieval times. For example, many states are "increasingly unable to meet the needs of their citizens," such as providing jobs for a growing population, resulting in large segments of the population being unemployed, leading to a growth of the disenfranchised and alienated segments of society, along with disputes over resources. While he draws on examples from Africa and Latin America, a comparable example from America is the growth of movements like the Black Lives Matter movement and the protests by low-wage Americans.

Williams also describes the development of alternative loyalties held by significant portions of the population to family, clan, tribe, ethnic group, religion or sect, which are sometimes led by warlords, who challenge the state's notions of public interest and collective identity. In fact, a growing number of criminal organizations and radical Islamic groups have developed from family ties or common ethnicity, even though groups become international through linkages with groups in other countries. As he suggests, these organizations with alternative loyalties will become increasingly important as the state increasingly is unable to provide adequately for its citizens.

At the same time, as the states are increasingly unsuccessful in providing for their citizens, this creates a pressure for citizens to get involved in criminal activities, or as he puts it: "Amid conditions of economic hardship, extra-legal means of obtaining basic needs often become critical to survival." The result is being drawn into the informal economy or the entrepreneurship of organized crime, which are increasingly "cooperating and collaborating with each other in networks that span national borders and include fellow tribal groups, criminal groups, and corrupt political elements."[14]

Williams also points out that the New Middle Ages resembles the past Middle Ages in the growing importance of cities. In the later Middle Ages, the towns and cities, though smaller than now, became centers of social activity and commerce and now it is possible that cities will increasingly become an alternative to the state for organizing economic, political, and social activities, even as the cities become increasingly ungovernable, due to their growing problems of crime, violence, widespread poverty, overcrowding, disease, and environmental degradation. A good example of this is the raging battle in San Francisco, as the city is transformed by "new moneys" from high-technology, resulting in sky high rentals and evictions of the formerly middle class but now new poor who can't pay the inflated rates for housing. The current housing crisis in many cities is the result of such developments, and it is only getting worse, due to the loss of jobs and business due to the pandemic. Though the stock market is up, while going through a series of dramatic ups and downs as of this writing, when the inevitable bubble bursts, as economists are even now predicting, there will even more economic chaos. This disruption has parallels with the economic upheaval hit in Europe in the 9th and 10th centuries resulting in widespread starvation, population declines, and higher taxes on the peasants by the wealthy landlords seeking to maintain their position in the face of declining production.

Williams additionally notes the many different forms that disorder in the cities takes, such as riots, contract killings, kidnappings, and child prostitution. Other modern examples could be the spread of sex slave trafficking, and the porous borders that encourage the flow of people, money, weapons, drugs, and contraband in global trade today. While the form of these activities may be different, they hark back to the rampant invasions, piracy, and banditry that marked the early Middle Ages, when the different nation states were being born in the battles of the feudal lords for territory and soldiers readily switched sides.

Unfortunately, this growing chaos could become even worse, creating a devolution to the Dark Ages after the fall of the Roman empire. As Williams concludes:

> It is not hard to envisage the transformation of global politics and an abrupt, nonlinear shift from the New

Middle Ages to the New Dark Ages. The 21st century will see a continuing dialectic between the forces of order and the forces of disorder. Within this co-evolution, the limits of state power will become increasingly apparent, while the empowerment of non-state actors will increase significantly...Moreover, many of these weaker states will be neutralized, penetrated, or in some cases even captured by organized crime, terrorists, militias, warlords, and other violent non-state actors...One of the corollaries of this is the spread of disorder from the zone of weak states and feral cities in the developing world to the countries of the developed world. Problems such as transnational organized crime, terrorism, and pandemics cold intersect and interact to create a tipping point from 'durable disorder' into chaos. When one adds to the trends already discussed the strains coming from global warming and environmental degradation, the diminution of cheaply available natural resources, and the proliferation of weapons of mass destruction, the agenda becomes even more formidable. As states go further into decline, some will inevitably collapse.[15]

In sum, we do live in frightening times today – times which politically, economically, and socially have many of the characteristics of the Middle Ages and could turn into the Dark Ages. A key quality that is contributing to the disorder and chaos and possibly leading to a New Dark Ages is the problem of inequality, for as the rich get richer, the poorer poorer, and the middle class is increasingly decimated to become the new poor, society is even more destabilized.

Thus, it is especially important to look at the ways in which society today parallels medieval society by looking more closely at this inequality and how it pervaded medieval times. Accordingly, the next section of this introduction is designed to present a more detailed discussion of the political, economic, and social characteristics of the Middle Ages before I examine the parallels between now and then in the rest of the book.

The Growing Inequality in Medieval Times

Numerous historians and economists have pointed to how a growing inequality spread through medieval society due to numerous factors, much like the Depression and World War II was followed by a growing inequality in the U.S. from the 1960s to the present.

Renee Doehaerd describes this situation well in *The Early Middle Ages in the West: Economy and Society*. A key reason for the increasing hardship for the peasants and growing consolidation of wealth in the hands of a wealthy class of landowners who formed the nobility and royal classes was a scarcity of production, combined with the continual warfare to consolidate territory and power. As Doehaerd describes it, this new system grew up in the chaos left behind after the fall of the Roman Empire in 476.Specifically what happened is that during the 5th century, Germanic peoples settled on parts of the territory in the western part of the Empire, where their kings seized power over these territories. Then, after the Empire collapsed in 476, these kings began to fight among themselves, and as they did the rigid, state-administered system which the Roman emperors used to maintain their power as the Empire began crumbling in the 3rd century disappeared or fell into disuse. What remained in the void were the villages, towns, and farms of an urbanized agrarian society.

The system which collapsed had provided a set of fiscal and administrative institutions which ensured that the machinery of production could produce enough goods so the state could tax enough of this to maintain itself. Within this system, the peasant farmer was bound to the land, while the artisan, ship owner, and merchant were bound to guilds at birth, and the state taxed part of the goods or services produced. Then, the state used these funds to set up its own system of production and distribution and supplied its own market. Or to quote Doehaerd: "In this way it fed, clothed and equipped its armies, supplied its own employees with provisions and sold in the towns, at prices which it fixed itself, the products which their inhabitants would buy and which were within the means of the humblest citizen." Through this system of taxation, it was able to ensure a diversification of production, which included selling the town's essential foodstuffs and goods and providing any arms or luxury clothing for the army or court. It also created its own systems of vouchers and coins which were tied to an official exchange rate fixed by the state and administered by the huge Roman bureaucracy and police force.

But then in the beginning of the fifth century, the collapse began, which is reminiscent of many of the conditions that exist today in the impoverishment and the dislocations of millions of people displaced by wars around the world. As Doehaerd describes:

> The beginning of the fifth century brought chaos to the Western Empire; peoples, soldiers, families, furniture and cattle moved along the roads and blocked them; these same roads carried from region to region hordes of pillagers who seized livestock, carts and boats, spread terror, cut off or temporarily occupied the towns, raided, took prisoners and drove the peasants from their villages. In the face of this flood, an exodus began: the richest people tried to reach the estates they owned in other parts of the Empire. They emigrated to Africa, to Carthage, Egypt, and Syria. The poor went where they could...
>
> This dislocation did not take place everywhere at the same time, but wherever taxpayers were leaving their estates, peasants were fleeing, and officials were leaving the towns, wherever roads were cut and the labor force departed, the levying of taxes became impossible and the supplying of the state shops was interrupted. [16]

In short, the economic life of the early Middle Ages was characterized by "insecurity, the scarcity of currency, the lack of a regulating institution for prices, (and) the disappearance of the authority which had constrained men to produce." The wars in Gaul (which later became France) and Italy of the 5th and 6th century essentially undermined any institutions which might have filled the void. Although, the image of lost order, texts of imperial legislation, and the role of the state in supporting the economic system continued to be a model through the early Middle ages for the Germanic kings who hoped to restore their authority.

Meanwhile, similar chaotic conditions occurred in the lands that would become England, Scotland, and Wales, since the disappearance of the Empire created a void there too, which tribes sought to exploit in their own efforts to take over, control, and expand different territories, leading to continual warfare which included battles to stave off invaders from other lands, such as the Vikings from the North.

It was these conditions that contributed to the increasing inequality that developed as growing class divisions emerged between the peasant farmers and the landowners who increased their holdings, controlled the military, and formed part of the new nobility and royalty that grew more unequal over the centuries.

According to Doehaerd, a key reason for this development was the scarcity of consumer goods in Frankish society and among other peoples left to fend for themselves after the Roman Empire. He writes: "The state system of the later Empire, which was designed as a means of lifting society above the level of scarcity, enforced production, enforced the circulation of goods, and guaranteed that non-producers of goods would be supplied. The disappearance of this system left men equipped only to provide for their own subsistence.[17]"

This was a very serious matter, since in those times, farmers could do little when faced with drought, rains, floods, plagues of locusts, diseases, and war. They suffered extreme losses, and a bad harvest meant famine, eating spoiled meat, and even cannibalism. One result of this scarcity, because most men had no reserves, is that under the threat of destitution, took on debts they could not possibly repay. Since all they could offer was their own and their family's ability to work, they sold themselves as slaves for basic necessities such as food or clothes, while the merchants who had foodstuffs effectively reduced them to slavery, and even the barbarian legal codes affirmed these practices. For instance, the Law of the Barbarians that a "poor man could retain his freedom and his possessions, unless he sold himself." In many cases, some starving men gave up their land in return for food.

In turn, these kinds of practices contributed to the growing disparity between those with land, goods, and money, and those without, and those with money used their increasing power to maintain these conditions and gain even more money for themselves at the expense of the poor. As Doehaerd observes:

> Who were these poor people who had to be supported by the rich?... These poor people in need of sustenance, as we have already seen, were the peasants themselves, that is to say the majority of men in a society composed almost entirely of peasants. It was they who had to be fed in times of famine, who had to be sustained when disaster struck; and it was they who gave away their land and who borrowed on the strength of the harvest to come.[18]

And those in power commonly used their power to exploit the peasants who became tenant farmers after giving up their land. A key reason is the poor productivity of the land, leading the rich to seek more and more so they could maintain their great estates and enjoy an increasingly high style of luxurious living. Even agents of the Church who were supposed to help starving paupers acted out of greed in support of their great estates. As Doehaerd explains:

> They were men of privilege, great landowners or the beneficiaries of the produce of great estates ... The peasant was poor and the rich man distressed because the land was unproductive – hence the extraordinarily large number of farms placed by the king at the disposal of his vassals: 200 to 300 farms! Does this not prove that to ensure his livelihood a man needed the revenue from enormous properties? The

hunger for land amongst those who held power or devoted themselves to the public service or to religion is no doubt explained as much by the low productivity of agriculture as by the desire to possess more. Scarcity also explains the priorities established in the value of things... Those men who exercised power at governmental level and who needed the collaboration of men who supply them with aid in the military or administrative field, ruled by distributing land with farmers settled on it. The society in which the bonds of vassalhood developed was a society of low agricultural production before it was a society of low monetary circulation. In exchange for a more or less guaranteed material livelihood a man could buy the freedom or the loyalty of others.[19]

As for the reason for this low productivity, it was due to the low quality of agricultural equipment, plus the usual practice of rotating crops twice a year. This common equipment included "spades, hoes, forks, sickles, scythes with metal blades, hand-combs for harvesting wheat, harrows, riddles, carts, heavy wagons, light vehicles drawn by a single horse, millstones, baskets and panniers, winnowing baskets for cleaning the grain, (and) horse-hair sieves which would allow only the wheat to pass through. As for fertilizer, farmers used human and animal dung and bird manure. Animals most raised included sheep, goats, pigs and cattle, with horses and cattle becoming increasingly important after the invasions. As the population increased, so did the number of rotations from two to three a year, so more work was required for crop-growing.

Meanwhile, the great landowners increased their wealth and power by the dues or rent they took from their tenant farmers, such as sheep, pigs, goals and even oxen. Plus, they also took in dues wheat, oats, barley, beans, and other crops. Later, when the landowners invested in large vineyards, they expected about half of the returns from production of that crop after the five-year period needed to produce a good yield.

Contributing to the growth of inequality in the early Middle Ages was the development of slavery in response to a decline in the population, primarily due to a decline in the birthrate caused by the poor conditions, the destruction of villages, and the continual wars for power during the 6th and the beginning of the 7th century. One source of these slaves were the captive prisoners sold by soldiers in the markets, many of whom were bought by bishops with Church funds. While the Church viewed its policy of buying back captives, especially Christian ones as an act of charity, it also gave the church control of a growing labor force, since not all of the captives who were bought were given their liberty. At the same time, the great landowners made use of these slaves to work their lands – a policy supported by the king himself. As Doehaerd writes:

> The scarcity of labor explains the new upsurge of slavery during the first centuries of the Middle Ages; it was a scarcity that put any man alone in peril; it was even necessary to forbid ecclesiastics to take part in raids to capture slaves...
>
> We can see the concern of Charlemagne over the vassals to whom he had granted land already under cultivation; for he saw them buying estates on which they put to work the slaves or laborers of the farms which he had entrusted to them...(So) Charlemagne ordered the managers of his villae to buy slaves for those holdings which were without farmers, and to inform him of any superfluous men they might have, with the obvious intention of placing them where they might have.[20]

In short, these various factors which contributed to depopulation, such as war, invasions, poor harvests, and famine, also contributed to the growing inequality in society, as landowners sought to tie both peasants and slaves to their land. As Doehaerd notes: "War and invasion created, over the centuries, relatively enormous gaps in the population map...The fact that the farmer remained tied to the land after the invasions and that the Roman law relating to marriage outside was one's own social position was maintained with the same strictness are sufficient evidence that during the period in question the scarcity of labor never ceased to be a problem.[21]" Meanwhile, to increase the acreage for their estates, many of the landowners, including the agents of the Church, engaged their laborers to clear their land, which enabled some peasants to gain an ownership of this cleared land, though they were still obligated to pay any taxes on the produce of this land. In short, whether by acquiring slaves or payments from tenant farmers, the landowners increased their wealth and power through the early Middle Ages, setting the stage for them to gain even more wealth and power with the rise of cities, trade, and new sources of landownership in later medieval times.

As for the cities in the early Middle Ages, although much of western society was being ruralized, most of the rich and powerful moved to the country in the fourth century and drew a majority of the working classes with them, although some rich people did remain. Also, the bishops of the Church continued to administer the estates, property, and land of the church, and taxed the individuals who still lived there. At the same time, large scale agriculture provided by farmers and farmer-landowners who lived in these cities provided food for the clerks, monks, and servants who lived there. And gradually merchants and craftsmen settled in the cities, too. But for the most part, between the 5th to 11th centuries, the main preoccupation of almost everyone was producing food; few people had the opportunity or the means to produce other goods, and those who owned the productive land opted to live on their estates and built powerful defense around them, while the markets for the limited good and produce sold were held in large villages or ports along the coasts and rivers. Mostly, though, the kings and counts avoided the cities to live on their large estates, while the bishops mainly controlled the cities.in the 8th to the middle of the 9th century, known as the Carolingian era.

Then, in the second half of the 9th century and 10th century a period of invasions ensued, led by raids by the Norsemen,

Hungarians, and Saracens, which led to the creation of new perimeter walls and fortifications, to protect both those in the cities and in the countryside. As Doehaerd describes it:

"These invasions did exert a marked influence on the development of the towns because of the threat they posed to the suburbs outside the walls. Everywhere, the raids of the Norsemen, the Hungarians and the Saracens caused the inhabitants of the suburbs to withdraw inside the walled areas where these were extensive enough to receive them. They also led to the restoration of the Roman perimeter walls and to the construction of new fortifications ... Villages were fortified and so were ports. And in these fortresses, from the tenth century onwards, the authorities organized the defense of the countryside ... In the following centuries groups of people seeking effective military protection settled in or near new towns just as readily as in the proximity of the ancient fortified cities ... The result of the invasions was therefore to increase the population within the fortresses, and in the case of the cities to eliminate or reduce in number the dwellings in their undefended suburbs.[22]

Then, in the late 10th and 11th centuries, as the population and trade grew, the Germanic kings and emperors gave the bishops the rights to extend their authority for several miles around the city, and as a result of the raids, the king or bishop who provided urban charters with the right to protect the city with a wall around it.

In sum, as Doehaerd concludes, the population of western Europe during the early Middle Ages dropped precipitously during the fifth and sixth century and remained low until the 7th century when the population began to rise again through the 9th and 10th centuries, resulting in the creation of new markets and trade, causing the growth of merchants' quarters outside the walls of the cities and fortified places in the 9th century and even more from the 10th century onward. But then the invasions led to an increase in fortifications. At the same time, agriculture was a "great devourer of land, which means that it was a great devourer of work," due to the poor agricultural techniques of the times, which contributed to the poverty of the peasants, as the wealthy landowners sought to increase their holdings and therefore their production.

These developments, in turn, contributed to the growing inequality, as the gap between the wealthy landowners and the peasants increased, and in time a wealthy merchant class developed that became part of this upper class. Moreover, the invasions contributed to strengthening the position of the wealthy, since they took on a warrior role to protect the people. The result was the creation of the military structure of knighthood, which became largely a preserve of the upper classes, while they recruited peasants to serve in their armies.

While Doehaerd's analysis is focused on Western Europe, and particularly the regions that became France and Germany, similar developments were occurring in England, too, as a landowning class developed in the chaos left behind with the collapse of the Roman Empire. England experienced the battles of the kings ruling small kingdoms for control followed by a consolidation of lands, followed by invasions, and the emergence of a central kingdom with walled cities. Peasants were increasingly driven into poverty by debts and high rents. Inequality thrived and spread everywhere, and as there were more goods available through trade, the wealthy used their power to live even more opulently, increased taxes to help fight their wars, and make the poor even poorer.

In fact, as trade developed, the landowners took a leading role in organizing trade. They not only produced these commodities, but they organized their transportation, so they essentially oversaw the supply chain. The Church too became part of this trading network through the hunting and fishing rights and other rights granted to them by the king. This control over trade and the proffer of gifts helped to cement relationships, giving the wealthy even more power over those under their control. As Doehaerd writes:

"Men accumulated consumers around them, people whom they fed and who became bound and loyal to them ... because in normal times the demand on the market for these common consumer goods was very uncertain."[23]

With the development of the warrior class and the organization of military service in response to the invasions, there was a trade in arms, since every free man might be called into the army and had to bring his own equipment. Then, too, a class of craftsmen emerged who worked in workshops or at home, some of them slaves or peasants' sons, and most of them joined the urban guilds, a position that was passed down from father to son. But pay was low and commonly the artisans had to pay dues in the form of manufactured products, services, or taxes in money to those in authority, which included both the landowners and the bishop of the local abbey, thereby giving the already wealthy still another source of income, although as trade spread after the 10th century, some merchants gained enough wealth themselves to live well and join the nobility. Some of these merchants even had shops in the cities where they sold luxury products to the nobility.

However, even the rise of markets contributed to the growing division between rich and poor, since the weekly market and annual fairs that were held were all at the prerogative of the power of the king, since the market was linked to the treasury which levied taxes on any commerce. As Doehaerd notes:

"The supervision of the markets was the domain of the ordinary or extraordinary agents of the central authorities. Royal permission was necessary even when the markets were to be created on the land of immune or tax-exempted churches and abbeys, where the taxes to be levied would go to these establishments.

"Anyone who hoped to do business of any kind would normally go to the market ... The market was the place where certain things such as slaves, horses and cattle could be sold legally…

"Numerous charters granting the right to hold markets or fairs must no doubt be explained by the desire to levy taxes from them….

"The increase in the number of country markets can only be a sign of an increase in agricultural production and of the commercial exchange of more goods."[24]

As trade expanded, increasing travel was necessary though at a high cost, given that they had to be undertaken by carts, horses, and ships. As a result, a class of merchants who could afford to possess their own means of transportation, beasts of burden, carts, and boats, and either own or hire the people to operate them was developed. In turn, even if a peasant owned a number of carts and some oxen, he couldn't travel very far from his village, so either sold it through local channels, or turned to the merchants to transport his goods beyond these local markets. Meanwhile, the wealthy – the nobles and the royalty – were major purchasers of these goods, along with the luxury objects, some of which came from Egypt, Byzantium, and the Orient, such as silk, gold and other precious materials, and ivory.

They were, according to Doehaerd, "with their new-found wealth, even more anxious to obtain these costly products than the nobility of the later Empire had been."[25] And besides products, many acquired slaves, while other slaves were shipped East as a result of the wars of conquest and internal wars, which led to the shipment of slaves there, since the Church forbade the sale of Christian slaves in the West. Indeed, the growing inequality in the Muslim world paralleled that in the West, as the Muslim world experienced its own industrial and agricultural expansion, its military machine similarly needed slaves. Concurrently, from the 10th century on, slaves were sold within the West because of the conquests from battles between the kings, nobles, and their forces for territory and power. Though much of the trade was in wheat, flour, clothing, wool, tin, and copper, slaves made up an increasing part of this cargo.

In sum, in response to the invasions of the 9th and early 10th century, and then as the economy expanded from the 10th century onward, inequality increased. As trade grew and the monetary supply increased, and the institution of knighthood emerged to fight for more power and territory, the wealthy landowners were able to increase their control and power increasingly at the expense of the peasants and slaves. Also, even as a class of merchants emerged to travel or open shops with goods, the king and nobles were able to place them under their control, through the use of charters permitting them to sell their goods as well as taxes on whatever was sold.

The Impact of Inequality on Society

This growing inequality gap has been widely analyzed by academics, not only in Western Europe and England, but in the Eastern Roman Empire, also known as Byzantium, that spread throughout the Middle East, and included the Crimea, Balkans, and Southern Italy.

For example, in a study of the average income and inequality in Byzantium around the year 1000, when Byzantium was at the peak of its power as the richest state in the Christian world, Branko Milanovic found a socially polarized society divided from the nobility which had about 100 times the income of those at the subsistence level.[26] At the time, the estimated population of these territories was between 12 to 18 million and the territory was under the strong rule of Basil II from 976 to 1025, a powerful emperor of the Macedonian dynasty. Basil's rule corresponded to a high point of Byzantine economic affluence, in part due to the military successes which led to greater security of peasants, resulting in greater harvests which stimulated the agricultural and urban economy. By converting Byzantine incomes into today's present-day incomes and subsistence minimums, he found there were vast differences between the classes. At the time, the rural population was about 90% of the total, made up of land-holding smallholders or peasants and tenants, though the pressure of taxation had led an increasing number of peasants to sell their land to become tenants who were tied to the soil and were similar to serfs. As he found, aside from the wealth landholding nobility, most of the population was living at close to subsistence levels. Among the rural groups, about two-thirds of the population was composed of small land-owning farmers, and another one third were tenant farmers, wage earners and slaves working on the large demesnes, but all of them lived at about the subsistence minimum. Among the non-rural groups, the city marginal and beggars were at the subsistence minimum. The other groups included a very small urban middle class earning about 6 times the subsistence minimum and an army of about 120,000 soldiers paid at about the same level as unskilled workers, both earning about 3 times the subsistence minimum. By contrast, the nobility's average income was pegged at about 100 times the subsistence minimum.

Eventually, his statistics work out to about 99% of the population living at the subsistence level and 1% sharing the entire surplus, resulting in a Gini coefficient[27] which measures inequality in a society at about 41 to 43, which is only slightly higher than in the U.S. or Russia today, and less than in South Africa in Brazil.

Why the similarity? Because as Milanovic concludes, "as mean income grows...there is more of a surplus to distribute and inequality may grow as well." In other words, he concludes that even "at this very modest (from today's rich world perspective) income level, income inequality was comparable to what it is in today's more unequal society," because this level of inequality is close to the maximum inequality that can exist where there is a guaranteed subsistence minimum for all.

In short, as the economy grows, so can inequality, because a small percentage of the wealthy can gain an even greater percentage of the available wealth, while the impoverished can survive at or near the subsistence level, back then, as well as now, when society has become wealthier than ever, and the top 1% of the 1% have gained an even greater share of increased wealth today.

The Continued Inequality through the Middle Ages

This income gap continued throughout the Middle Ages, even as the economy expanded. Towns and commercial activities expanded, since the wealthy classes, which now included the wealthier merchants, expanded their power, not only economically, but politically.

For example, Cliff T. Bekar and Clyde G. Reed discuss how between the eleventh and thirteen centuries, the English peasants faced large income shocks leading them to trade small parcels of land to reduce their risk. Then, inequality increased in the distribution of their landholdings, since many peasants became landless or had to supplement the income from their harvests with a wage income.[28]

Using a simulation analysis, Bekar and Reed found that "the development of land markets increased the absolute and relative size of the smallholder/landless category of peasants (and) forced the poor into dependency on the labor market."[29] They concluded this after finding that in the 11th century, at the time of the Domesday survey, about 10% of the peasants were classified as servi": individuals who did not hold land and worked exclusively for the lord of the manner. But then, by the time of the Hundred Rolls survey, the number of landless or near landless men grew steadily over time. A key reason was a combination of population growth and commercial development, leading peasants to reduce the subsistence crisis by buying and selling small parcels of land in order to buy food, especially in response to a bad harvest. The result was the larger landholders gained more land and income – thereby contributing to increased inequality, polarization, and poverty in society. In terms of numbers, this worked out to less than 2% of the landholders holding more than 2 acres of land, and the wealthiest families, which experienced the greatest population growth, since they could afford larger families, held even more.

In turn, these developments contributed to the further polarization and splintering of communities, as the wealthiest landowners sought to improve their position even more at the expense of the peasants who had small holdings or had become landless. As

Phillipp R. Schofield observes in *Peasants and Community in Medieval Community 1200-1500,* "It is easy to imagine the splintering of communities, divided along lines of vested interest, with the wealthy promoting an active market through their various machinations including economic and political pressure exerted upon lord and village community alike, while the poor offered resistance in whatever form that presented itself."[30] And Christopher Dyer, author of *Making a Living in the Middle Ages* similarly saw a breakdown in traditional manorial norms and customs as the wealthier minority took advantage of the less advantaged. As he noted:

> In many ways the rise in population and commercial activity threatened to weaken the community. Many of the changes of the period, such as the growth of the land market, encouraged selfishness among a minority, who took advantage of their poorer neighbors.[31]

At the same time, as Cliff T. Bekar and Clyde Reed note, this increase in inequality based on the growth of landholdings by the few helped to set the stage for a commercialized agriculture that contributed to the later Industrial Revolution. These changes also created a large population of landless wage laborers that contributed to the decline of serfdom.[32] Yet, despite these changes, the gap between rich and poor established in medieval times continued.

From Inequality to Control of the Reins of Power

This growing inequality economically was reflected politically, just as today, where the wealthy are able to drive the political agenda with their contributions to established politicians already in office, as well as their own political campaigns since they can buy advertising and gain access to the media to increase their visibility and ultimately obtain more votes. It's a dynamic which James Masschaele notes in his dissertation "A Regional Economy in Medieval England." As he notes, "as political and economic entities grow in complexity, they inevitably develop hierarchical structures to mediate power and wealth," and one of the most important structures developed to do this occurred on the regional level in the two centuries preceding the Black Death. Before the 12th century, trade primarily occurred between towns, and from the last quarter of the 2th century to the first quarter of the 14th, the rural and urban economies became more integrated, primarily by filling in the countryside, as the separate villages expanded and connected with each other. Concurrently, the towns "bustled in the new prosperity and prospered in their expanding role in local economies," though most grew less quickly than the villages.[33]

This growth led to village society becoming increasingly stratified due to differential access to land, leading to increased economic differentiation, and alongside this an increasingly stratified local power structure both in the villages and towns. The local merchants, village craftsman, and peasant farmers were the ones whose patronage determined the success of a market. They provided the services and facilities that fueled this expanding economy, and maintained the local roads and bridges, yet the nobles and lords quickly jumped in to participate in order to maintain their privileged position.

The result was that the elites of society continue to maintain their privileged position generation after generation in an extremely hierarchical medieval society. Initially, the root cause of inequality in the village and rural countryside was economic, due to an imbalance in access to basic resources, especially land. A relatively small number of families dominated the lands in most villages. For example, in one village, less than 20% of the total population, about 175-200 people, supported themselves from 1080 acres, while the remaining 800 or more people had little more than 500 acres.

Later, these economic inequalities translated into political control that helped to maintain the dominance of the wealthiest families. For example, as Masschaele notes:

> The families who dominated landholding also dominated the offices of juror and aletaster... (They) were the

families that reproduced themselves in the village, generation after generation…. (They were regularly the ones paying the highest amounts in lay subsidies, which is tantamount to saying that they had the highest levels of wealth in the village.[34]

With the development of the regional economy the village elites were not only the ones most responsible for its creation, but they were the ones who most benefited from it. This occurred because the wider market access gave them the opportunity and incentive to make the most of their already privileged position in the village. Additionally, this wider market access "gave them more ways to erect social barriers, partly by the possession of distinctive types of material goods, but more importantly by the possession of a more expansive experiential basis to their social existence."[35] In other words, they had more income to spend to enjoy a more luxurious lifestyle, much like the luxury living elite, such as the Kardashians, high paid film, music, and sports stars and business billionaires live in a superwealthy universe today.

Then, after the Black Death decimated about a third to a half of the population throughout Europe, the revival of the economy contributed to even greater inequality throughout Western Europe, as well as in Eastern Europe, as described by Jean Batou and Henryk Szlajfer. According to Batou and Szlajfer, the 13th century marked the height of the medieval economic development of Western Europe and set the stage for its future collapse. Some of the key reasons are that the large-scale rural settlement went beyond the zones fit for farming, and a balanced proportion between cultivation and animal husbandry was undermined. At the same time, this growth depended on low wages paid in both the town and rural area, on the "steady deterioration in the living conditions of the peasants, and on the poverty of a part of the artisans," which in turn was due to an abundant supply of labor and from price rises.[36] So, most of the population lived in "very hard circumstances" with a high death rate.

Then came the Black Death, which was especially hard on the lower income classes, followed by another period of expansion, marked by the growing power of a central authority, as the kings consolidated their territories and gained even more power, along with the support of a court of nobility and military that helped to sustain their power.

Though the economies and political structures of Eastern Europe, such as in modern Bohemia and southwest Russia, were slower to develop, they followed a similar pattern. For example, as Batou and Szlajfer point out, most towns in Eastern Europe were:

> ...small agglomerations near the castles of princes and their officials, inhabited by populations of craftsmen and traders who were chiefly concerned to satisfied the needs of the restricted groups of the ruling class...The inhabitants were obliged to supply the prince and his followers with the products of agriculture and domestic industry...During the tenth, eleventh and even the twelfth centuries...everywhere in the east tributes in mind and labor services predominated...Wars and invasions provided princes and lords with a source of revenue...these states were not only fighting for the land. Each invasion brought the victors a certain number of captives. During the eleventh century and certainly in the preceding century, these prisoners were installed as serfs on the domains of the conquerors.[37]

Then, in the 13th century, even as the economies expanded, the situation of the peasants became even worse. Again, to quote from Batou and Szlajfer:

> In the course of the twelfth century the state and the aristocracy had succeeded in driving the great majority of the peasants in these countries [Bohemia, Hungary, and Poland] into serfdom...(Then) internal and external circumstances and the rising cultural level required increases

in the revenues of the aristocracy. They had to extract more work from the serfs.[38]

At the same time, the wealthy were doing even better due to" the abundance of grain and mineral wealth which increased the power of the great lay and ecclesiastical lords and of the rich merchants of the towns. Later, as the rich merchants earned even more from the expansion of trade, they tended to join the nobility in these eastern regions in the 16th century. Over the centuries, things became worse for the lower income classes. For example, in Poland, during the beginning of the fifteenth century, the economy of the nobility experienced a crisis, leading the nobles to introduce a system of labor services called "the second serfdom." It was a process that lasted over a century, and it ruined most of the peasants and undermined the economic life of the towns, especially the smaller towns tied to local markets, where industry and small scale commerce disappeared. Yet, at the same time, this process further increased the power of the nobility.

Throughout Eastern Europe, as in the West, the growing economy further strengthened the position of the wealthy classes, while the position of other classes declined, as the peasants variously reduced their holdings or lost their lands and supplemented or replaced their lost agricultural labor with wage labor. But regardless of the form of their work, they lost ground compared to those with wealth – the nobility, royal aristocracy, high church officials, and increasingly wealthy merchants. And even though the increasingly dire condition of the lower classes was a breeding ground for revolution, ultimately, the wealthy classes, with their greater access to power put down these recurring revolts that occurred in the 14th through the early 16th centuries.

The Revolts in the Late Middle Ages

As conditions for the peasants and wage laborers declined in the late Middle Ages, uprising and rebellions that commonly involved the peasants in the countryside, workers and sometimes the small and growing middle class in the towns rose against the nobility, kings, and abbots. These revolts expressed a growing frustration and rage over the unfair and unequal conditions experienced by the lower income classes while the wealthy lived in splendor, with their armies to protect them at home, as well as wage their wars to maintain or expand their territory. The revolts occurred all over central Europe, England, and the Balkans.

As described by Michel Mollat and Philippe Wolff in *The Popular Revolutions of the Late Middle Ages*,[39] a key reason for these revolts was that the social gap between rich and poor had become more extreme. According to Norbert Elias in *The Civilizing Process*,[40] starting in the 12th century, the concept of nobility developed, whereby the nobility developed their own distinct appearance and behaviors, in terms of dress, manners, courtesy, speech, diet, and education, and by the 14th century, this difference was very distinctive, much like the superwealthy elite live a very different life today, fueled by their vast fortunes reflected in their huge mansions that are like modern day castles, jet-setting to events around the world, akin to the transport by horse and carriage with footman in the late Middle Ages, and far better diet and education. Then matters became even worse for the peasants and wage workers, because the nobles experienced a declining income in the late 13th century due to inflation, caused in part by the growing population, and as the cost of goods and services increased from inflation, the nobles' incomes declined, especially for those who charged fix rents. This put pressure on the nobles to gain even more income from the peasants and wage workers, since they were now used to living a luxurious lifestyle. So as Mollat and Wolff describe, they gouged the tenant farmers by illegally raising the rents, and they also cheated, stole, and sometimes used violence to take the money or foodstuff's they wanted. They were like the modern-day Mafia, making as much as they can from those in their debt.

Adding even more pressure to the mix was the additional taxes by the kings to support their wars of conquest, which the nobles participated in, too. So not only were the peasants and wage laborers recruited to help fight these wars, but they had to contribute money, and with the increase in inflation, as the kings used less precious metals to cut their silver and coins, the tax rates went up. Plus, in the 14th century, on top of the wars, there were more pressures from famine and plague.

Meanwhile, as a counterpoint to the traditional Christian teaching that supported the rigid medieval hierarchy that one's station in life was a fixed according to the great chain of being which descended from God, a new popular teaching spread by the Franciscans was that wealth and inequality was against the teachings of God. A modern day comparison might be with the teachings of the Protestant preachers of the success gospel who embrace success as a sign of God's favor and the religious ministry serving the modern day poor in the inner cities preaching that seeking excessive wealth at the expense of others is a form of greed, which is a sin.

Thus, for many reasons the 14th through the 16th century was a time when the spirit of revolt spread through the land, pitting the poor against the superwealthy of the day – the kings, nobles, and high-living abbots. Before the 14th century, there had been some occasional local revolts, such as against an oppressive lord of the manor. Moreover, before this time, society had been divided into three main orders – "those who work, those who pray, and those who fight."[41] Even the peasant was viewed as being "next to God, just like the other orders." But increasingly, the peasant was seen as a lower form of being, even almost subhuman, as someone to pay as little as possible to work, while the royalty, nobility, and high status clerics enjoyed their privileged high-style life.

But then, fueled by a desire to share the wealth, status, and good fortune of the more fortunate, in the 14th century, the revolts began and spread throughout Europe and England. Among them was the peasant revolt in Flanders from 1323 to 1328, which began as a small number of rural riots around the countryside in 1323 and then turned into a full-scale rebellion for the next five years. Another revolt was the St. George's Night Uprising of 1343 to 1345 in Estonia and the even better known Jacquerie from 1356 to 1358 in northern France, which erupted during the Hundred's Year War, which was a contributing factor, due to the higher taxes and calls for more and more peasants to join the battle.

Then came the English Peasant's Revolt of 1381, sometimes known as the Great Rising, which was the best-known revolt of this period. As Jeff Hobbs writes in "Peasants' Revolt: 14th Century Poll Tax Riots," this began as a local revolt in Essex and quickly spread throughout much of the south east of England, and some peasants even went to King Richard II in London to present their grievances.[42] It initially began when peasants in Brentwood began by protesting and resisting the poll-tax collectors, and then peasants in neighboring villages joined in. Soon armed bands of villagers and townsman began attacking manors and religious houses, and then some rebels from Essex and Kent marched on London, where they were joined by some of London's poor and then began attacking political targets in the city. For instance, they burned down the Savoy Palace, the home of Richard II's uncle John of Gaunt who was probably the most powerful figure in the real. They also "set fire to the Treasurer's Highbury Manor, opened prisons and destroyed legal records." Yet, while a delegation of peasants met King Richard and a small group of lords and knights, pledged their allegiance, and handed him a petition in which they asked for "the abolition of villeinage, for labor services based on free contracts, and for the right to rent land at a the rate of four pence an acre, to which the king agreed, other peasants attacked the Tower and executed the Archbishop of Canterbury, the Chancellor and John of Gaunt's physician, considering them traitors engaged in corruption and extravagance. And the next day, some peasants had more extravagant demands, including an end to all lordship beyond the king, the confiscation of the Church's estates, and a division of them among the larger populace, and that there only be bishops throughout the kingdom. But soon after that, the tide turned against the rebels, when the rebel leader, Wat Tyler, insolently addressed the king, whereupon the Mayor of London pulled Tyler off his horse and a squire killed him. Though a crowd prepared to rush the king, he convinced them to follow him, and soon after that the Mayor recruited a force of men in the city who surrounded the rebels, whereupon Richard pardoned them and declared they should return peacefully to their homes, which they did. So the revolt in London was effectively over, and after that, the other revolts around the countryside were over as well, and for the most part the main leaders of the revolt who weren't already dead were executed.

This was a similar pattern elsewhere throughout Europe, where the peasant revolts lasted a short time and were then quelled by the superior power of the kings and nobles. Though the specific cause or triggering incident might differ, in general the basic inspiration for these revolts was the poor condition of the peasants. For example, in the case of the 1381 English revolt, Hobbs writes:

> The targets that the peasants attacked, plus the demands that they made to the King, show the pressures they faced at the time. The immediate cause of the revolt was the unprecedented amount of taxation the peasantry faced from the Government. The poll tax of 1389 was three times higher than that of the previous year, and unlike its predecessor, taxed rich and poor at the same rate. Hence, it was very unpopular with the peasantry. However, the main call of the peasant rebels was for the abolition of serfdom. This was because, since the middle of the century, their lords had prevented them from making the most of the changing economic conditions.[43]

A key reason for these changing economic conditions is that visitations of the plague between 1348 and 1349 had reduced the population by a third to a half, so labor was scarcer, so wages rose. But the landowners passed legislation through Parliament that kept the wages low and restricted the serfs from moving freely. Plus, the local manorial lords tried to increase the feudal dues the serfs were obligated to perform for them. Thus, the resentment of the peasants grew, and the rebels targeted "symbols of lordship and lordly authority, such as the manors and manorial records," in their revolt.

A list of these major revolts over the next two centuries – at least 20 or more — shows how this pattern continued in other areas. Among these are the following:[44]

- A revolt against the Queen of Hungary from 1382 onwards.
- The Imandino Revolts in Galicia in 1431 and 1467.
- The Budai Nagy Anal Revolt in Transylvania in 1437.
- The Kent rebellion of 1450 headed up by Jack Cade.
- The Rebellion of the Remences in Catalonia in 1462 and 1485.
- The Cornish Rebellion of 1497 in Cornwall and London.
- The 1514 peasant revolt in Hungary
- The Slovene peasant revolt of 1515 throughout Slovenia
- The Knights Revolt of 1522-1523 in Germany
- The German Peasants' War of 1524-1526 in the Holy Roman Empire
- the Pilgrimage of Grace in England in 1536.
- The Dacke War of 1542 in Sweden
- The Wyatt rebellion of 1554 in England
- The Prayer Book Rebellion of 1549 in Cornwall and Devon.
- The Croatian-Slovene peasant revolt of 1573 in Croatia
- The Cudgel War uprising in Finland in 1596.
- The peasant wards in 17th century Russia led by Ivan Bolotnikov and Stenka Razin
- The Swiss peasant war of 1653.

The Lessons to be Learned for Today

In short, the same basic conditions, poverty and high taxes at the hands of a royalty that lived a very separate and luxurious existence by the 14th century, prevailed throughout Europe, England, the Baltic regions, and Eastern Europe leading to the spread of the peasant revolts. But then these were all overcome by the wealth and power of the king and nobility. They had the weapons and armed forces, and as necessary, they used them to eliminate the rebel leaders and diffuse the revolt.

In turn, what is especially significant about these developments is the parallels with the inequality crisis of today, where the super-wealthy live an increasingly separate life from the rest of the population, and where the decline of the middle class driving more people into the new poor, as well as the long-term poor are triggering a growing resentment. The last decade has witnessed a growing number of these movements These include that movements like the Occupy Wall Street, Oakland, and other city protests that began in 2011 and continued for several years that are like the spread of revolts through the towns around the countryside during the English Peasants Revolt of 1381. Additionally, protesters revolted against fast-food and chain retail stores, seeking to overturn the current low minimum wage of about $8-9 for a $15 an hour wage. It is a protest that has spread to dozens of major cities around the U.S., such as protests organized against McDonald's and other fast food restaurants since late 2012 and the advent of the Fight for 15 Movement. These protests have amounted to a combined $68 billion raise for 22 million low-wage workers in both the public and private sectors.[45] And more recently, the Black Lives Matter movement has turned into a widespread protest against racial injustice and economic inequality.

In the modern day, these protests are accompanied with or followed by lawsuits to try to increase the minimum wage. But just as the kings, nobles, and high ranking clerics were able to beat back the protests in medieval times, so they may attempt to do so today, such as with the police to constrain protests and batteries of lawyers and lobbyists to fight off the claims of the protesters with their own arguments against increased wages, such as the claim that an increase in pay will result in a decrease in jobs, especially since higher labor costs can lead to more automation, higher costs to consumers, and reduced sales.

At the same time, if demands aren't met, the protests can not only spread but become increasingly violent, much like some of the protesters in medieval times resorted to burning down the residences and official buildings of the nobility and sometimes carrying out executions, though many protest leaders ended up being executed themselves.

The verdict is still out, but one of the lessons from this growing divide in medieval times and the growing resentment, protests, and rebellions it triggered as a result could lead to a similar scenario today. Certainly, conditions are different and any rebellions will take other forms – from the use of more sophisticated weapons to legal weapons used in the legislature and courts. Despite this, if the underlying conditions triggering growing poverty and a growing rich, the seeds of resentment, protest and rebellion are likely to grow, and just like plants spread out their roots and seeds, triggering new growths, so these protests today are apt to spread.

Will they get snuffed out like the protests of yore? Or can they mobilize for change?

That is the big question as the protests are likely to spread, given the continuation and growth of the underlying conditions.

This book is designed to look at the parallels between the Middle Ages and today to contribute to this important discussion. As the book illustrates, now as then, a growing inequality has led to an increasing social separation, as well as an economic one, between the superwealthy and their luxurious lives as part of today's worldwide elite culture and both the long-term poor and the new poor made up of the declining middle class, due to the loss of jobs and homes. Yes, since the darkest of times in the Middle Ages resulting from the Black Death gave way to the Renaissance, maybe there is cause for hope today that American society will experience a similar rebirth.

The next section looks at the problem of inequality today – and then the rest of the book focuses on comparing the economy and society of the Middle Ages to conditions today.

CHAPTER 1: THAT WAS THEN; NOW THIS IS NOW

In America today, stories about inequality and the growing divide between rich and poor are increasingly in the headlines as the middle class slips away. The next chapter presents a stark portrait of what is happening through a statistical roadmap showing the growing disaster created by this great divide in incomes between the superrich who are like the royalty and nobility of the Middle Ages and the lowly peasants just scraping by. Unfortunately, more and more Americans are falling into this "just scraping by" class.

Some of the stories in the news as of this writing illustrate this divide, like the earth separating after an earthquake creates a huge and expanding fault line through the ground. On the one hand, news stories reflect the glamorization of the wealthy lifestyle and the expensive entertainments where the wealthy can participate and everyone else just watches; on the other hand, some recent stories show what it's like for once successful families to be struggling, downsizing, and falling into the ranks of the impoverished. These all reflect parallels with life in the Middle Ages, where the superrich royals and nobles lived in huge estates, financed their lavish lifestyles through the work of the poor peasants and artisans, and used the military to control the lower classes.

The following chapter features these stories which highlight this wide class split – the contrast between the elaborate manors of the modern-day royals and the people losing their homes and now living in very small ones, the sport of billionaires today, and the growing protest against the superrich that might lead to a modern-day revolution if things don't change.

Living Rich and Large

Today, many films and the lifestyles of the A+ list entertainers in films, TV, music, and sports serve to glamorize the way the super superwealthy live. Although the hands of most of the big movers and shakers with money and power are wielded behind the scenes by the financial wizards of Wall Street, the politicians and lobbyists of Washington, and the multinational billion dollar corporate owners, the very prominent entertainers are like the public face representing this elite way of life that still seems to fuel the American dream. Yet, it is increasingly unobtainable, since mobility in America is at an all-time low, far behind the mobility possible in other industrialized countries, though the lottery and success on reality shows offers a kind of instant shot at fame and glory, though it is only fleeting for most winners.

Several films and TV series of the past decade, such as *The Crown*, *Downtown Abbey,* and *Succession* reflect the glamour of the lavish lifestyle of the super-wealthy – as well as providing a subtext critiquing this lifestyle for its superficiality and dangers to society. Take *The Bling Ring*, a film released in June 2013, based on a real world story chronicled by Nancy Jo Sales in an article in *Vanity Fair*: "The Suspect Wore Louboutins" and later published in a paperback as *The Bling Ring: How a Gang of Fame-Obsessed Teens Ripped Off Hollywood and Shocked the World*. The original story dates back to October 2008 through August 2009, when a group of seven teenagers and young adults living in and around Calabasas, California, burgled the homes of several celebrities, including Paris Hilton, Lindsay Lohan, and Orlando Bloom, and stole about $3 million in cash and belongings. Led by Rachel Lee, a student at Indian Hills High School; Nick Prugo, a once shy lonely teen; and others who were drawn into the group. They learned when the targeted celebrities would be out of town for celebrity events through celebrity gossip websites, Facebook, and Twitter, and found their houses using Google Maps and the website celebrityaddressaerial.com. Gradually, they turned their fascination with being in the celebrities' homes and feeling like a celebrity with their clothing and jewelry into an organized criminal enterprise where they sold many of the items for cash. After being caught on surveillance video, an anonymous tipster informed the police that Lee and Prugo had committed the burglary at Lohan's house, and after links between Lee and Prugo were shown on Facebook, the police arrested Prugo who soon confessed to the crime, after which evidence of the burglary was quickly obtained by the L.A.P.D. exercising search warrants on all of the ring participants, who were soon arrested and sentenced to various penalties.

But while Coppola's film reflects this story, it also provides a loving glimpse of the lifestyles of the superwealthy whose homes were burglarized, especially the home of Paris Hilton, whose home was burglarized repeatedly and who willingly invited the film crew into her home. Repeatedly, the film shows the teenagers fascination with looking through the closets and draws, pulling out and trying on clothes and shoes. It shows them gazing at themselves in front of mirrors and preening in front of each other. Their excitement is even greater when they go into Paris Hilton's house several times and enter her huge room with hundreds of designer dressers and her racks upon racks of high heel shoes in an array of colors. Then, behind a door, they discover the entrance to a treasure trove of glittering jewels and make off with all of them.

While the stories in the press and police reports may highlight the extent of the robberies, the dozens of homes burglarized, and the ability of the thieves to go undetected for so long, the film exalts in presenting these homes, often high on hillsides like the castles of old, with protective shrubbery, fences, and walls around them, like medieval moats and stockades. These palatial homes are very much characters in the film who are under attack from the teens like the olden barbarians and pirates escaping with their booty and going back to their hideaways to count up and distribute the loot.

For example, even though the thieves may have made off with dozens of her best dresses and shoes, she still has hundreds more, and many viewers may wonder about the need for all of this collect-ing. After all, how could she possibly wear all these dresses or shoes, and why would she need to, especially since many look very much alike? In fact, there are so many, the collection almost looks like the racks of a store, not the collection of a single person. Perhaps the money for such a huge collection of clothes, shoes, and jewelry – presumably in the multi-millions might have been better spent helping to improve the lives of the growing number of sufferers from poverty today. But then, the superrich don't commonly think that way. They are enjoying their superrich lifestyle with other superrich, which might include supporting a few pet causes with charitable fund-raising events, but not thinking about how their liv-ing large lifestyles contributes to the growing inequality in America and the misery of the super poor.

Another example of both glamorizing and critiquing the superrich lifestyle is the documentary, *Queen of Versailles,* directed by Laureen Greenfield and released in 2012, about the billion-aire couple David and Jacquie Siegel, who were made rich by the housing boom, decide to construct the biggest house in America a 90,000 square foot palace which is modeled after the royal French Palace of Versailles. The palace was the center of power from 1682, when Louis XIV moved from Paris until the family was forced to leave in 1789 with the beginning of the French revolution. Quite fittingly, then, the Siegels chose to create this building, which not only is a glamorous construction showing of extreme wealth, but was a symbol of the Ancient Regime's system of absolute monarchy that represented a consolidation of monarchy power dating to the Middle Ages.

At the time the Siegels began their palace, their company Westgate Resorts, had become the largest privately owned time-share company in the world.[46] It specialized in selling time-shares to individuals who were eager to live the wealthy lifestyle to the extent they could in expensive properties – but ones they couldn't afford on their own. But at least they could get a piece for a time of this American dream of living like royalty, and so in catering to them, Westgate Resorts made billions for the Siegels. So what was more fitting than for a couple who made their fortune helping buyers achieve the royalty dream to create their own royal palace and to use it to flaunt their great wealth through both the house and its elegant furnishings and artwork?

But after they got about half-way through building it, the real estate bubble collapsed, and along with that the couple's ability to keep building the house and pay off the loans on it, leading to them eventually having to lay off thousands of employees and put the house on the market to keep the banks from taking it over. However, since the film was released, the Siegels have sued the filmmakers for defamation, by claiming the Westgate Resorts company is "currently financially sound and very profitable," so that the company has paid off the loan and has resumed construction. Whatever the status of the house now, the film shows the effort of a then superrich billionaire family to build a mansion as befitting the wealthy today, an example of the nouveau riche writ large, since Jackie as a former model and David as a once struggling real estate developer did come from humble beginnings. Then as billionaires they joined the new royal American upper class.

Finally, one more film, this one a fictionalized biopic – *Behind the Candelabra*, released in 2013, directed by Steven Soderbergh and starring Michael Douglas and Matt Damon, is an example of celebrating this luxurious lifestyle today. The film is based on the autobiography of Scott Thorson, who had a fairly tempestuous relationship with Liberace from 1977 to 1986, the film celebrates the gaudy elegance of Liberace's flamboyant style of dressing in expensive attire with a dramatic flair and his massive residence filled with fancy French furniture, as if pulled from the Versailles playbook. So even though the relationship implodes as Liberace tires of his young boy toy, amidst accusations of unfaithfulness and Thorson's lawsuit over unkept promises that Liberace would adopt and take care of him in the lifestyle to which he had become accustomed, Liberace's elegant home and lifestyle of servants and limousines play a central role until the end, even as Liberace lies dying of AIDs and Thorson visits him one last time to say goodbye.

In short, this rarified lifestyle played out in the palatial mansions of the superrich provides a kind of modern-day American dream that replaces the once middle-class aspiration for the comfortable house in the suburbs. But since it is a dream only a small percentage of the 1% can realize, these films become a way to both savor the glory of the dream, while getting some satisfaction that this unrealized dream can bring with it many problems (such as thieves who might strike in the night, financial difficulties, and emotional conflicts) that help those who can't live the dream feel better about their own station in life.

Living Poor and Small

The other side of the equation of the rich getting richer is the middle class and poor becoming poorer, so that many are losing their homes or having to move to much smaller quarters, whether they rent or buy. While assorted government programs have resulted in some banks changing their policies to enable certain homeowners to obtain lower mortgages and payments, reducing the number of homes in some state of foreclosure from its peak of 3 million in 2010 to 624,753 properties in 2018, the lowest level since 2005.[47] The foreclosure crisis has continued for many homeowners, like a scythe cutting homeowners out of their homes. In turn, they have joined the ranks of the newly poor, resulting in higher rents in many cities and a growth of a new tiny homes movement, for those who can no longer afford or acquire a mortgage. The process is similar to what peasants in the Middle Ages were hit with: more taxes to pay for the continuing battles of the kings and lords over territory or forced out of their homes when rival lords raided and burned their villages and farms.

An example of this kind of transformation of the housing market as the rich get richer and poor get poorer is what happened to an elderly Chinese American couple and their daughter in September 2013 San Francisco. Even though their threatened eviction brought out hundreds of protesters to try to save their home and point out the unfairness of the system, it was to no avail and the eviction is expected to go through.

The couple, Poon Heung Lee, an 80-year old retired hotel housekeeper, his wife, and disabled daughter, were caught in the maelstrom of the conversion of rental housing to more expensive tenant-in-common units, due to the tech-fueled housing boom in San Francisco bringing in thousands of high-paid tech workers seeking a place to live. Over the course of a year their eight-unit complex in the Polk Street area of San Francisco near Chinatown was emptied of its other occupants after the building owner sent out notices to all the residents under the state's Ellis Act, which gives him the right to force tenants to leave if he doesn't rent to someone else but moves his own family into them or sells the units such as to the new tenants-in-common owners. However, after living in their two-bedroom apartment for 34 years, the family didn't want to leave, and he couldn't afford the rent increase from $778 for his rent-controlled apartment to the average $3206 rent for an equivalent two-bedroom apartment. Even with $22,000 in relocation costs for the move, the couple, who lived mainly on Social Security checks, would soon go broke.[48]

The Lees were not the only ones affected, since at least four other Ellis Act evictions were in process in the neighborhood to make way for the more expensive condos and tenant-in-common apartments being built, along with the upscale restaurants catering to this wealthier class of residents. This eviction process was completely legal, so the landlords desire to make money was gentrifying the neighborhood, with the result that low and middle income residents were being pushed out. As a result, though several hundred protesters blocked the doorway to the Lee's building, the sheriff's office was poised to return to carry out the legal eviction order, much like a medieval sheriff might force peasants out of their homes at the bequest of a noble who owned the land, whatever the reason for the eviction.

The Rise of Tiny Homes

In recent years, the growth of tiny homes is another response to the increase in inequality, as once middle-class and poor people are being pushed out of traditional homes or unable to pay increasing rents. Such homes provide scaled down and less expensive living accommodations. So instead of moving in with parents, doubling up with roommates and housemates, or ending up in homeless shelters or on the streets, a new industry and new type of community has developed based on living in homes which are about the size of an RV. It's a house that can be easily moved to a wide variety of locations, including backyards, RV parks, rural settings, and even in a national park.[49]

In contrast to the typical American home that is around 2600 square feet, the tiny house is around 100-400 square feet and can be built for around $30,000 to $60,000, though it can cost as little as $8000 to $150,000 depending on the size, building materials, and extras, such as stainless steel appliances.[50] While some drawn to these houses are seeking a smaller space and simplified living out of environmental concerns, a key motivator is the financial savings, along with the additional time and freedom from living with lowered expenses and fewer possessions in a house that can be moved.[51]

Such housing is especially appealing to the largely well-educated, older adults, who now live on a low income, who make up a large part of the tiny homes market. For example, recent research indicates that 68% of the tiny house people have no mortgage compared to 29% of all U.S. homeowners, and they spend on the average about $65,000 to build the home, compared to the $320,000 cost of an average home, about 40% of the homeowners are over 50, and the tiny house people also have less credit than the average America, while 65% have no credit card debt. Their per capita income is about $42,000 per year.

In short, these tiny homes have become one option for people squeezed out of traditional home ownership, because of the decline in housing prices, the loss of homes to foreclosure, and the low income of people facing retirement. While, such living small isn't the optimal solution for everyone, it is a growing response to the increasing disparity of the rich in their big houses and many middle class and poor being forced from their homes into the modern day equivalent of the tiny one room homes that were common for the peasants and artisans of medieval times.

The Sport of Billionaires and Kings

The America's Cup is a prime example of a sport that only the wealthiest billionaires can compete in, while ramping up the excitement of millions of followers of all classes, from those who follow the sport in the papers or as spectators on the shores to the wealthy sponsors and city officials who raise or contribute funds for the event in their city. Since the Cup came to its conclusion in San Francisco with a win of the team sponsored by Larry Ellison of Oracle, one of the wealthiest billionaires in the world, the number of entrants declined from 15 to 4 because of the huge expense of building and maintaining teams for these big boats. Ultimately, it was down to teams from Sweden, Italy, New Zealand, and America.

A little history shows the sport's royal bloodline from its founding in 1851, when the Royal Yacht Squadron arranged for a race around the Isle of White in England. Even Queen Victoria came out to watch the race. But then a schooner named America sponsored by the New York Yacht Club, an organization patronized by the New York elite, won the race, which was then renamed the America's cup after the yacht, not the country. According the America Cup's history, this win and the change of name "symbolized a great victory for the new world over the old, a triumph that unseated Great Britain as the world' undisputed maritime power."[52] After that, the syndicate of owners who sponsored the race donated the trophy to the New York Yacht under a Deed of Gift in 1857, which stated that this would be "a perpetual challenge cup for friendly competition between nations." Ever since, the winner of the cup determined where the next race would be held, for the next 26 challenges over 132 years, the cup stayed in the U.S. Australia won the cup in 1983, so the next race was in Western Australia, though the winning San Diego Yacht Club brought the 1987 race back to the U.S.

Meanwhile, the boats began to become larger and incorporate new technologies for yacht designed, such as a revolutionary winged keel and a hull of fiberglass, rather than aluminum and wood.[53] Then, over the next two decades battles over boat sizes were played out on the water and in the courts with challengers like the American billionaire Bill Koch, Italian billionaire Raul Gardini, Patrizio Bertelli of the Prada fashion house, Larry Ellison of Oracle, and Swiss Bio-Tech entrepreneur Ernest Bertarelli. For a time, after Bertarelli's win in 1995, the battle for the cup played out in Europe, but then Larry Ellison's BW Oracle team, racing a trimaran with a powerful wing sail, won the 33rd, which set the stage for the 34th match in San Francisco in 2013.

But before the match could even go forward here, there were all sorts of back-room deals with the city to line up support, as well as attracting wealthy local sponsors to provide backing and arrange for TV coverage to turn racing in the Bay, rather than in the ocean, into a reality TV show. As described in a San Francisco Weekly article by Joe Eskenazi: "San Francisco poured millions into the event in hopes of catching crumbs off the table of a megalomaniacal billionaire. New Zealand, meanwhile, directly subsidized its yachting team with government funds, buying something akin to partial ownership of the product."[54] For example, to offset city costs to underwrite the boat race, a private America's Cup Organizing Committee claimed to obtain over $16 million, and the city struggled to sell bleacher tickets of $70 to $110, since most spectators watched from in front of the bleachers or on TV – an estimated 100,000-250,000 viewers.

In the end, it turned into an odd battle played out mainly in the local press, as one sailor from the Swedish Artemis team was swept overboard and drowned after being trapped under the boat, as the Italian Russo team sought rule changes to make the huge boats safer and protested when it lost its case, and many boats ran earlier heats without any challengers, until the finals led to a two-boat match between Oracle and the Kiwi team, with local San Franciscans commonly supporting the Kiwis against the Oracle team financed by a corporation helmed by a very rich and very unlikeable billionaire.

In a way, the race seems a fitting symbol of the class division and inequality separating the very rich from everyone else in this modern day American Middle Ages. On the one hand, the demands for bigger and bigger boats, now the size of 13-story buildings with more speed and danger, like high-tech brutes in modern-day sci-fi action movies, has meant that fewer and fewer teams can afford to compete. That's why this race was down to only four competitors, rather than the 15 originally expected. Only the very rich could compete or as the SF Weekly article so aptly describes it:

> The America's Cup is one of the least egalitarian sporting competitions on the planet. The winners choose the host ventures and craft the rules to suit themselves, and wealthy syndicate-owners can, intuitively, buy better boats. The sums thrown about by Ellison and his billionaire cohorts are a shade greater than those expended in the past. The ceiling has been raised, just a bit.[55]

So the high price of entry kept many entrants and their fans away, though by setting up TV coverage of the event, Ellison did provide a way for the masses to see the spectacle and the local San Francisco Chronicle did provide an extra page encasing each edition during the race with details on where spectators could go to watch the races, even for free.

In sum, the America's Cup race provides a perfect example of the great divide, where the very rich participate in a sport as captains, owners, sponsors, and movers and shakers getting the media and cities internationally to provide a forum for their sport. Meanwhile, others become observers of the wealthy at play, while a chosen few are like the knights of old participating in jousting and other types of combat contests for the pleasure of the king.

CHAPTER 2: WHO HAS THE MONEY?

This divergence of wealth between the superrich and everyone else is reflected in the statistics that show a growing divergence in the U.S. since the 1970s and exacerbated even more by the Great Recession that began around December 2007 with an even more precipitous drop in September 2008. Since 2019, the income disparity gap is the largest it has ever been.[56]

A Measure of Inequality

This growth of inequality is shown by a Gini index in which income inequality is shown by a single number, based on a scale from 0-1; while zero represents perfect equality where everyone has exactly the same income, 1 represents complete inequality, where one person has all the income, and commonly the scores are multiplied by 100 to make them easier to understand. It's an index that can be used to compare inequality within and between countries by race, gender, and employment, before and after taxes, and over time.[57] As much as I might like to claim this index as my own since the focus of this book is on the inequality that has created a society that parallels the disparity of income in the Middle Ages, it was actually created by an Italian statistician and sociologist Corrado Gini and originally published in his 1912 paper: "Variability and Mutability." It's a rather complex formula, but basically it is based on the Lorenz curve which plots the proportion of the total income of the population that is cumulatively earned by the bottom percentage of the population. The Gini coefficient represents the ratio of the area that lies between the line of equality at 45 degrees and the Lorenz curve under the line of equality.

Reduced to a single figure, the Gini index shows the growing inequality in the U.S., which is now fourth among the OECD or developed countries with high-income economies, according to the Organization for Economic Cooperation and Development, which is composed of 34 countries, founded in 1961, to stimulate world trade and economic development.[58] As of 2018, its pre-tax Gini coefficient was 41.4. Meanwhile, the index has increased from .44 in the early 1980s to this higher level today.

The Source of Inequality

This great divide today between rich and poor has been triggered by a number of factors, including the high-tech transformation of the economy rendering some industries and jobs obsolete, the outsourcing of many middle class occupations to other countries, the disintermediation of management for increasingly educated knowledge workers, and the growth of low-pay service jobs. Perhaps more than anything, it has been due to the deregulation of the financial industries and the changing tax structure to reduce capital gains taxes, which has led to those in the financial industries and those with investments in financial properties to reap a fortune, at a time when the salaries and benefits of a small number of corporate owners, CEOs, and entertainment tycoons have become greater than ever, contributing to the great wealth divide. In medieval times, the huge gap was between the king, nobility, and Church on the one hand and peasants on the other; but now this gap has been increasing between the super-wealthy, with earnings from these sources, and everyone else. Moreover, they have been able to increase their earnings by exercising their power in Washington to change the laws in their favor to the detriment of others. For example, many of the very wealthy have found loopholes in the tax laws, such as through tax havens and tax shelters, reduced capital gains taxes, and the ability to roll over property taxes from one sale into the purchase of another property. Meanwhile the full brunt of taxation falls most heavily on everyone else, much like it was in the Middle Ages, when the very wealthy landlords imposed ever steeper taxes on the peasants.

The Growing Inequality of Wealth in America

Numerous reports show this growing concentration of wealth among the already wealthy in the U.S. expressed in various ways. Here are some of the major measures that show this, suggesting that the U.S. today is increasingly similar to the Gilded Age of inequality, which proceeded the stock market collapse of 1929, and may portend another financial collapse since the spread of inequality has slowed the economic recovery, increased the misery for the less fortunate, and inspired a growing protest movement by the Occupy and Housing Crisis demonstrators. These articles from 2010 to 2020 reflect the grim trend to inequality, even before the Great Recession hit and exacerbated this trend even more.

For example, in an article that compared inequality to Gilded Age levels, Alexander Eichler reported that a study by the Congressional Budget Office, released in October 2011, found that income was "dramatically concentrated, shifting heavily toward the top earners between 1979 and 2007," and while "income at all levels have risen some, they've skyrocketed for the very wealthiest of earners." The income for those in the top 1 percent did even better, since their income spiked 275% in this period. Since their relative income increased so much more than for others, their share of the nation's total income more than doubled to just over 20%.[59]

This expanding income inequality, sometimes described as the "Great Divergence," has meant that as of 2016 the richest 5% in the United States controlled two-thirds of all the wealth, and even more in 2020. A key reason for this control of the wealthy is because of stock ownership and capital gains, according to an August 2020 Trader Talk article. While 55% of U.S. households do own stock according to a Gallup poll, in fact, "the very wealthy…"control almost all of this asset." According to a Federal Reserve report, the top 10% of all households based on their net worth control 87.2% of the equities in the country, and the top 1% have controlled 70 % to 80% of the stock market value since 1989, when record-keeping for these figures began.[60]

In turn, the U.S. has become more like the less developed countries, such as Uganda, Cameroon, and Rwanda, in its gap between its richest and poorest citizens. In turn, this great inequality has contributed to holding back the economic recovery with the result of increasing the suffering for the millions of out of work Americans and the 46.2 million living in poverty – more than ever before.

According to Josh Bivens, an economist of the Economic Policy Institute, a major reason for this growth of inequality is the deregulation of the finance industry. Those in the industry have experienced the largest increase in income, and thereby taking a larger and larger share of the economy, though this return comes from financial manipulations rather than producing any kind of actual product or service.[61]

As an increase in equality develops, American is turning into a "patchwork nation," in which entire communities are becoming winners or losers. In more than half of the different types of counties, 7 out of 12, the median family income in 2010 was lower than in 1980, based on estimates from the firm Geolytics, a company that specializes in providing demographic data drawn from the census in an easily accessible form. While the most populous county types in the country, including the Monied Burbs, Industrial Metropolists, and Boom Towns, all saw growth the hardest hid communities were the agricultural areas, called Tractor Country, the areas with high concentrations of Latinos, called Immigration Nation, and the small town Service Worker Centers primarily due to the loss of small manufacturing. Overall, due to these changes, "the already wide income gap between the wealthiest county types in Patchwork Nation and the poorest grew by more than $4,400 in the last 30 years in inflation-adjusted dollars.[62]

Other researchers have identified this growing inequality as a "middle class crisis," described by Derek Thompson, a senior editor of *Atlantic* magazine, as "the most important economic story of our times," as he illustrates in an annotated slide show, drawn from the 2012 edition of the State of Working America from the Economic Policy Institute, a non-profit, non-partisan think tank, which conducts research on the economic status of working America, with a view to considering the needs of low-income and middle-income workers. As Thompson points out, the income of a typical working-age family grew considerably in the late 1990s from about $62,000 to $69,200. But then around 2000, it stopped growing and started falling in 2007, from $68,900 to about $64,000 in 2010, even though productivity grew steadily in the 2000s, yet compensation didn't. The big change was that the gains from productivity went to the top, since household income, adjusted for inflation, grew 12 times more for the top 1% than the middle 20% and 24 times more than the bottom 20%. At the same time, the big source of income growth for the top 1% was at capital income from assets like houses, stocks, and bonds, a trend going back to 1979. Since that time, the top 5% gained more than half of the total income growth, while the top 1% gained nearly 40% of that growth.[63]

So, what was the source of this big difference? As Thompson's charts illustrate, between 1979 and 2007, about 60% of the increase in the top 1%'s share of the total income came from the expansion of the financial sector and the explosion in the amount of executive pay. At the same time, the effective tax rates on the richest of the rich went down, largely due to U.S. laws providing a tax advantage to income from capital gains, a big plus for the top 1% who have controlled over 40% of the stock market wealth since the 1980s.

As the very rich have benefited, the earnings for those on the bottom have gone down. In 1964, the minimum wage was about 50% of the average worker's hourly earnings; but by 2011, that wage was only 37% of these earnings. At the same time, the wages went down for those in manufacturing jobs, because of the competition with cheaper goods at lower labor costs from less developed nations and the decline in the power of unions, from representing 27% of the workers in the early 1970s to only 13% in the late 2000s, thereby reducing the ability of middle class workers without skills to obtain higher wages, since those without unions had less bargaining power.

The implications of this growing gap are huge, because of its effects on the health and life expectancy of those on the bottom. As described in an *Economist* article: "Your Money, Your Life," income inequality in American is at a level not seen since the 1920s, and new research finds "a link between America's wealth inequality and the life-expectancy gap." On average, individuals in wealthier counties live longer lives because wealth pays for numerous goods that result in a longer life, such as better health care, more leisure, more exercise, and less unhealthy fast food. The result is a 5-10% increase in life expectancy for wealthy seniors.[64]

The growing inequality gap has also triggered a growing movement against it that could turn revolution. For example, the World Economic Forum, independent international organization committed to improving the state of the world by engaging business, political, academic and other leaders of society to shape global, regional and industry agendas, recently rated "severe income disparity" as one its top global risks for 2013. Oxfam, an international confederation of 17 organizations in more than 90 countries, who have come together as a global movement for change to build a future free from the injustice of poverty, has called for "a new global goal to end extreme wealthy by 2025" as part of its fight against income inequality and poverty (www.oxfam.org). In the past, the group has focused on ending extreme poverty, without much concern for extreme wealth, considering it either irrelevant or a prerequisite for the growth that would also help the poorest through a trickle down approach, but now the group's focus has shifted and an international movement against income inequality has been gaining momentum with the problem of inequality in the U.S. seen as part of a growing tide bringing more wealth to the superwealthy all over the world.[65]

As Olga Khazan writes in a January 20, 2013 *Washington Post* article: "Can We Fight Poverty by Ending Extreme Wealth?" in the United States, "the share of national income going to the top 1% has increased to 20%, from 10% in 1980. Globally, 1% of the population have seen their incomes rise by 60% in recent years". In turn, this vast concentration of wealth could itself end world poverty, in that the $240 billion which the top billionaires added to their wealth in 2012 would be "enough to end world poverty four times over" and if this inequality problem isn't addressed, it could contribute to social instability. Or as Khazan puts it: "Oxfam's idea is basically the opposite of the trickle-down theory: Rather than creating jobs and lifting others out of poverty, the group says, super-rich minorities cause social unrest and depress demand for goods and services, limiting growth and innovation as a result." Although some wealthy billionaires, such as Bill Gates and Warren Buffet, have made a similar argument and have created foundations to donate much of their wealth to charity, other billionaires simply seek to make more and pass on their wealth to their family. While Oxfam may be proposing various tax remedies to reduce inequality, such as closing tax havens around the world, reversing the trend towards more regressive taxation, a limits to bonuses and the amount people can earn as a multiple of the earnings of the lowest paid, limits to capital accumulation, and increased investment in free public services and safety nets for people out of work or ill, those are not policies that the U.S. or other governments are willing to endorse. That's because in the most unequal countries, governments won't be willing to "risk angering their wealthiest citizens in order to improve life for the poorest." But then that response evokes the risk of growing social unrest that could lead to revolution, as more previously middle class but now poor individuals join with the already poor feel they have less and less to lose and so are willing to resist more.

Still another consequence of the march to increasing inequality is a reduced mobility between classes, thereby undermining the American dream of equal opportunity based on the potential for rising to the top based on hard work and a bit of luck.[66]

The Growing Poverty in America

The figures on poverty in America in the face of huge accumulations of wealth paint a bleak picture of life for the growing class of poor in America today. While the superrich and highly paid professionals and their kids have access to the latest high-tech gadgets from an exploding high-tech industry, the poor are left out of the equation, akin to the struggling peasants and artisans of medieval times. For example, citing newly released census figures, Salvatore Barbones reports the following "More than 46 Million Americans Still in Poverty," posted on Inequality.org.[67]

According to the U.S. Census Bureau, in figures released September 10, 2019, 11.8% of the U.S. population, more than 38 million Americans, live in poverty, below a poverty line set in 1969, when the poverty rate was only 12.1%. More than 16% of all children live in poverty.

Turned into dollars, the 1.65 million households with 3.5 million children suffering in extreme poverty with incomes of less than 12% of the poverty-line income are living at $2.00 or less per person per day, as described in an article by Gilbert Mercier. The two key factors reducing the social safety nets were the Clinton administration's welfare reform of 1996 which ended the only cash entitlement program for poor families with children and replaced it with a program that provides only time-limited cash assistance, along with a requirement that able-bodied recipients have to quickly rejoin the work-force. But then, due to the Great Recession, the growing number of unemployed and desperate were left on their own. As Mercier describes his take on the situation:

> Wealth inequality … in the U.S … has never been as great as it is today … This concentration of wealth, or share of it owned by the wealthiest one percent, rose sharply … to peak at about 40% of the total wealth right before the crash of 1929 and onset of the Great Depression. Thereafter, wealth inequality gradually decreased until the late 1970s, but it began to increase again in the 1980s. For example, between 1983 and 1989, the share of wealth held by the wealthiest one percent grew from 33 to about 38 percent. The most pronounced increase in US wealth inequality occurred

between 2001 and 2007 when the wealthiest one percent managed to take a phenomenal 43 percent of the country's total wealth. In 2013, only seven percent of the wealth is left to the bottom 80 percent. The middle class have become poor, and the poor are now destitute.[68]

A Portrait of the Super-Poor

So where are the superpoor? According to a Brookings news report,[69] described in a Guardian article: "US Poverty: Where Are the Super Poor?", about 6.7% or 20.5 million Americans are the poorest of the poor, who are those at less than half of the 46.2 million people below the poverty line. In 2010, the poorest poor individuals earned $5570 or less, while a family of four scraped by on $11,157 or less. This 6.7% in the super poor category is the highest in the 35 years the Census Bureau has maintained such records beginning in 1975. In turn, these super poor tend to be concentrated in certain geographical areas – the highest concentration since 1990, due to high unemployment and rising energy costs. More specifically, these concentrations include the following:

- Following the 1990s economic boom, the proportion of poor people in large metropolitan areas jumped from 11.2% in 2000 to 15.1% in 2010.
- Extreme poverty is especially prevalent in the industrial Midwest, including Detroit and Akron, Ohio, because of a decline in manufacturing, and the growth in high-poverty areas is especially high in the new Sun Belt metro areas, including Las Vegas and Cape Coral Florida, after the housing market collapsed, reducing home values and construction jobs.
- While blacks and Latinos make up the largest group in the extreme-poverty neighbors, between 2005 and 2009, the residents were more likely to be white, reflecting the spread of poverty throughout the U.S. population.[70]

The Reasons for the Growth of Inequality and Poverty

A key reason for the spread of poverty is not just high unemployment, but low wages for those who do have work, especially for African American and Hispanic-American workers out of more than 34 million Americans living in poverty, according to the U.S. Census Bureau.[71] This number represents about 10.5% of the U.S. population in 2019. While this rate decreased to the lowest level since the estimates were first published in 1959, it is expected to increase substantially in 2020 and 2021 due to the pandemic resulting in millions of claims for unemployment averaging about 8-9 million a week, according to the U.S. Department of Labor[72] and the increase in homelessness in major cities across America.

Low wages for millions of workers has contributed to poverty too for decades. As described by David Coates, the typical Walmart employee earns $8.81 an hour and grosses an annual income of under $16,000, which is "well below the poverty level for a family of three – and Walmart is currently America's largest employer." Moreover, he points out that at least 1.65 million households survive on less than $2 a day "subsistence-level incomes", and the Pew Research Center reported that nearly a quarter of the Americans they recently polled said "they had trouble putting food on the table over the past year." Besides the low wages, the poor and their children are affected by the distributional rules, such as the compensation packages, taxation, property rights, and inheritance rules that "disproportionately favor the rich," in contrast to other industrial economies that have more egalitarian distribution systems.[73]

Another key reason for the rise of poverty along with the increasing income for the superrich is the policies of the U.S. government, which favor of the super elite, because that's what the super-elite want, as pointed out by Barry Ritholz, an economic journalist and financial strategist. The tax breaks under the Trump administration have only continued this trend noted by Ritholz in his 2013 blog:

- According to a report by the non-partisan Congressional Research Service in 2012, the U.S. income distribution is among the most unequal of all major industrialized countries and it has been experiencing the greatest increases in the various measures of income, including average household income before taxes and share of income after taxes compared to 1979.
- The richest Americans captured 121% of all income gains during the first years of the recovery between 2009-2011, according to research by Emmanuel Saez, an economics professor at the University of California at Berkeley. So the result was they became 11.2% richer while the bottom 99% became .4% poorer.[74]
- Inequality in America is now not only worse than in Gilded Age America, but worse than in modern Egypt, Tunisia, or Yemen, many small republics in Latin America, and twice as bad as in ancient Rome which was built on slave labor.
- While it might appear that new consumption boom has contributed to the revival of the economy, the overall retail statistics are misleading, since there has been a mini-boom in upper-end consumption, while the retail chains catering to the lower and middle income consumer have declined. For example, sales at luxury and high end retailers, such as Tiffany, Saks, Ralph Lauren, Nordstrom, Michael Kors, and Coach, increased 30% after inflation during the five year period from 2007 to 2012, while the discounters and mid-market department store chains, such as Wal-Mart, Target, Sears, J.C. Penney, Kohl's and Macy's, experienced a decline of 3% in sales from $405 billion in 2007 to $392 in 2012.[75]

Another report on poverty in America: "21 Statistics About the Explosive Growth of Poverty in America that Everyone Should Know" presents an even more daunting picture beyond those stats already described, and again, these findings of poverty continue today. Some of the disturbing statistics presented in this report are these:

- According to the U.S. Census Bureau, approximately one out of every six Americans are living in poverty, and more than 146 million Americans are either "poor" or "low income."
- Approximately 20% of all children are living in poverty, and 57% of them are living in "low income" or impoverished homes. Over 2.8 children are living on $2 a day or less; an increase of 130 percent since 1996.
- About 40% of all unemployed workers in America have been out of work for at least half a year, and one out of every four workers has a job paying $10 an hour or less.
- More than 100 million Americans are enrolled in at least one welfare program run by the federal government, excluding Social Security or Medicare.
- An all-time record of nearly 48 million Americans – one in six Americans — are on food stamps, in contrast to the 1970s, when only about one out of 50 in the 1970s.[76]

The Effects of Government Policies and Financial Institutions Controlled by the Rich

In turn, the reason for this growing divergence of rich and poor today is because of government policies which allow wealth to be concentrated in the hands of what has become an oligarchy in America.

According to Barry Ritholtz, one key reason is the big banks "literally own the Federal Reserve" and the Washington, D.C. politicians. Numerous top economic officials and researchers, including two International Monetary Fund (IMF) officials, the head of the Federal Reserve Bank of Kansas City, and Moody's chief economist have said that the U.S. is controlled by an "oligarchy" or "oligopoly" and the big banks and giant financial institutions are key participants in that oligarchy, which is why the government saved the big banks at taxpayer expense.

All of the monetary and economy policies have helped the wealthiest individuals while penalizing everyone else. An example of this is "the biggest transfer of wealth in history, as the giant banks have handed their toxic debts from fraudulent activities to the countries and their people." A result of this transfer due to the bank rescue plans has been a "massive redistribution of wealth to the bank shareholders and their top executives," according to David Stockman, the former White House budget director under Ronald Reagan. His view is that monetary policy has become "an engine of reverse Robin Hood redistribution ... by creating opportunities ... for speculative gain in the Wall Street casino."[77]

Still another economist, Joseph Stiglitz, a professor at Columbia University, a Nobel prize winner for Economic Sciences in 2001, and author of the 2012 book *The Price of Inequality*, has pointed to the use of money to influence government policy to benefit those with money. Through what economists called "rent-seeking", these policies are designed to produce income not from creating wealth but from "grabbing a larger share of the wealth that would otherwise have been produced without their effort," such as by selling services and products above market prices or obtaining the government tolerance of monopoly power.

In effect, the wealthy have the power which enables them to acquire even more wealth. As Stiglitz further states:

Wealth begets power, which begets more wealth ... Virtually all U.S. senators, and most of the representatives in the House, are members of the top 1 percent when they arrive, are kept in office by money from the top 1 percent, and know that if they serve the top 1 percent well they will be rewarded by the top 1 percent when they leave office. By and large, the key executive-branch policymakers on trade and economic policy also come from the top 1 percent.[78]

Yet another reason for the shaping of money to favor the rich, as Ritholtz has pointed out in his blog, is that the financial industry spends hundreds of millions on campaign donations and lobbying for each election to maintain the subsidy to the banks by the public. Moreover, as the banks have grown increasingly large over the last few years, there is a sense that they are too big to fail, thereby providing supports for the banks from the government treasury.

A further reason for wealth concentration is that the government is prosecuting almost no financial criminals, with a few rare exceptions. Thus, the financial manipulators feel they can readily line their pockets at taxpayer expense.

Then, too, the Fed's focus on boosting the stock market has benefitted the wealthy, because "stock market gains go disproportionately to the wealthiest 10% of Americans, who own more than 80 percent of outstanding stock." As reported by Bob Pisani in an August 27, 2020 Trader Talk article, the top 1% owned nearly 52% of the stocks, while the top 10% owned 88%. The bottom 50% owned only 12% of the stocks.[79]

This is a continuation of a pattern noted by Professor G. William Domhoff, a professor of sociology at the University of California at Santa Cruz. As he describes in an article on "Wealth, Income, and Power," as of 2007, the bottom 50% of the U.S. population owned only one-half of one percent of all stocks, bonds and mutual funds, compared to 51% owned by the top 1%, a divergence that has only increased since 2007, while the richest 10% own 98.5% of all financial securities. As he explains:

> The top 10% have 80% to 90% of stocks, bonds, trust funds, and business equity, and over 75% of non-home real estate. Since financial wealth is what counts as far as the control of income-producing assets, we can say that just 10% of the people own the United States of America.[80]

Another government policy favoring the rich to the detriment of everyone else is the way taxes on capital gains and dividends are figured. As described Thomas L. Hungerford of the Economic Institute the changes meant that the wealthy benefitted from lower tax rates on investment income, causing their wealth to grow faster.[81] The tax code now strongly favors capital gains, increases in the value of assets such as stocks and real estate, over ordinary income. Not only is the capital gains tax rate far below the top tax rate on ordinary income, but taxpayers can delay paying taxes until they realize their capital gains (usually when they sell assets).[82]

The Role of Unemployment and Low Wages

Changing employment patterns have contributed to the growing inequality divide as well. The three factors here are unemployment, underemployment, and low wages, and government policies have contributed to the declining economic fortunes of the middle and lower classes, a pattern that continues today beyond those described in a blog on poverty written over a decade ago.

- According to Ritholz's blog on poverty, while economists claim a recovery in June 2009 following the deep 18-month Great Recession (although the date of this recovery is much disputed), economists at Northwestern University found the that 88% of the growth in real national income was reflected in corporate profits; while wage and salaries only amount to 1% of that growth, an unusually tiny share of the growth in national income during this recovery.
- According to John William's Shadow Government Statistics, the number of workers who gave up and dropped out of the labor force has mushroomed since 2009, which is much higher than the official labor force statistics. A key reason is they have been discouraged in finding jobs.
- The earning power of the middle and lower classes has declined, since most newly created jobs have been low wage jobs, primarily in the leisure and hospitality, health care and social assistance, and retail trade fields, as pointed out in a September 7, 2012 article by Tyler Durbin: "Where the Jobs Are: Low Wage Sectors Add the Most Jobs in the Past Year."
- According to Ritholz, unemployment at of July 2011 was around 9.1%, which is higher than it was after the previous three recessions in the U.S. when the average was about 6.8%. A key factor contributing to U.S. unemployment is the

trend for corporations to hire overseas. For example, in 2010, according to the Economic Policy Institute, a think tank based in Washington, DC, American companies created 1.4 million jobs overseas, compared with less than 1 million in the U.S. In turn, the U.S. government policy contributed to this unemployment, low-wage situation for U.S. workers by encouraging American companies to move their facilities, resources, and payments abroad, because these companies pay less taxes there. Some big taxes actually have a negative tax rate, which means they not only pay no taxes, but get a tax refund, encouraging further expansion overseas to the detriment of American workers.

- Other factors contributing to the lower income for most Americans were higher gas and food prices.
  - The contrast with the increase in pay for high end jobs couldn't be more striking. For example, according to a New Times Study conducted by Equilar, an executive compensation data firm based in Redwood City, California, the median pay for top executives at 200 big companies in 2010 was $10.8 million, representing a 23% gain from 2009. Moreover, many executives benefits by receiving stock options in 2008 and 2009, at a time when the stock market was way down, so now that the market has recovered from its decline due to the financial crisis, "many executives are sitting on windfall profits," while cash bonuses for the highest-paid CEOs are "at three times prerecession levels."
  - It's a pattern that has increased even more in the last decade. As a report by the Economic Policy Institute noted, the CEO compensation grew 940% since 1978 while worker compensation rose only 12% during this time. As a result, the average pay of CEOs at the top 350 firms in 2018 was $17.2 million, with stock options making up a large part of their pay package. As a result, the typical CEO compensation level relative to the compensation

of a typical worker is about 278 to 1. In turn, this increase in CEO and executive compensation compared to the lower growth of income for ordinary workers has led to an even economic gap between the highest earners and the bottom 90%.[83]

Summing Up

In short, as this statistical and economic portrait of the distribution of wealth in the United States had shown, there is a massive divide between the very wealthy and the rest of America, which is growing wider due to a variety of factors, from the power of the banks and superwealthy to influence government policy to their benefit to the problems of unemployment, underemployment, jobs going overseas, and an increase in lower-wage jobs. A failure to prosecute the financial criminals has contributed to the problem, too, because of the influence of the super elite.

So increasingly, the US has been turning into an oligarchy, with many parallels to the social structure and conditions of the Middle Ages, and just as the detrimental conditions for the poor and downtrodden in medieval times contributed to a growing resistance, so it is today. Anger is rising, reflected in groups like the Occupier movements. As noted in a Huffington Post article by Robert Reich, "Why the Anger," posted on August 12, 2013, "by almost every measure, Americans are angrier today. They're more contemptuous of almost every major institution – government, business, and the media. They're more convinced the nation is on the wrong track. And they are far more polarized." The reason is because "the middle class has been losing ground" for the last three and half decades, so that the median wage of male workers is lower than in 1980, adjusted for inflation. At the same time, income, wealth, and power have become more concentrated at the top than in 90 years, going back to the 1920s, just before the stock market crash.[84]

The result of this inequality, Reich predicts, is deeply dangerous, for many Americans "have come to believe the deck is stacked against them," such as the Tea Party and Occupier movements which both began with the bailouts of Wall Street, when both concluded that "big government and big finance had plotted against the rest of us." While the Tea Party blamed government, the Occupiers blamed Wall Street.

Today, these movements, and others spawned by their anger against inequality have emerged, and this anger is likely to continue as long as the conditions of inequality remain, since, according to Reich, political scientists have discovered "a high correlation between inequality and political divisiveness."

The following chapters will explore these themes in more depth and will point out the parallels between the social structure, society, and culture that have emerged from this Great Divide today and that in the Middle Ages. For despite the high tech transformations, globalization of society, and new products, services, and occupations in modern society, the underlying social dynamics and divisiveness have led to a new Middle Ages. This recreates many of the same social patterns that existed in medieval times and could contribute to the emergence of a modern revolution in America, much like the spirit of revolution has spread through the Middle East, Africa, and other countries where a wealthy powerful elite is increasingly divided by its wealth and power from the vast majority of society. The potential for revolt increase the more this divide occurs. I is only a question of when and where someone will light the match.

Chapter 3: Creating the Kingdoms

During the Middle Ages, there were numerous competing feudal territories, ruled by lords who sought more and more power and engaged in continual wars to gain dominance. Gradually, kings like Alfred in England won their battles through strategic alliances until they created their kingdoms. This process is much like the battles for dominance in different industries that have created huge economic kingdoms, ruled by modern day kings like Larry Ellison of Oracle, who sponsors races for the rich like America's Cup.

The same kind of process happens in any industry or territory, where an old order is disrupted by new technologies or more efficient ways of doing things. Gradually, the old is undermined by the new, and in the period of transformation, a kind of vacuum is created in which new participants become both competitors and collaborators in the struggle to replace the old with the new. So, for a time there is a free-for-all in which many new contenders battle it out to gain dominance. Then, over time, as the old withers away, a period of consolidation follows, whereby the strongest of the new contenders gain dominance and other wannabes fall by the wayside, until one, two, or sometimes three, of the very strongest remain as the new kings.

It is a process that played out in American history during the Gold Rush, which gave birth to some of the big retail giants who served the miners like Levi Strauss; during the age of the Robber Barons, which gave rise to the big industrial magnates like Carnegie; and in the last few decades, with the rise of the big software, Internet, and social media giants, like Microsoft, Apple, Google, and Facebook.

Likewise, the process occurred during the Middle Ages in the emergence of the new kingdoms in the vacuum which became Western Europe and Britain, after the decline and fall of the Roman Empire from about 350 to 1050 A.D., give or take several decades according to different historians. What is the modern-day equivalent to the fallen Roman Empire? As I read about the struggles of the battles of the tribal chieftains to ward off barbarians from outside their borders, defeat nearby competing tribes, and overcome betrayals from competitors within their community, I thought about how the U.S. Post Office has been gradually declining in the past few decades and possibly nearing its end, as the cost of postage goes up and service declines to different neighborhoods. While the U.S. Post Office has been spun off to become a self-sustaining profitable private enterprise, it increasingly cannot be, because the essence of this service has been taken over by new technologies and services. For example, more and more people don't send letters; they send emails or text messages, people increasingly don't use the post office to ship packages; they send manuscripts, books, and photos by PDFs and JPGs via email or post files on Dropbox. Then, too, people increasingly use private services like UPS or FedEx for physical deliveries or they communicate in real time via online or crowd-based webinars, such as GotoWebinar and GotoMeeting. So more and more, the United States Postal Service is becoming an anachronism in response to new technologies and competing providers of communications. And recently, the alternative providers with new communication platforms have been battling out among themselves to determine the new e-mail, online, and social media kings.

These company battles call forth parallels with the battles for territory, wealth, and power in medieval times. At time the Church was one of the participants in these medieval battles, as well as a force that created alliances to help favored tribal chieftains in their quest for power, much like the modern media has undergone its own struggles to gain or retain power, while providing a media platform to cover the battles of the communication providers.

Meanwhile, today as then, one outcome of these struggles is the concentration of wealth for the winners, while those who lose out or depend on the combatants for jobs and income are increasingly part of the lower-income masses. And today, as in the Middle Ages, the income of those who lose out is on the decline.

In what ways do these modern-day struggles hark back to the battles for dominance in the early Middle Ages? Here's a brief introduction to medieval history and a discussion of many of these modern-day battles to illustrate the parallels.

The End of the Roman Empire

The ending of the Roman Empire provided the foundation on which the New Middle Ages was to rise. As described by Brian Tierney, author of *Western Europe in the Middle Ages: 300-1475*, at the height of its power, the Empire stretched from the Mediterranean to north Britain, the coast of North Africa, and through what is now Asia Minor, Syria, Palestine, and Egypt. While its center of power and wealth was concentrated around the Mediterranean Sea, its power stretched outward through its well-organized administrative apparatus, which provided governors and military support to its outer provinces. In turn, the leaders of the newly conquered people commonly took on the ways of the Romans, and in each area, local citizens eagerly participated in this local administration, while the support for the empire's power and wealth came from its legions of Roman warriors and the taxes and food supplies provided by the lowly farmers.[85]

However, beginning in the middle of the 4th century, the Huns, Goths, Vandals, Burgundians, and other tribes invaded and plundered throughout the empire, undermining the established authority and institutions. At the same time, as Tierney notes, the Empire was weakened by other de-establishing forces, such as the loss of popular support due to the spread of Christianity and various economic problems. Among them were a barely sufficient agricultural output, a growing unemployed population in the cities, the large armies needed to defend the frontiers, and the extensive bureaucracy to maintain the central government.

As the Roman emperors tried to deal with these problems, such as by upping taxes on the small farmers which the wealthy upper classes had to collect for the emperors, the middle class was gradually undermined and society became more stratified as the richest aristocracy grew richer. This system then contributed to undermining the economy of the towns and the ruralization of society, as many wealthy Romans retreated to their rural estates, further decentralizing society. Eventually, two major tribes successfully settled in the lands they carved out of the Roman Empire – the Franks, who settled in Gaul, and the Angles and Saxons, who sailed to Britain.

Many of the conditions that contributed to the rotting away of the Roman system might be compared to the upheavals and transformation in the U.S. economy today that portend worse times ahead. For example, just as the Roman treasury was undermined by the cost of maintaining its hold on the frontier provinces, so the U.S. debt has been increased by paying for foreign wars, such as the troops sent to Iraq, Afghanistan, and elsewhere in the Middle East. Likewise, just as the Roman system contributed to a growing inequality between the wealthy aristocrats and other groups, so in the U.S., inequality has increased since the 1970s. Now new government policies are contributing to the disparity, such as legislation to slash funds for food for the poor and continued attacks on the Affordable Care Act, which was designed to expand health care to all. So just as these social and economic changes contributed to undermining the strength of the Roman Empire, so they could imperil the U.S. economy today.

Preparing the Way for Something New

As the Roman Empire was dying, small seeds and structural changes were occurring that would prepare the way for something new, much in the way that companies like Microsoft, Apple, Twitter, Facebook, and Google started small, gradually building a growing network of users, as old ways of communicating by letters and land-line phones declined, and people sought new ways to connect with others and find information online.

One of these seeds that was to sprout into a mighty tree was Christianity, which began as a small sect within Judaism, when Jesus began to teach at a time when Herod, backed by Rome, ruled Palestine. According to the Gospels, when Jesus was around 30, he was baptized by John the Baptist, had a vision in which the Holy Spirit of God spoke to him, and began preach his message of hope, love, and caring for the poor. Also, he shared his vision that a new age was at hand, the kingdom of heaven, which would be brought to the world through a Messiah, God's son. But after his popular-ity grew with the help of his 12 apostles who traveled with him, spreading the word, the Romans authorities, led by Pontius Pilate, the Roman procurator, had him crucified around 30 A.D. While his death might have been the end of the movement, his message was spread by Peter, one of the first 12 apostles, and then Paul of Tarsus, whose vision of Jesus on the road to Damascus, led him to spread the word.[86]

So gradually over the next few centuries, the new faith spread, with a particular appeal to the poor and powerless, because it offered a message of hope, meaning, and purpose, and it helped followers feel a sense of belonging. At first, people met in small groups in private homes with little distinction among rank among members. But during the first century of its existence, a hierarchy emerged, which helped to standardize the beliefs and practices of the faith. At the top was the bishop, "the highest authority on ques-tions of faith and practice," and under him the priests and deacons administered the everyday operations of the church. Over the next century, this hierarchy expanded even further, so that the church government was structured much like the Roman administration. Each priest led a parish, and coordinating these parishes, was a bishop who oversaw a diocese or region containing several parishes.

Each city usually had its own bishop and several priests, and several of these dioceses were combined to create a province, governed by an archbishop.

Though initially the bishops of Rome, Constantinople, Antioch, and Alexandria were equal in status, later the bishop of Rome claimed the supreme title of pope. In effect, the Church, like Roman state, had parallels with the modern corporation with its branches or franchises radiating out under the leadership of a CEO and its top officials, such as the CIO and CFO.

For a time, the Roman state saw the Church's growing popularity and power as a threat to the Roman state at a time when the empire was under other destabilizing pressures. As a result, Rome conducted numerous crackdowns to squelch the Christians, including unleashing lions on many Christian leaders which only turned them into martyrs. Yet, as the Roman Empire was increasingly crumbling, the Christian faith continued to grow, until by the beginning of the 4th century, most people in the empire had become Christians.

Finally, as Tierney points out, as if recognizing the inevitable, and perhaps to help strengthen the fading empire, the pagan Emperor Constantine officially granted tolerance to the Christian religion, as well as other religions in the empire, with the Edict of Milan, issued in 313. For a time, Christianity continued to exist alongside the pagan state religion and other regions. Then, in 395, the Emperor Theodosius the Great made Christianity the Empire's official religion, which gave it special privileges, including the right to receive legacies, and its clergy no long had to pay taxes. Meanwhile, the Christian church went through its own process of formalizing its doctrine, such as by overcoming the Arian controversy based on the notion that only God was eternal, while Christ was the highest of God's creatures. But at the Council of Nicea in 325, the Arian doctrine was forever condemned and Jesus Christ, as the son of God, was declared as "of one substance with the Father," a doctrine that later became incorporated into the Nicene Creed, which set the stage for the further growth of the Christian Church.

Over the next century, the Christian church underwent its own internal upheavals that paralleled the battles between the barbarian tribes for primacy, which were fought out by the bishops of Constantinople, Alexandria, Jerusalem, Antioch, and Rome. Eventually, Leo's argument that he was the heir of St. Peter and that Christ had appointed Peter to head the entire universal church won out. As Leo asserted, since all the other apostles were subordinate to Peter, all the bishops were subordinate to the popes who succeeded to the office of supreme government which Peter received from Christ. This doctrine in turn contributed to the separate development of the Christian Church in the West after the empire collapsed, while the eastern Roman Empire followed a separate path where both the structure of the empire and the orthodox Christian church remained strong.

However, these efforts to provide a religious support did little to stave off the end of the Empire, given the many other pressures undermining it, such as the Germanic incursions, declining tax base, growing independence of the provinces, and reduced military support. Rather, these developments helped to build up the Christian Church as an institution, which could help fill the vacuum after the Empire's collapse, during which the tribal chieftains fought among themselves and began to build up and consolidate their own kingdom over the next centuries in this political vacuum created by the empire's collapse. At the same time, Christian church in the West went through its own period of decentralization and reorganization, with the rise of the monastic movement, which created a network of monasteries throughout the Empire, at the very time that the Empire was weakening.

As Tierney describes it, the tradition of monasticism began early in the development of the church, when individuals pursued their own path to live lonely, isolated, and frugal lives of prayer and contemplation. But then in the early fourth century, St. Anthony and St. Pachomius in Egypt began organizing communities of monks, who were required to obey their superiors who were subject to the local bishop. After St. Basil expanded on the ideas of Pachomius to create a community of monks based on the ideal of living a "simple, chaste, frugal life devote to hard work" with others, St. Athanasius brought the ideal of monasticism to the Western church in 340. Eventually, St. Benedict established the form of monastic life that came to dominate in the West in the beginning of the sixth century, based on the ideals of poverty, chastity, and obedience, under the direction of an abbot, who was elected by the monks but had the full authority over them.

Given the chaos of the declining Roman authority and the continual battles for territory and power by the tribal groups left in the vacuum when Rome collapsed, it would seem the monasteries played a stabilizing role over the next centuries. As Tierney points out: "Each abbey was endowed with enough land to support the monastic community. The Benedictine abbey was thus as self-sufficient, autonomous community capable of sustaining its own orderly life however much the surrounding society might disintegrate." [87] Thus, as the Benedictine Rule spread to hundreds of monasteries around Western Europe which were self-sustaining communities with their own resources, internal government, and ordered everyday routine, these monasteries were strong units of Christian culture that helped the Church as it grew to play an increasingly powerful role as new leaders emerged to unify different kingdoms in Western Europe and Britain.

The Battle to Create the New World Order

In 476 A.D., the Roman Empire finally came to an end, after a brief reign by a figurehead king, Romulus Augustus, the 13-year old son of Orestes, who had become a supreme commander of the Western Roman army. Within a few weeks of his coronation, Odoacer, a barbarian mercenary, led a revolt by the army, which killed Orestes and captured Romulus, who had to abdicate. Though Odoacer advised the then Eastern Roman Emperor Zeno that he would rule the West in Zeno's name, in effect that was the end of the Western Roman Empire, which no longer was ruled by an emperor.[88] Instead, the empire was divided into many smaller kingdoms and the barbarian tribes engaged in a series of battles to gain power and territory.

Meanwhile, the Eastern Roman Empire thrived as the Byzantium Empire that had been established in 330 A.D. by the Emperor Constantine. Conditions there could not have been more different from the chaos in the West, since the Eastern Empire was led by an all-powerful emperor, who was considered the highest being of all since he was the closest person to God. As such, he lived a life of luxury and ceremony, surrounded by many courtiers and advisers, and he was considered superior to the Patriarch of Constantinople, who was a counterpart to the pope in the East.

However, until the time of the Crusades beginning in the 11th century, when warriors from the West went to convert the infidels in the East, the two worlds largely developed separate histories. So the focus here will be on developments in the remains of the Western Roman Empire which gave rise to the new nations in Europe and Britain during the Middle Ages, and on the parallels with the New Middle Ages of today in America.

In a sense, this upheaval in the West after the collapse of the Roman Empire might be comparable to the collapse of any old technology, system, or service that is replaced by the new, since the vacuum unleashes a wave of new innovation and creativity. Or consider the process much like the opening of any new territory or frontier, such as in the beginnings of the Gold Rush or the discovery of 3D printing. There is a surge of new settlers, inventors, and investors, all trying to gain dominance based on employing the new methods or a new model for making money that will lead to gaining power and success, until one to a few participants achieve dominance.

The high-tech world has experienced this process again and again. Some examples from the beginning days of the tech revolution include the battle between VHS and Betamax to be the new video standard, which VHS ultimately won because of better marketing and promotion, though Betamax was the better format. Another big struggle was over being the platform for sharing information and creating an online community, which Facebook ultimately won after other contenders like MySpace and Friendster dropped out. Still other example are the struggle to be the online source of auctions, where EBay ultimately prevailed; and the fight over dating rights, which have been claimed by eHarmony and OKCupid and later by still other dating sites: Elite Singles, Zoosk, Match.com, and several others. Similarly, a struggle occurred when live-streaming video first became possible, initially made popular by Periscope, after which competition followed, and now the major players include Instagram, TikTok, and Snapchat, with Instagram, now owned by Facebook,

The twists and turns along the way were quite different for the modern day contenders, since the life and death fight in the online and media world is an economic one. By contrast, the battle for territory, wealth, and power during medieval times often turned into a life and death struggle, marked by betrayals, attempted assassination, brutal torture, and murder. But the process of winnowing through the chaff to come up with one or a small number of winners is similar.

During the early Middle Ages, the first phase of this struggle went on from about 476 to 800, which is sometimes called the Dark Ages by historians, since it was especially tumultuous and the medieval church was still in its formative stages. But then this struggle continued on through the next centuries until about 1050, when the Norman king from France began a new dynasty in England after the 1066 Battle of Hastings, and the European kings launched the Crusades to exert their power over the infidels in the lands that had once been part of the Eastern Roman Empire.

The next chapter will focus on these struggles to carve out the new medieval kingdoms in these two periods to 1050 in the vacuum left by the fall of Rome.

CHAPTER 4: MAINTAINING AND EXPANDING THE KINGDOMS

Much like in any start-up, the role of the first leader is to create the vision and bring others together around that, and commonly this first leader is powerful and charismatic, which leads others to want to follow. Then, the next phase involves consolidating the success, delivering on that vision, and expanding to new territories and defeating competitors. Often a struggle to maintain one's power ensues, as followers compete among themselves to stay in charge or remain part of the powerful faction seeking to maintain control, while outside competitors look for a weakness they can exploit to take over, if the newly powerful organization or community created by the first leader falters.

This process is much like what happened in the early Middle Ages, after the first kings acquired and consolidated large territories in the regions that would become France, Spain, Germany, and England. This chapter focuses on these developments from about 500 to 850, though the dates vary somewhat, before the now Christian kingdoms in Europe and England launched the Crusades to battle what was now perceived as a threat to their kingdoms – the growing power of the Muslims and the Byzantium Empire in the East. Meanwhile, as these battles erupted among the royal courts and knights of the times, the wealthy nobility increasingly gained wealth and power, while further oppressing the peasants and workmen who formed the lower classes, as they helped the kings and nobles further enrich themselves and fight their wars. The use of taxes and land confiscations helped to contribute to this growing inequality of rich and poor back then, paralleling the same processes occurring today.

The Battle Begins: Creating New Kingdoms in the Early Middle Ages

Initially, the collapse of the Western Roman Empire left a land ripe for looting. While some of the Gallo-Roman aristocrats remained on their manors, they were soon replaced or taken over by the Germanic tribes who were led by a warrior elite. With the major controlling institutions of the Roman Empire gone, the farmers and peasants who remained were now at the mercy of waves of marauding barbarian tribes and their warrior elite, who sought to conquer the lands and fought against other barrier tribes to keep their own territories or conquer others. A modern parallel might be a city suddenly undergoing bankruptcy like Detroit or a city devastated by a flood or earthquake. Many modern-day movies, such as Elysium and World War Z, portray this situation where a decimated city is now vulnerable to gangs of predators.

In Europe, the first major figure to emerge was Clovis, the ruler of the early Frankish kingdom. Like the head of a Mafia family seeking to control an ever-widening territory, from 481 to 511, Clovis gained power and easily engaged in treason and murder, if that was what it took to make his conquests. When it suited his purpose, Clovis used Christianity to help him in battle. Then, once he established his power in the territory that became modern France, the invasions ended, and he allied himself closely with the Christian Church at Rome, so the two great powers of the new emerging Europe – France and the papacy – grew in tandem. You might think of Clovis as much like a modern-day don of the Mafia.

According to Tierney, Clovis gained his pinnacle position as a result of several strategic moves, much like a modern CEO might strategically plan a campaign to raise his own position within a company and in relationship to competing companies, such as when Steve Jobs masterfully maneuvered his way back into Apple by driving out John Sculley, the CEO who he had brought into the company though later Sculley betrayed Jobs and forced him out. Likewise, Clovis managed to strategically take over the kingdom of Syragrius in 486, making him one of the most powerful Germanic rulers in the West."[89] Then, he launched a career of conquest and successfully used his alliance with the Church and the murder of other Frankish kings to make sure that he and his descendants would rule over the Franks. It was the beginning of the Merovingian dynasty.

Likewise, Steve Jobs' firm rule over Apple killed off any competition, and his insistence that Apple have a closed platform led to the committed loyalty of its developers and customers. This approach, along with great products, helped to build the Apple kingdom, much like Clovis created a unified Frankish kingdom that became the foundation for modern France.

In England, a similar battle to unify the country went on after the Roman troops were pulled out by the emperor in 410. After that a number of smaller kingdoms faced numerous external challenges from different tribes, including the Picts, Saxons, Angles. But gradually, the Anglo-Saxon invaders won over more and more territory, until by around 600 A.D., most of England was controlled by the Anglo-Saxons, who carved England into seven major kingdoms – East Anglia, Mercia, Wessex, Northumbria, Kent, Essex and Sussex, each with its own king. Over the next two hundred years, until Alfred the Great unified nearly all of Anglo-Saxon England under his rule, these kings, who were like tribal chieftains, fought incessantly with each other, as one, and then another, gained power over the others, only to lose it again, when other kings fought back.

Once a unified kingdom was finally created, the struggle continued to maintain and expand it. It was the kind of battle for dominance that has occurred again and again not only over territory, but whenever there is an innovation or change in an established system, opening the door for new systems and social structures. As in medieval times, the same sort of struggle to take charge has been played out in the modern-day economy, leading eventually to the vast corporate empires of giants like Apple, Microsoft, Google, Facebook, and Oracle. And now that fight has shifted to building mobile empires, controlling the cloud, and winning the 3-D printing wars. Though the battle is focused on controlling markets and sales rather than land and people, the process is much the same as the battles between chieftains and their tribes to control increasingly large territories to create new kingdoms. In both cases, as kingdoms become larger and larger, the inequality between the victors and loyal followers and the rest of the population grows, then as now.

From Clovis to the Carolingians and Capets in France

While Clovis had the power to keep the Frankish empire together, his death in 511 led to a power struggle, after the kingdom was divided among his four sons, according to the custom in Germany, before the principle of primogeniture led to keeping the kingdom together under a single heir. A modern equivalent might be the early death of Steve Jobs at Apple or the departure of Bill Gates at Microsoft to pursue more philanthropic ventures, leading to a leadership vacuum in the company they left behind. This transition also paved the way for other companies to begin invading the Apple and Microsoft kingdoms with new platforms and products, now that the visionary powerful leaders had left their kingdoms in the hands of less bold successors, more skilled in management and monitoring the bottom line, than willing to take the risk of developing new breakthrough products as Jobs and Gates had done in establishing their kingdoms.

From Bureaucrats to Kings

These intercine battles led to a weakening of the Merovingians rulers, and perhaps that is why the heirs of Clovis' sons were considered "politically feeble" and "incompetent as rulers," so they became known as the "do-nothing" kings. As a result, while they battled among themselves for power during the seventh and eighth centuries, the local nobles took control of many of the lands and ignored most of the king's commands. In response, the weakened Merovingian kings turned over more and more of the kingdom's operations to officials called "Mayors of the Palace," who originally gained their position of nobility by caring for the kings' horses and stables. In effect, they were the power behind the throne, which set the stage for one family, which passed the position from father to son, to become the new king, with a little help from the mounted army and the Church. As Tierney describes it:

> "During the last century of the Merovingian age, the power of the kings declined greatly. The last of Clovis' dynasty who ruled vigorously and effectively was Dagobert (the son of Clothar II) who ruled from 629-638. After his death, the kingdoms of Austrasia and Neustria were again divided, and in the middle years of the seventh century, their rulers were often at war with one another... The last Merovingian kings were remarkably short-lived. Under a succession of minor kings, real power passed to the chief officer of the king's household, called the *mayor of the palace*, who exercised the royal authority on their behalf."[90]

As such, these palace mayors were both gatekeepers and decision makers, since the mayor-controlled access to the king, so anyone wanting to speak to the king had to first gain the mayor's approval. In addition, the mayor was the key decision maker on the kingdom's policy and procedures, so that all of the counts, called *comites*, who were in charge of administrating different organizational units in the kingdom, such as finance, justice, and the army, had to report to the mayor. Meanwhile, as the mayor gained behind the throne power, so did the counts. As Batchelor notes:

> "Over time the comites grew into incredibly powerful and influential people. The Merovingian kings could make as many decisions as they liked, but they were unable to implement any of them without the comites."[91]

In effect, the mayors and the counts were like the heads of any major bureaucratic organization today, from a city or county government to a large corporation, where the official mayor or CEO is like a figurehead, who energizes and inspires the people. But a behind the scenes organization is running the show.

Yet, while these mayors of the palace may have held the reins of power behind the scenes, they were very strategic in determining when to act, much like a modern day board member planning a coup to take over a company, but waiting to line up sufficient disaffection against those in charge to support for the change, such as when Steve Jobs engineered a coup against John Sculley, then the CEO of Apple, to prepare the way for his triumphant return to restore Apple to its glory days. In the Merovingian case, the mayors of the palace simply waited until it was strategic to act. Their strategy was to leave the Merovingian king on the throne, because the Germans had long believed in the sacredness of the king, and the mayors felt usurping the king could result in a failure to gain the support of the people.

The Rise of a New Empire

Finally, as described by many historians, after another round of palace intrigue, in 714, one of the mayors, Pepin of Heristal, paved the way for his illegitimate son Charles Martel, who was born to one of his concubines. Though only another mayor of the palace, Martel, called Charles "the Hammer" because of his great success as a general, became the Duke of the Franks and consolidated the Frankish state's political power over new territories through a series of foreign wars. Once in power, he decided who would receive church and political offices, and he sowed the seeds of feudalism, since he gave out land titles to pay his warriors in return for their loyalty. With the help of the Church, he also provided funds for an army of nobles on horseback who could attack with swords, in addition to the traditional Frankish army of men on foot, which was the beginning of the armies of mounted knights. Also, he used personal oaths of loyalty to bind these men to him – an approach that became the basis of feudalism in the 9th century.

After his death in 741 and still another succession battle, his grandson Charles became the new emperor and was known as Charles the Great or Charlemagne, since he proved a ruthless effective leader who created the vast Carolingian Empire. It stretched from the Iberian Peninsula that became modern day Spain and Portugal to the border of present-day Germany. Charlemagne achieved this success by uniting all the small Germanic kingdoms through over 50 military campaigns in which he took over one territory after another. His actions might be compared to the actions of the leader of Google, Yahoo, or Facebook buying out many competitors with their greater access to funds and making those companies part of their territory or abolishing them to get rid of the competition.

Then, to help solidify his position as king, Charlemagne created a close alliance with the Church, and eventually was crowned by Pope Leo in Rome as the "Holy Roman Emperor" in 800. This close alliance with the Church might be compared to the way modern day corporate titans have gained increased influence through a close relationship with the media that keeps them in the news or as guests on major talk shows to demonstrate their power to the masses. Charlemagne's success as a leader also has parallels with the success stories of many modern day corporate and political leaders who have risen to the top. Throughout his reign, he was almost constantly at war, and his successes led him to constantly win more territory, expand his kingdom, and defend it from internal and external attack.

As emperor over the next years until he died in 814, Charlemagne created some systems which helped to create a strong, solid empire, ruled by the king and nobility, with the support of the Church. Among other things, he created a new economic system and bureaucracy to run the empire, rather the local dukes and barons who swore their allegiance to him. Much like the systems which structure a corporation or any large organization today, he divided the empire into many divisions – in this case 300 districts or counties, headed by a count in charge of secular business, a duke handling military affairs, and a bishop dealing with spiritual matters. To maintain control, Charlemagne closely monitored all the administrators with the help of inspectors and punished anyone who did not follow orders. A modern-day parallel might be any of the huge, modern corporations that have become multi-nationals and are divided into different operational units in charge of different functions, such as finance and operations, under a CFO and CIO (much like a medieval count), product development, acquisitions, and international expansion (much like the duties of a duke), and human relations and public relations (equivalent to the role of the bishop).

Additionally, Charlemagne was instrumental in setting up a system of education, in part to train the clergy, as well as teach the seven liberal arts and theology to both the nobles and the poor. While the main school was the Palace School in Aachen, many other schools were opened in cathedrals and monasteries, and the new emphasis on learning led to a renaissance of scholarship and learning. The influx of artists, writers, and intellectuals to Aachen was a little like the influx of artists, writers, and high-tech entrepreneurs to the Silicon Valley and San Francisco today, which has contributed to the gentrification of many neighborhoods and to the growing inequality of rich and poor. So, it was in the Middle Ages, and so it is now.

Similarly, in England, as in Scotland and Wales, the kings of the seven major kingdoms established by around 600 A.D. – East Anglia, Mercia, Wessex, Northumbria, Kent, Essex, and Sussex, battled it out for primacy, until Alfred the Great unified most of Anglo-Saxon England under his rule. These continual battles for dominance and control among the royalty and nobility within each kingdom and against other kingdoms and invading forces went on in a kind of parallel universe to the mundane, hard-scrabble lives of the peasants.

As on the Continent, the Christian Church was a unifying force. Once the Anglo-Saxons gained control over most of England, the

Catholic Church, sought to bring the English back into the fold through a series of missions beginning in 597 through the seventh century, until all of Anglo-Saxon England was converted, despite some remnants of pagan worship, mainly in the countryside.

Finally, after 200 years of the English kings of the individual kingdoms fighting each other and the Viking invaders to stay in power, the king of Wessex, Alfred, later known as Alfred the Great, was able to defeat the Vikings. He then became England's first true king as the "King of the Anglo-Saxons," though initially his kingdom only included southern England, since the Danes were still ensconced in the north. Over the next 150 years, this newly solidified England prospered under Alfred and the kings that followed, until 1066, when the Norman invaders defeated the Danes at the Battle of Hastings and united all of England under King William. Perhaps a reason for the success of Alfred and his successors is that the English created created an effectively organized administration, in which the old Anglo-Saxon territories were organized under the lords of the manors, and the newly occupied Danish lands, that had been a land of independent farmers, were organized into new counties. Another reason for success is that the king owned estates all over England, and every Englishman was required to fight if able to do so, if summoned by the king. So the king, as needed, could call on a retinue of loyal subjects to fight on his behalf.

Again, these long battles between kingdoms and against invaders in England as on the Continent might be comparable to the fights today between the many start-ups seeking to create kingdoms in new industry. After a time, the strongest consolidate and expand after a shake-out eliminates the weakest, while many of the defeated who are still standing make the best possible deal to be acquired by the corporate raiders, who are the modern day Vikings of today.

Comparing the Creation and Expansion of the Kingdoms to the High-Tech Wars of Today

Intriguingly, these wars between and within these medieval kingdoms at a time of rampant inequality between royalty, the nobility, and the church leadership on the one hand and the peasants and independent farmers on the other echoes the same kind of battles today. The earlier battles when the medieval kingdoms first emerged might be parallel to the early days of the high-tech revolution. But this later period of maintaining and expanding the kingdoms might be compared to the battles between the major players that emerged from the earlier struggles for dominance to gain even more control over the marketplace. Then, too, the internal struggles over succession from one king to another might be comparable to the internal struggle in companies where the original founders left due to various reasons – from illness (as in the case of Jobs at Apple), to disappointing results (in the case of HP), or the founder's decision to become a philanthropist and contribute to worthy causes (in the case of Microsoft). Another parallel is that these battles for physical territory in the Middle Ages and market territory today occurred on the level of a ruling class with money and power, while the rest of the society – the masses or 99% if you will – were more like bystanders. In the one case, they were peasants living on the land and paying taxes, in the other they were part of the mass market, paying for products offered through the vast new tech empires.

These kinds of internal and external battles for dominance in the kingdom and in competition against competitors occurred again and again. Take what happened in Twitter. As described in a new book called *Hatching Twitter* by Nick Bilton,[92] Twitter was co-founded by Noah Glass, who had previously founded a pod-casting start-up called Odeo in 2005. Then, he teamed up with a then friend, Jack Dorsey, who helped create the original Twitter concept, along with Evan "Ev Williams," a farm boy from Nebraska, who had successfully created Blogger and sold it to Google, and Christopher "Biz" Stone, who played the diplomat in the struggle for control over the company that ensued as it grew. In brief, what happened is that Glass came up with the Twitter name in 2006 and was the influential co-founder in the early days when he helped Dorsey build upon a general idea of what to do. The two then presented the concept to Evan Williams, who had the money to help develop the project. Then, as Twitter grew, the four founders fought for money, influence, publicity, and control, and they turned on each other, much like the brothers fought for control over a kingdom after a king died and split up the kingdom among his sons, as was the custom, before primogeniture helped to keep the kingdom in a single line of succession.

Initially, Glass took the lead, though soon Dorsey became the lead engineer and subsequently sought to oust Glass, telling Williams that "Glass had to go or he would," whereupon Williams told Glass that he needed to quit or be fired. Ironically, that night, Glass met with Dorsey at a local bar, where he told Dorsey of William's ultimatum, and Dorsey acted like he didn't know anything and blamed Williams. Then, two weeks later, Glass was forced out of the company, and Dorsey soon became the new CEO. But after that, Dorsey was forced out himself, and Williams became the CEO, but not for long, since Dorsey acted to get Williams replaced as CEO, whereupon Dick Costolo, and 50something former comedian, took over the reins of power.[93]

The saga reads like a palace struggle among the nobility or the heirs of a medieval king who died to become the next king, though after the new king was determined, the fate of the loser might have been banishment to a distant plot of land and manor, an assignment to a military campaign to fight for the king, a referral to become a monk at a monastery, or even death as a traitor or pretender to the throne. But in the modern-day battles, the losers in one struggle often got back on their feet and could start again. For example, after he left Twitter, Dorsey co-founded the payments company Square, and he still owns a 4.9% stake in Twitter worth about $400-500 million, while Williams still holds 12% of the company's stock and is likely to become a billionaire when the company has its first IPO. Only Glass ended up getting the short end of the stick, since he was reduced to earning the wages of one of the many IT workers who are more like the peasants and farmers or yesteryear.

The same kind of battle for control of the empire can be seen in the early days of Facebook when Zuckerberg first developed the project at Harvard. Supposedly, the two Winklevoss twins claimed they created Facebook and Zuckerberg stole the idea from them, although their battle played out in the courtroom, after Facebook had become a $50 billion dollar business. As the story goes, the Winklevoss brothers and their classmate Divya Narenda conceived of a social network for Harvard students called the HarvardConnection to help the students better connect with each other. After their first programmer left, they hired another programmer to work on the site. Then, they claimed that after they hired Mark Zuckerberg to work on developing source code for their website, he took their idea and developed it into Facebook. So in 2004, they filed a lawsuit against him, which eventually was settled in 2008, with a $65 million legal settlement in which they got $20 million in cash and $45 million worth of Facebook shares. The suit was even featured in a major Hollywood movie – *The Social Network* – featuring rising star Jesse Eisenberg in the role of Mark Zuckerberg. However, in 2010, they sued again, claiming they were given fewer shares than they were entitled to in the settlement, on the grounds the shares which they thought were worth $35,000 were actually worth much more.[94] But the judge thought they were sophisticated enough to understand the deal they had settled for, and even had the help of five lawyers from two firms to advise them so "Too bad." Then, of course, Zuckerberg turned Facebook into the multi-billion-dollar business it has become today with over 2.6 billion users as of March 2020 according to Facebook's quarterly earnings report.[95]

While the battle may have played out in the court, it has some parallels to Alfred's struggle to claim the English throne and maintain it in the face of competing nobles and attacking Danes. After succeeding in fending off the competitors, he skillfully created an organizational structure throughout the country to solidify his holdings, bind the nobles and others to the English state, and keep his treasury strong so he – and later his successors – could maintain and extend his power, much like Zuckerberg has expanded the Facebook platform by opening it up to other developers of apps, such as game producers like Zynga, and advertisers for numerous products and services.

A similar power struggle that played out in Apple between Steve Jobs and John Sculley reads like the battle between brothers or potential heirs to the throne to eliminate a rival. As the story goes, Steve Jobs co-founded Apple with his friend Steve Wozniak in a garage in the Silicon Valley, California in 1976, much like carving out a small manor or estate in the Middle Ages. Over the next years, the estate grew, as Apple gained more success in the marketplace and went public in 1981. But two years later, after Apple gained entry to the Fortune 500, Jobs decided it was time to bring in a CEO with marketing experience and he recruited John Sculley, then the head of Pepsi-Cola, to take over the position and persuaded him to do so by presenting this as an opportunity the change the world, not just sell sugared water. Meanwhile, Jobs took on the role of Apple's chief visionary and took charge of the team developing the Macintosh computer. As such, Jobs had his own team and building to create the product, and he even flew a pirate flag over the building, expressing his independence from the rest of the company. [96] It was a little like carving out a sub-province, much like there were a few independent domains among the seven main provinces of England, before Alfred united most of the provinces in southern England and his successors united them all.

However, after the Mac was introduced in 1984, it had disappointing sales, despite its rave reviews, which led to a conflicted relationship with John Sculley. Making matters worse, Sculley got complaints from Mac team members about Jobs being overly demanding, since he drove people too hard to realize his vision. One might compare him to a noble leading his knights into battle and forcing them to fight even harder than usual to win the battle for the whole kingdom of which the Mac team was still a part.

Then the conflict with Sculley turned into a power struggle, where Sculley appealed to the Apple board, which sided with him and removed Jobs from overseeing the Macintosh group in the spring of 1985. As a result, Jobs lost his responsibilities and Sculley assigned him to an office, which Jobs referred to as Siberia – a move Jobs considered a betrayal, as he told his closest friends and colleagues. A medieval comparison might be where one heir to the throne gains the support of the nobles to be the king and sends his rival to a small estate or even to an enforced captivity in a small part of the palace.

Well, just like banished royals or noble seeking the throne could not accept remaining out of power and so launched a rebellion, that's what Steve Jobs did. After a few months in a kind of purgatory, Jobs left Apple in the summer of 1985 and spent the next few months deciding what to do. Essentially, like a medieval royal or noble, he turned to a trusted associate and decided to launch a new challenge to the Apple kingdom by starting a new computer company, NeXT, as well as the Pixer Animation Studio. Meanwhile, Apple under Sculley began struggling over the next decade, while NeXT and especially Pixar became more successful, so in 1986, Apple acquired NeXT, which returned Jobs to the company, and the following year, he became Apple's CEO and Sculley was out. The rest is history. Over the next two decades, under Jobs' leadership, Apple became more and more successful, as it further developed an expanded the McIntosh line and expanded into other product lines, such as the iPhone and iPad, and created a network of Apple stores to sell its products. In turn, its growing penetration of new markets and increasing profits might be compared to the expansion of a medieval kingdom like Wessex to Southern England and then to the rest of the island, including modern-day Scotland and Wales. And creating the Apple stores and network of distributors was like setting up a system of shires and counties under a network of administrators to rule their subjects, while sending their receipts and profits to the king.

Meanwhile, besides the internal battles to control the kingdom in the Middle Ages and in modern times, the continual battles to expand these kingdoms continued today as in medieval times, as these high-tech companies battled against others with competing products and software platforms. Over the last four decades, since the computer-software battles began in the mid-1970s, numerous contenders have fallen by the wayside with names long forgotten, much like many smaller provinces, counties, and shires were conquered by larger and more successful kingdoms leading to the emergence of kingdoms in England and France by the middle of the 11th century.

Even now these battles for primacy continue between the major high-tech companies that have emerged. An article in Computerword: "Battle of the Media Ecosystems: Amazon, Apple, Google, and Microsoft," reflects these modern-day battles between the largest kingdoms, while smaller kingdoms, such as Pinterest, The Chive, Digg, Reddit, and many others, engage in their own battles to appeal to a growing and often fickle audience to replace or diminish the larger kingdoms with their own. As the authors note, the battles between Amazon, Apple, Google, and Microsoft and their competitors have led them to become vast ecosystems that include hardware, software, and online services and now they are battling among themselves for primacy. Participating in these battles is much like the kingdoms of the Middle Ages continued to battle among themselves and occasionally formed alliances in an ever-shifting fight to best their rivals. As the article authors: Michael deAgonia, Preston Gralla, and JR Raphael observe: [97]

> Once upon a time, tech behemoths such as Microsoft and Apple battled to persuade businesses and consumers to purchase their computers, mobile devices, or software packages...Those days seem so quaint now...Today, the battle is on a much larger scale. It is a war between vast ecosystems made up of hardware, software and online services, not just individual pieces of hardware and software. Purchase an iPhone, for example, and you're buying into the entire Apple ecosystem, including operating systems, apps, add-ons, music, movies, books and more. The big money isn't in your single purchase, but in encouraging you to purchase only products and services that interact with each other – and your wallet...Each offers a vast array of products – and

because there are strong differences between them, each offers distinct advantages and disadvantages, depending on which part of the ecosystem you're examining... But one way or another, they're all locked in a death match."

Much the same could be said of the medieval kingdoms. Until the 800s, when Charlemagne united the provinces of France and Alfred the Great united the counties and shires of southern England into a larger kingdom, these territories were composed of smaller units battling it out. Under the weakened kings following Charlemagne, the smaller units returned to fighting again, before they were once more united after more internal conflicts led to the emergence of the Capetian kings.

Then as now the process is the same, though the details might differ. Throughout nature, there is this conflict for domination, control, and power. It's the age old struggle out of which the victor gains the spoils, and the loser usually ends up banished or dead, though sometimes as in the Apple case, the loser creates another army to start again and eventually topple the older regime.

Though the specifics vary, in the Middle Ages the internal and external battles for control led to a few key kingdoms that were to control the destiny of historical development, along with the help of the Christian Church, that emerged as a powerful kingdom, too. And each kingdom was supported by an administrative and military network to administer the kingdom, collect taxes, and maintain control Now a similar process has played itself out to create the major computer, software, and media empires of today, with the support of the traditional and social media that has helped to spread and reinforce the message, much like the Christian Church once did in days of yore.

Subsequently, as described in the next chapter, this pattern continued through the High Middle Ages of the 11th through 15th centuries, as the major kingdoms continued to reinforce and increase their power over the territories they already controlled and the new ones they added to the mix.

CHAPTER 5: BATTLING FOR CONTROL

While the 10th century may have ended with most of England consolidated under Alfred and his descendants and most of France united under the Capetian kings, any peace didn't last long. Rather, the history of the late or high Middle Ages from about 1000 or 1050 to 1300 or 1450, based on how various historians divide up these events, is one of constant war and struggle. There are battles within each kingdom over succession and repeated efforts to fight off internal rebellions by nobles to break away from the kingdom or take it over, as well as a few peasant rebellions over feeling exploited and oppressed. There are battles with the church over who is really in charge, the king, or the pope. There are battles from invasions from the north by the Vikings or Northmen, and from the east from different groups of Muslims and Asian nomads. There are Crusades and other battles to convert or conquer other lands. And often new technologies, such as the stirrup and longbow, contribute to the ability to win a battle, even in the face of daunting odds.

Meanwhile, the peasants, who are variously small independent farmers or serfs reduced to being slaves on the land, are like a perpetually exploited underclass. A few may sometimes escape their position by serving well in the military and gaining entry to the ranks of nobility as knights or dukes. But for most peasants, it is a hard life of eking out a living, while being taxed heavily by the king and nobles for the money to contribute to their luxury lifestyle and frequent wars.

A comparison with the world of today might be with the battles over succession in the big high-tech companies who have largely vanquished the competition and now dominate, the efforts of these companies to encroach on each other's territory, their expansion into other spaces, such as mobile apps and the cloud, the eruption of big patent wars, and the use of the media to build an audience and gain their support in the various wars for control, much like the kings often turned to the church to sanction and support their efforts.

This chapter explores these developments and comparisons in the late Middle Ages.

Fending Off the Invaders

These outside invaders might be comparable to modern-day corporate raiders. Through the 8th to 10th century, the new kingdoms not only had to beat off internal challenges from warring nobles and claimants to the throne after a king died, but the threat of external invaders seeking plunder or territory. Primarily these invaders were Vikings, once part of the Germanic tribes, who settled in the lands that would become Denmark, Sweden, and Norway, who began raiding England in the 8th century and created settlements on the coast of what became Ireland. For a time the Vikings even had a treaty with Alfred the Great, who united southern England, to control northeastern England, so they would stop their raiding, resulting in the creation of the Danelaw kingdom, though they continued to fight the Anglo-Saxons for the next 100 years, and in the 11th century, a Danish king, Canute, even ascended to the English throne.[98]

Still other Viking troops conducted raids in the lands that became modern France. Besides attacking farms, they robbed and destroyed many of the monasteries and convents, until one of the Carolingian kings, Charles the Simple, gave a group of Vikings some land, later called Normandy, if their chief Rollo was baptized as a Christian and agreed to defend France against attacks by other Vikings.

Finally, after the 11th century, the Viking raids ended with the Vikings absorbed into the rest of the Christian culture.

In turn, these continual raids by the different groups of invaders might be compared to the actions of the patent trolls of today – the lawyers who use legal attacks against already established company kingdoms, like Google, to extract monetary settlements. Like the invaders of yore, they engage in their incursions to come away with booty or perhaps carve out a little territory, though in the end, the kingdom has the power to ultimately defeat them. For example, in an article "Patent Trolls Are Damaging Our Economy" in the San Francisco Chronicle, Caleb Garling writes that Rockstar Consortium, a patent-trolling company representing Microsoft, Apple, Blackberry, Ericsson, and Sony brought a lawsuit against Google claiming it infringed on six search-related patents. The suit was launched after Rockstar bought up the patents for a bankrupt Canadian company Nortel for $4.5 billion in 2011, presumably to gird itself with the patent armor to do battle, like the knights of yore. Still another patent troll, Intellectual Ventures, headed by Microsoft's former chief technology officer, Nathan Myhrvold, has acquired over 70,000 patents. Meanwhile, Google has armed itself to defend itself against such lawsuits, such as by paying $12.5 billion for Motorola Mobility and its patents.

The battles of the patent lawsuits sound a little like the medieval kingdoms preparing to call up soldiers and arm them with the latest military equipment, while the invaders have equipped themselves with the most powerful ships and weapons, too. But even if the invaded kingdoms win, the battles still take a terrible toll on the people in their kingdoms, much like the patent trolls have not only chipped away at the power of the attacked companies but generally damaged the economy today. As Darling observes:

> These sorts of lawsuits, especially with patent trolls, are harming our economy in ways that are often hard to see … Companies have to spend millions of dollars (and uncountable hours) on lawyers, and potentially billions in damages. That cost does find its way into the prices of products and services, one way or another … Those are dollars

that could be directed toward research and development – making your gadgets more usable and intelligent."[99]

An example is the Oracle v. Google battle which has gone on for nine years, beginning in 2012 over whether Oracle could claim a copyright on Java APIs, and if it could, whether Google infringed on these copyrights. While one judge, Judge William Alsup of the Northern District of California, ruled in May 2012 that APIs are not subject to copyright, Oracle appealed, and a Federal Circuit Court reversed that decision in May 2014. But then in October 2014, Google filed a petition asking the U.S. Supreme Court to review the Federal Circuit Court's decision. Then, after the Supreme Court denied Google's petition and the case was kicked back to the district court, a jury agreed that Google's use of the API was far use. But that wasn't the end of it, since after further lower court rulings, Google again filed a petition in January 2019 asking the Supreme court to review the earlier decisions. Now after hearing oral arguments in October 2020, a Supreme Court decision is expected to be issued in June 2021 in the case, now known as Google v. Oracle.[100]

And this is just one of many high-tech battles over who owns or has rights to use the latest digital and other technologies.

The Development of Castles and Feudalism to Defend and Protect the Realm

During the Middle Ages, a common way of fighting back was getting out the troops to defeat and kill the raiders. But these battles also led to other developments that helped to structure medieval society, such as building fortified castles or creating a feudal system based on the loyalty of vassals who would fight for their lord, when required to do so, usually to repel invaders – though later the system was used to recruit soldiers to attack enemies and claim new lands, such as during the Crusades. While modern companies might use legal countermeasures to avoid hostile takeovers and corporate raiders, such as poison pills, permitting shareholders to buy discounted shares if a shareholder buys a certain percentage of shares, golden parachutes, giving employees extra compensation if their employment is terminated, and increases in debt levels of the corporate balance sheet, in the Middle Ages, kings and nobles used on the ground practices to fortify the land or gain more fighters.

One approach was building increasingly stronger castles and more of them as a barrier to invaders, a little like homeowners today may take steps to fortify or "harden" their target to ward off home invasion robberies, such as by putting in grills on the doors or setting up an alarm system connected to a home protection service or the local police. In the Middle Ages, the strategy for protection was using towers, strong walls, and a moat of water with a drawbridge to pull up when invaders threatened.

For example, soon after King William's Norman Conquest in 1066, castles began springing up all over England, including the White Tower of London, built in 1078. Aside from transforming English society by introducing French culture, eliminating the old Anglo-Saxon aristocracy by giving their lands to Norman or Norman-friendly nobles, reducing the power of the earls so they could control at most one shire, transferring control of local areas to local towns and boroughs under an organized central administration, and creating the Domesday book in 1086 to assess the total wealth and tax due to the king, William created a network of castles to maintain his authority of all of England. Plus, he used these castles to gain more territory by building castles in his enemy's territory.

Typically, these castles were built on top of a large hill in a structure which included the living quarters, stables, and well for water, surrounded by a deep moat filled with water to keep out enemies, since the moat could only be crossed by a drawbridge lowered from the gatehouse in the inner wall of the castle. Eventually, turrets were added to the tops of these walls, so guards could observe the surrounding area and if attacked, they could use clubs and arrows and drop rocks, boiling water, and other objects on the attackers below. Besides being used for protection or to claim new territory, the castle was a social and political center for the rich and powerful. The kings and lords lived with their entourage in the largest tower called a keep, and they conducted all their business and administration there. Plus, they received visitors and held feasts and revels in the castle.

Intriguingly, some of the big corporate headquarters today are a little like these keeps with surrounding walls and gates to admit only those with employee, security badges, and day passes, and keep others out. For example, the Google campus, featured in the film *The Internship* with Owen Wilson and Vince Vaughn, has that kind of modern-day castle look, and all sorts of amenities, from a gym to a cafeteria to a gift shop, are the main building is like a medieval keep, so a Google employee never needs to go outside during the day. Or at least that was the case until the pandemic, leading many companies, including Google, to permit or require most workers to work at home. In fact, Google one of the first big companies to advise employees in early March 2020 that they could work from home to prevent the spread of COVID-19. Then in July, the company announced it was extending its global voluntary work from home option until June 30, 2021.[101] So much like the Black Death in the Middle Ages led many people to withdraw to their homes for fear of being infected, many workers have found ways to stay at home to work, though today, the new technologies have helped to make that possible by enabling people to work together by phone, email, and online connection and communication technologies.

Besides the fortified castle, the other big strategy for defending against invaders as well as conquering new territories was the feudal pyramid. Apart from being an economic system that helped support the king and nobility through the taxes the peasants paid in money or produce, this feudal pyramid created a system of obligation, so that the vassals who were indebted to the lord above them had to provide military service. This meant they were not only required to fight to protect their lord and his lands when under attack, but they could be called upon to fight to acquire territory, such as when called upon in the 11th century to go on Crusades.

A modern-day equivalent might be the hierarchy of employees at one of the big high-tech companies or any big corporation, who are required to help the company fight back when attacked by corporate raiders or by companies with competing products, such as through ad campaigns, so consumers will buy their products, not those of a competitor. Or the company might plan a campaign to introduce a new product or technology and position its employees to provide customer support to appeal to consumers and thwart any attacks on that product by rivals.

In any case, the feudal system evolved from its early beginnings in the 8th century to become an elaborate system with a hierarchy of titles and a complicated arrangement of the privileges and responsibilities of lords and their vassals. For example, the nobles who gained titles to the land became known as dukes, counts, viscounts, and barons, depending on the size of their estate and power, and they had complete control over the people, houses, and villages within their territory. Those with enough power could even initiate war, mint coins, collect taxes, and enter alliances with other nobles, though they still had to offer military assistance to their own lord when asked to do so. Plus, the vassal had other financial obligations, such as paying to ransom a lord who was captured by an enemy or contributing to a lord's marriage ceremony or a daughter's wedding feast. Then, when a vassal died, he passed the rights and obligations associated with his own fief on to his children. Yet, the big caveat was that the land belonged to the higher lord, so if he was displeased with his vassal's service, he could always opt to take away that right to the land.[102]

Over the years, the development of a fighting force to ward off invaders and gain more territories for the king developed into the system of knights, who had their own hierarchy and code of honor. It became a very prestigious, yet dangerous calling, that could enable a successful warrior to advance into or through the ranks of nobles to a higher position with more land, money, and prestige, although the downside was that the fighting was very dangerous, as were the entertainments that featured fighting between knights.

A comparison might be with some of the physical combat sports of today, most notably boxing and football. While well-known athletes, such as Mike Tyson, Floyd Mayweather, Jr., and Manny Pacquiao in boxing and Tom Brady, Patrick Mahomes, and Russell Wilson in football, can rise through their performance to make millions, they also can suffer from precipitous losses after their careers end and they end up broke; or they may suffer from major injuries from concussions to broken bones, resulting in disabilities in later life or an early death. But while the money and fame last, the top athletes can savor the fruits of living among the ranks of the rich and famous with big mansions and large retinues of employees, much like their medieval counterparts.

But to return to the system in the Middle Ages, after the invasions of the eighth through the tenth centuries ended, the nobles began to fight among themselves about land, rights, and kinship, and in time, the art of fighting became a recreational activity. Moreover, this sport became increasingly dangerous and deadly, as the knights gained more and more sophisticated weaponry and armor. A comparison might be with the upping of the danger level in some sports today, such as turning regulation boxing matches with rounds, padded gloves, and rules about where to hit, such as no hitting below the belt, into extreme fighting, where opponents fight with bare fists until they achieve a knockdown. On TV, some of these battles have become even more elaborate and dangerous, such as on shows like, *The Challenge* and the *Ultimate Fighting Championship*. Typically, these shows attract lower-income and working-class individuals hoping to score big with a win; but most go home without much if any prize money and nursing any injuries sustained in the battle.

In the early Middle Ages, the warriors wore only padded leather coats and metal helmets, but once the stirrup spread and warriors faced each other on horseback using spears or arrows, they needed more protection. At first, this protection took the form of small iron rings sewn into the padding. Then these rings were linked together to form chain mail for more protection, and after a while, the knights wore armor, and in time, their horses wore armor, too. The shields also became heavier, and a design called a "coat of arms' was used to identify the knight, and in time was handed down from one generation to another.

But much like the technology wars of today, where one improved technology replaces another and updates continually improve a software program, so it was with the knights. At one time, a knight on a horse could effectively win against a man on foot, and a knight with the heavier armor and larger shield commonly had an advantage against a knight with lighter armor. Then, the crossbow, originally invented in China, could be used by a foot soldier to fire a metal bolt to pierce the knight's armor, though it was limited by its awkwardness and short range. After that the longbow was developed to fight back against the knights. Though it couldn't penetrate the armor like the crossbow, when a large number of arrows were fired, the longbow could upset the horses and disperse a charge or cause a knight to fall off his horse. Then, once they were on the ground, the knights were disadvantaged by their heavy armor, which made it hard to move around and fight.

These knights not only fought in real wars to defend or conquer territory. They also engaged in mock battles, which were called jousts between two competing knights, and they participated in tournaments, in which teams of knights fought against each other. While these jousts and tournaments served as a kind of training ground for the real thing, much like the modern military may engage in war games where each team uses guns with paint pellets or blanks to defeat the other in a simulated battle, they also became a sport for the upper classes who observed the battle. While the goal of a joust was for one knight to unhorse the other as they sped towards each other with their lances raised, many knights were actually injured or killed[103]. But then that was the risk of the sport, and to the victor went the honors, much like in a modern-day boxing match, where the gloved hand of the winner is raised in victory, and the loser is led out of the ring and down a path of shame through the crowds, often bleeding profusely or lying on a gurney. And afterwards, it can take days or weeks for a boxer to heal, and some even end up dead, much like the losing knights in these jousts, though even the winners may get injuries, such as piercings from a lance – and after winning one match, until they retire, they have to fight again and face the same risks of being injured or killed.

Deciding What to Do About Succession

Besides fending off invaders, creating large fortress castles, administering the feudal system to defend and protect the realm, and trying to expand through crusades and internal conversions, the other big development to consolidate the kingdom and retain control was determining the succession. This way, the present king could set up an orderly transfer of power to his chosen successor, usually a first-born son. At one time, the usual practice was to divide up the land between the king's children, but this was possible at a time when the kingdom was expanding through conquest and opening up previously undeveloped lands. But by the 11th century, most of the land in England and Europe was spoken for, so the most sensible approach was to pass on the rule of the kingdom to a single successor. Ideally the choice was the king's first son if he had heirs, and if, the succession would usually go to a close relative, such as a brother or male cousin, and in some cases, a wife, sister, or female cousin, if there was no likely male heir. Then, once the expected next king was selected, the current ruler's other children were given other roles, such as a male child being groomed for the priesthood or a female child being promised for a future auspicious marriage with a high-placed noble or ruler of another kingdom to create a solid alliance. In effect, these royal or noble children were moved around like pieces on a chessboard to create a strong network of alliances to protect not only the current king but set the stage for the rule by another successful king, though sometimes overly eager prospective heirs jumped the gun by working out plots to kill off the current king, so they could step into that role and put their own loyal courtiers in place to protect their rule.

This need for an orderly succession existed whether the current ruler died from a natural death of illness or old age, was killed in battle, or in some cases was assassinated. In turn, the selection of a successor triggered an ongoing series of battle for the throne throughout the Middle Ages, especially after the 11ᵗʰ century when the kingdoms were consolidated, since previously the succession was determined by strength on the battlefield and there were fewer candidates, and in some cases, any succession battle for a throne was diffused by dividing a kingdom into smaller subkingdoms, each given to a single brother. For example, after Charles Martel died, his kingdom was divided between his three sons and later consolidated under his grandson Charlemagne. This kind of concern for success in the Middle Ages can, in turn, be comparable to the concern for succession in the high-tech giants, like Microsoft, Google, HP, and Apple.

Battles over succession reflect the kind of planning and struggling over succession in some of the high-tech companies that have become modern-day kingdoms. Much like in the Middle Ages, a smooth succession has contributed to a company's continued success, as occurred in Apple and Microsoft, while in other cases, as occurred in HP, a series of executives contributed to a confusion about the direction of the company and the loss of power on the high-tech stage.

For example, in an article on the success of Apple's succession planning, "Behind the Scenes, Apple Planned Jobs' Succession by the Book," Jonathan Barr writes that "succession planning is a mundane by necessary aspect of corporate life. When done well, transitions go smoothly. When neglected, the results can be disastrous."[104] Thus, while both Hewlett-Packard and Yahoo!, now struggling companies, fired their CEOs without a clear succession plan in place, Apple, a supersized success, carefully planned what to do.

A key reason that Apple started early succession planning is because of Steve Jobs' health problems, due to the grim prognosis for pancreatic cancer. While Jobs tried to minimize his health problems by publicly claiming he had a rare but less deadly variant, the concerns about his health increased after the news came out that he had had a liver transplant and because of his continued gaunt appearance in public. Meanwhile, Tim Cook was groomed to succeed Jobs, in keeping with the Wharton's business school recommendation that companies should "promote from within and take time to introduce a soon-to-be leader to stakeholders." In Cook's case, he first joined Apple in 1998 and slowly climbed the corporate ladder, serving in various capacities, including being Executive Vice President of Worldwide Sales and Operations from 2002 to 2005 and then taking charge of Macintosh hardware engineering and becoming the company's Chief Operating Officer, responsible for all company's sales and operations. In fact, according to Barr, Jobs showed he had selected Cook as the heir apparent in 2009, when they appeared at a press event and Cook wore Jobs' trademark outfit of black shirt with jeans.

Additionally, besides selecting, and grooming Cook to take over, Apple set up a management school using Steve Jobs' views about management to help prepare the company to continue its success under future leaders. As explained in an article by Josh Bersin: "The Real Succession Plan for Steve Jobs: Apple Thinks Different with Apple University," Jobs' style of leadership "created a strong sense of execution and excellence at the company — but will also be hard to replace." However, to counter this succession problem, besides working closely with Cook on the company's supply chain to give Cook a deep understanding of the company's internal operations, Jobs developed a long list of philosophies about management and supported a project to capture the essence of his management philosophies for future generations. To this end, as the Dean of Apple University, a former Yale Business School dean, Joel Podolny, worked on building a leadership curriculum to continue Steve's leadership model after he left the company."[105]

The result was that Tim Cook experienced a great success. Among other things he built on the success of the iPhone, boosting Apple's market value to over $1 trillion in early 2020. Then, he created a new path for growing the company beyond the iPhone.

Among other things it created iCloud storage, App Store Sales, and Apple Music, and it received billions from Google to be the default search engine when a buyer purchases a new Apple product. It has even created a growing wearales business, such as with its AirPods and Apple Watch.[106]

This kind of nurturing of the future leader is much like what happened in a number of instances during the Middle Ages, when the son of a king was groomed for being a future ruler by serving alongside the current king as a junior ruler. Or if he was too young to immediately take command, a future king would be taken under the wing of a regent.

At Microsoft, too, there was a smooth transition when Bill Gates turned over the rein to Steve Ballmer in 2000, and much as in medieval times, Jobs carefully groomed Ballmer for the role of becoming a future king. Initially, Ballmer joined Microsoft in 1980 as Microsoft's 30th employee and the first business manager hired by Gates.[107] He also acquired a stake in the company when Microsoft was incorporated in 1981, so he held an 8% ownership in the company. In effect, he was like a courtier in the royal court of the king of England or France.

Then, much as a king might send off his nobles to represent him on crusades or in negotiations with foreign leaders, Gates appointed Ballmer to head several Microsoft divisions, including operations, operating systems development, and sales and support. Ballmer also acquired various titles along the way, such as being the Executive Vice President of Sales and Support starting in 1992, and later he became the Senior Vice President of Systems Software and the Vice President of Marketing. Then, in 1998, he was promoted to the President of Microsoft, a position he held until February 2001, making him in essence the second in line to the Chairman and CEO. In January 2000, he was named the CEO and put in charge of the company's finances, though Gates stayed on as the Chairman of the Board and remained the company's chief software architect, until he stepped down from that role in 2006, though he remained the Chairman of the Board. So now Ballmer was in effect the new company king, since he had the ability to make major management changes at the company.

His reign, in turn, proved very successful for the company. While during the Middle Ages, success might be measured in terms of lands conquered and territories controlled, in corporate America – as well as in other countries, success is measured in annual revenue and stock prices.[108] As Ashley Vance writes in "Steve Ballmer Reboots" in *Bloomberg BusinessWeek,* under Ballmer's reign as CEO, annual revenues increased from $25 billion to $70 billion, while its net income increased 215% to $23 billion, due to gains from its long established line of Windows and Office products and Ballmer's ability to fight off threats from cheaper competitors, such as Google Docs, Linux, and other open-source operating systems.[109] In effect, Ballmer's battles against such competitors was reminiscent of the way many medieval kings held onto their power by sending their armies off against external and internal threats, such as during the Crusades or Britain's efforts to take lands from France and France's fight to get it back during the 100 Years War.

But in 2013, Microsoft faced succession crisis when Ballmer announced his retirement in a year without a successor in place, leaving a vacuum, as well as a company in trouble, due to declining sales as a result of a slump in the PC market and Microsoft's failure to become a major player in the mushrooming mobile-computer market. Perhaps a medieval equivalent might be the devastation caused by the Black Death, as it swept through England and Europe in the mid-14th century, leaving the population decimated and the countries facing revolutions by the peasants soon afterwards – the Jacquerie in France, the Peasant Revolt of 1381 in England. In any case, Ballmer's decision to leave with 12 months' notice and no successor in place was widely described by the business media as a succession crisis. For example, in a *Bloomberg* article, "Ballmer Exit Leaves Microsoft Searching for Hero in Slump," several reporters had this to say:

Chief Executive Office Steve Ballmer's retirement leaves the world's largest software company in a succession crisis amid the worst slump in history for the personal-computer industry it helped create...Ballmer's planned departure follows a management revamp, the company's biggest earnings disappointment in a decade and the fifth-consecutive quarterly drop in PC shipments. Meanwhile, Microsoft remains an outsider in a burgeoning mobile-computing market led by Apple...and Google. [110]

While some authors praised Microsoft for lessening the uncertainty that can accompany a CEO's resignation by announcing it in advance and providing details for interested parties about the coming transition,[111] others pointed to not naming a replacement as a big flaw. For instance, Anne Marie Squeo, writing in a *Forbes* magazine article: "Microsoft's Lack of CEO Succession Plan a Lesson for Other Companies," pointed out that "It's a bad idea to announce someone's retirement. It's equally bad when companies announce a new CEO and then delay the effective date for months. Either scenario results in confusion among employees and paralysis among senior executives about whose approval to get for key decisions."[112]

But later it turned out that Ballmer paved the way for the success of Satya Nadella who became the next CEO, since he placed an early bet on doing business in the cloud which led to the company's great success. For example, when he left in 2013 the company's market cap was only $245, but as of 2018 it was $700 billion. As Eric Jackson explains, Ballmer "was a bridge between the old Microsoft, which was focused on desktop PC software, and the new Microsoft. There'd be no Microsoft Azure cloud or Office 365 without Ballmer's decision to invest in the cloud."[113] Thus, in effect, as in the Middle Ages, when a king died, sometimes due to being killed in a battle, without leaving an heir, there was a period of uncertainty and struggle in trying to choose a new heir. But a good choice could help to carve out a new path to success — both in medieval times and now.

Yet, while success was possible if the new ruler proved up to the task, during the Middle Ages, many of the kings tried to avoid this problem of who would be the successor in two key ways. One was dividing the land between their sons; another was preparing their oldest son to be a successor by selecting him as a co-ruler or appointing a regent to train a young son who wasn't old enough to rule. But in other cases, when the king had no sons or tried to arrange for a succession by marrying a wife from another country, battles broke out between contenders and supporters over who would be the next king, especially in England. There the fight over succession was especially contentious, and a series of dynasties ruled due to winning a succession fight, whereas in France, the Capet kings or their cadet branches ruled the country for over 800 years through the Middle Ages and until the French Revolution in 1848 got rid of the kings.

This problem of not having a clear succession in modern times is shown in the case of Yahoo and Hewlett-Packard, two companies who have struggled with a series of leaders, in part because the company ran into hard times under one leader, didn't adapt to the times, and had trouble finding someone else to take the reins.

For example, in an article on "CEO Succession Planning: What HP Can Learn from IBM, Apple," The Var Guy writes that "Hewlett-Packard – a poster child for poor succession planning – can learn plenty of best practices amid the CEO transitions at IBM and Apple." Whereas both IBM and Apple had a clear plan of passing along the mantle to insiders who worked their way up in the company, HP had a series of CEO hires after Lewis Platt stepped down in 1999, with several leaving under a cloud of controversy. Among them was Carly Fiorina, CEO from 2000-2005, a controversial leader, since she had a background in sales, but paid insufficient attention to manufacturing; Robert P. Wayman, who was just an interim CEO for two months in 2005; until Mark Hurd became CEO from 2006-2010, when he was fired for sexually harassing a former actress who worked for HP as a marketing consultant and submitting inaccurate expense reports of $20,000 to conceal his relationship with the actress.[114] After that, Cathie Lesjak was another interim CEO for three months, followed by Leo Apotheker from November 2010 to

September 2011, and finally Meg Whitman took over in September 2011 after having a great success at PayPal though she stumbled in trying to run for governor of California that year. Why so many CEOs? The problem, according to the VAR Guy, is that since 1999, HP had no internal succession plan, and its Chairman Ray Lane suggested that HP insiders were not yet ready to lead the company. So HP looked outside for its CEOs, much like when the kings in the Middle Ages were too young, so a regent was brought in to rule in their stead, but not always very successfully[115].

Numerous other business writers and commentators have pointed up HP's lack of a succession plan for its difficulties. For example, soon after CEO Mark Hurd left, Dr. John Sullivan commented in an article: "Learn from HP's Errors – A Checklist for Designing an Effective Succession Plan," that "Hewlett-Packard deserves some sort of award for completely blowing it." Among other things, the issues leading up to Hurd's departure came as a complete surprise to the board, and they had no succession plan in place. The results of this situation were devastating to the company, because "within five days of Hurd's separation, HP had lost nearly $11 billion in market value and become the corporate punching bag for reacting stupidly."[116] The medieval equivalent might be a king being killed in battle and the whole army having to retreat, such as when the kings went on Crusades in the Holy Land and their armies sailed back to their country after the king was killed, since they now had no one to lead them in battle.

The departure of Hurd was especially devastating for HP, as noted by several *Wall Street Journal* writers[117], because he suddenly resigned after successfully slashing costs and acquiring other companies, including Electronic Data Systems Corp. and Palm, Inc. the smartphone maker, adding to the HP portfolio of personal computers and printers. Moreover, under his reign, H-P regularly beat Wall Street's earnings expectations, so his departure led to questions about H-Ps strategy and what was to come now that he was gone.

Then H-P faced another crisis after its CEO Leo Apotheker did an incredibly bad job, leading the stock to plunge 47% under his leadership. Also, many Board members didn't like his shift of focus in buying a software maker Autonomy for $10.3 billion, a price considered too high, and in seeking to lessen the company's reliance on its low-margin consumer products, such as printers and computers, that had been the heart of its business and shifting to more profitable servers, software, and network services. Part of the problem was the changing tech landscape with new cloud-based and mobile applications that were challenging H-P's core business, but Apotheker failed to respond to these challenges and provide a better vision for the company. As one banker who helped manage $9.5 billion for the Fiduciary Trust in Boston, including H-P's shares, put it: "They have to go back and redefine what they want to be as a company, go back to the drawing board." [118]

And that's what it did. It shifted away from a business based on large format printers to creating a new market for supplies, such as replacement inks and industrial grade 3-D printing. Plus it developed a strong executive staff working together as a team taking into consideration the priorities of its customers, employees, and investors.[119] In the process, it split into two parts in 2015 — a PC and printer business known as HP Inc., led by Dion Weisler, and an enterprise service business called HPE, led by former HP CEO Meg Whitman, until she left the company in 2015. Then in November 2019, Enrique Lores took over.[120]

So now after stumbling for a time, HP finally found its way under strong leadership, like a medieval kingdom finally finding the right leader after a succession crisis. As of March 2020, it reported revenue of $6.95 billion.[121]

Likewise, Yahoo had its own succession crisis with five different CEO's within as many years. As Paul Strebel commented in an IMD article: "Pitfalls in CEO Succession," it's a problem when you have such a rapid succession of CEOs within a year, because "you get a company that is schizophrenic, like Yahoo that doesn't know whether it is a media or a technology company."[122] The shakeup began when Yahoo founder Jerry Yang was CEO and refused an attractive takeover offer from Microsoft, thinking Yahoo could do better. But Yahoo could not and his rejection of the offer was widely criticized, so he was forced to resign. Then, after the new CEO Carol Bartz was unable to find investment partners to make media acquisitions, an activist investor Daniel Loeb engineered Bartz's firing, after which Scott Thompson became the new CEO in January 2013, after heading up eBay's PayPal division and holding other technology and IT positions. But when Loeb discovered inaccuracies in Thompson's bio for claiming a computer sciences degree from Yale when his degree was in another field, Loeb engineered Thompson's firing[123], and eventually the Board brought in Marissa Mayer to be the CEO and reposition Yahoo as a technology company. But after the company went through turbulent times, she left when Verizon bought Yahoo for $4.48 billion in 2017,[124] a little like one stronger medieval state taking over a weaker one and installing its own ruler for the to take charge of the kingdom.

In sum then, just as in the Middle Ages, a clear line of succession helped to maintain the strength of the company, and success in building the company or kingdom contributed to the power of whoever was CEO or king. Conversely, when the company or kingdom faced hard times, this weakened the power of the CEO or king, and a lack of a clear line of succession further weakened the company or kingdom, due to a great uncertainty and a lack of clear direction.

Chapter 6: The World of Work

Both in medieval times and today, the wealthy had plenty of time for leisure, obtaining their money from passive sources of income such as taxes or produce contributed by those who worked their lands, while the lower and working classes had to put in long hours to make a living. For example, in the Middle Ages, the wealthy got much of their income from crops grown on their lands and taxes on the peasants, while today much of their income comes from stocks, bonds, derivatives, other financial instruments, and running or owning shares in major companies. In fact, much like the medieval royals and nobles, the CEOs, business owners, and top level managers commonly earn huge incomes from capital rather than wages, such as bonuses and stock, in additional to high salaries, resulting in them earning hundreds of times the hourly wage of those working for them. And while they have varied jobs involving extensive wheeling, dealing, and leisure time often combined with business, such a day of golf or hunting, wage earners often have deadly, routine, low-income jobs in manufacturing or retail businesses, such as fast food restaurants and mega-stores with rock-bottom prices.

Thus, in many ways the work and wage disparity of today mirrors conditions in the Middle Ages, especially with the increasing divide between those on top and the struggling masses. This chapter illustrates these differences.

The Division of Classes and Labor in the Middle Ages

During much of the Middle Ages, there were essentially two main classes – the kings and nobles, whose ranks were measured in terms of land ownership, and those who worked the land as vassals, serfs, and slaves, plus some artisans providing craft services, sometimes as a side occupation to working the land. However, in the later Middle Ages, a merchant class grew up made up of traders who bought and sold merchandise and small shopkeepers who established shops in the towns, some of which developed into cities. For a time, these merchants led a precarious life, since they were subject to many dangers on the roads they traveled, especially a potential attack from pirates that roamed the roads. But gradually, the more successful merchants created their own hierarchy based their earnings from trade, so some became like a parallel bourgeois nobility based in the cities, while some of the skilled craftsman developed their own power in forming guilds to represent their trade. In turn, there are parallels today to the medieval class structure in today's mass of non-unionized workers in low-paid routine jobs and farm labor, in the skilled workers who have formed unions, such as of transportation and ironworkers, and in the super-wealthy, who have gained their money through inheritance, company leadership, or special abilities propelling them into the ranks of highly paid entertainment, media, and sports figures. The specific positions might differ, but the social positions based on wealth and work roles had parallels between the then and now.

The Everyday Work of the Peasant

Even as the towns grew in size and influence in the Middle and late Middle Ages, from about 1000 AD on, the peasant remained at the heart of the medieval economy, since the produce of the farms and the taxes on these crops kept everything else going, including the increasingly lavish life of the kings and nobles. Yet the contributions of the peasants were ignored, and most were stuck at the bottom of the economic pyramid, though some were able to do better than others, such as by having larger fields with more crops and more animals. Some peasants were even able to get a few peasants to work for and contribute crops to them, much like a foreman of a team of field hands or factory workers today. But they remained peasants, split from the upper classes by vast differences in wealth and family connections.

A few medieval writers have pointed to this firm social cleavage, adding a third division to include the priests and clerks of the Church. For example, one 13th century poem *Miserere*, translated into English, describes this hierarchy, pointing up the role of peasant in providing the food for everyone:

> The labor of the clerk is to pray to God,
> Of the knight to do justice,
> And the laborer finds their bread.
> One provides food, one prays, and one defends.
> In the field, the town, and the church,
> These three help each other with their services
> In a well-ordered scheme.[125]

Another medieval writer compared society to a human body, in which the priests and clerks were the head and eyes, providing the spiritual guidance; the nobles were like the head and arms, acting as the protectors and defenders; and the peasants were "the feet and legs, for it was on their labor that the whole of society was based."[126]

Yet, while everyone depended on the fruits of the peasant's labor, their "betters" readily took advantage of and exploited them, since the peasants were at the bottom of the pyramid that formed medieval society. At the top, the king was considered the owner of the entire land, but he granted certain portions of it to his most powerful great lords – the dukes, marquises, counts, and princes — in return for certain servicers. Then, these lords could grant portions of their land to the lesser lords, who would subdivide it among knights; and sometimes in England, these portions of land were further subdivided to squires. As previously described in Chapters 3, 4 and 5, these services often involved going to war and fighting on behalf of the king to defend or expand territory, or the nobles fought among themselves for power and land, and sometimes to usurp the king. However, these strugglers for power and the trappings of the royalty, nobility, and the Church went on in a kind of upper class bubble, removed from the day to day concerns of the peasants and artisans who did the work that enabled the rest of the system to keep going.

For example, in *The Middle Ages*, Dorothy Mills describes how the medieval lords oversaw the manors where the peasants worked. Though the manors might differ in size and some lords owned several estates in various parts of their domains, at the core of each estate was the peasant who performed the work. As Mills describes it:

> A manor was nearly always self-supporting. Grain and vegetables were grown for food, cattle were raised for the meat..., and sheep for the wool. The men and women on the manor did all the work, built the houses, made the tools, and did the spinning and weaving.[127]

Typically the peasants lived on the manor in small huts, which were simply furnished with only a few pieces of furniture, usually a wooden table, a few chairs, and a pallet for a bed, in contrast to the lord's large stone manor, which became larger and grander over the years, turning into the huge castles of the middle and late Middle Ages. It was from these huts that the peasants traveled to their fields and usually used a two or three-field system to rotate the crops, whereby one field was used for winter crops, another for summer crops, and a third lay fallow or uncultivated, so the soil could regain its nutrients, at a time when farmers didn't know about fertilizer.

Commonly, the peasants were call serfs, since most were tied to the land, in a system in which each field was divided into strips, and the serfs each had their own strips to farm, along with rights to the common pasture lands, where they were allowed to keep a certain number of cows, sheep, pigs, and poultry. Plus, they had access to the common woodlands where they could gather fuel, although they weren't allowed to hunt game, which was considered the crime of poaching. Only the lord of the manor and his guests had the right to do that.

Under the laws of the day, a serf couldn't freely take off and leave the land, though there were a few exceptions, in the form of landless men who lost their lands, so they joined the ranks of the homeless and sometimes lived as outlaws, who had an even more difficult existence, much like the situation facing the homeless individuals and criminals of today. But mostly, the serfs lived a highly controlled and routinized existence, living in a hut and working the fields. A serf even needed the consent of the lord of the manor to marry, and his wife and children were trapped, too, in working the fields and having nowhere else to go. It was a miserable, impoverished existence. As Mills describes this daily grind:

> The serf was not a freeman; he belonged to the manor and could not leave it without the consent of the lord. In theory he was secure in the possession of his hut, miserable and poor as it often was, and of his strips in the fields, as long as he paid service for them ... A serf had to give three days' work a week in the lord's fields and special services and payments, generally in kind, certain seasons. He was required to convey produce that might be sent to be sold at fairs ... He would have to use his own ox or horse to convey such produce, and if he were too poor to own an animal, he would have to shoulder the load on his own back.[128]

Moreover, the serf could not even do what he wanted with his own produce. Rather, he had to have all his flour ground in the lord's mill and his bread baked in the lord's oven. Then, he had to pay for these services with his own money or a percentage of his produce. He also needed the consent of the lord to marry, and his children needed the lord's blessing as well.

One of the famous 14th century poems written by William Langford between 1360 and 1387.*The Vision of Piers Plowman*,[129] describes this difficult routine of the serf very well. In answer to the question, "Now Plowman, what work do you do?" the Plowman answers:

> I work very hard. I go out at dawn driving oxen a-field and yoke them to the plow. For fear of my lord I dare not say at home even when the winter is very cold. Every day I must plow a full acre or more...I have to get hay for the oxen, water them, and clear out the sheds.[130]

Plus, making matters worse, as the peasant complains: "I am not free."

Likewise, the peasants who worked as shepherds had a hard life, too, as described in a medieval Nativity Play, the *Second's Shepherd's Play*, written in the early 15th century. As two shepherds have a conversation on one winter's night, one complains to the other:

> We are so lamed,
> So taxed and shamed,
> We are made hand-tamed
> With these gentlery-men...
> Thus we live in pain, anger, and woe.[131]

Later, when manors grew larger, a few officials supervised the administration of the properties. The most immediate supervisor was called the bailiff, and his job was to oversee the work of the serfs by surveying the woods, corn, pastures, and meadows, and he was in charge of disposing of any surplus produce, as described in a 13th century book called the *Seneschaucie*. In addition, there was a seneschal in charge of all the manors of a single lord, and he had to visit them regularly to make sure everything was in order. In addition, some other workers of the times included the plowman and wagoner, who had to work with the oxen and horses used in plowing and take the food to the lord or the market.

It was a hard life. Commonly, the medieval villagers would harness and hitch up the plows to their animals and travel in the morning in a cavalcade to their fields, which were divided into strips, consisting of long and narrow sets of furrows in two or three fields, since one always lay fallow. Each strip was about a half of an acre, representing the amount of land which the peasant could plow in a day. However, the number of strips each peasant owned varied, from a few to many fields that were scattered and intermingled, as Frances and Joseph Gies describe in *Life in a Medieval Village*. Yet, while the peasants had individual plots of land for growing crops, their work was heavily regulated. As Gies describe it:

> The strips of plowed land were held individually, and unequally. A few villagers held many strips, most held a few, some held none. Animals, tools, and other movable property were likewise divided unequally. The poor cotters eked out a living by working for the lord and for their better-off neighbors who held more land than their families could cultivate, whereas these latter, by marketing their surplus produce, were able to turn a profit and perhaps use it to buy more land.
>
> How much time a villager could devote to cultivating his own tenement depended partly on his status as free or unfree, partly on the size of his holding (the larger the villein holding, the larger the obligation), and partly on his geographical location. [132]

This obligation to the lord who owned the manor and village varied from lord to lord, though typically it was about two days of work a week, though less for the free tenants and very little for the cotters who held little or no land. For the most part the main work consisted of plowing each day throughout the agricultural year, and commonly the peasants shared their plows and plow animals to work in teams. When it was time to harvest the crops, the peasants had to variously cut, gather, stack, and thresh their grain crops – mainly wheat, barley, and oats, and harvest their vegetable crops.

The peasants essentially were tied to the farmer's year and had regular tasks each season. As Morris Bishop, author of *The Middle Ages* describes:

> All the villagers followed the ritual of the farmer's year: in the spring plowing, sowing, and harrowing; in the summer weeding, manuring, sheep shearing, tending the lord's gardens, cutting and storing hay; in the autumn reaping the grain, threshing and storing it; in winter house repairing, tool making, and odd jobs.[133]

Plus, the peasant was regularly recruited by the bailiff to work on the lord's demesne – commonly for two or three days a week – and he had to put his work for the lord before working his own fields. By contrast, the freeholder paid for his land in rent, although some had to occasionally offer their services to the lord, too.

After all this work, with all their obligations, peasants had little left over. As Frances and Joseph Gies describe it, the average peasant on a manor in England "might feed a family of three, pay a title to the church, and have enough grain left to sell for twelve or thirteen shillings, out of which his rent and other cash obligations would have to come. If he was required to pay cash of his labor obligation, he would need to make up the difference by sale of poultry or wool, or through the earnings of wife or sons." In short, the peasants were "slaves to the crops as much as to the nobility."[134]

At the same time, the cotters had it even worse since they didn't own plows or animals for the plows. Instead, they were the medieval equivalent of handymen, who did a lot of handy work, such as sheep-shearing, bean-planting, ditch-digging, thatching, and brewing. Often, they were hired by the wealthier peasants at harvest time and got paid with a percentage of the harvest – about 5 to 10%. Their wives and daughters typically helped with weeding and other chores.

As Bishop describes them, the cotters got their name since they occupied a cot or hovel rather than living in a house, and they were economically inferior to the freeman or serfs. While some might possess a small plot of land, they supported themselves by casual labor for daily wages. Among their most common tasks were herding cows and pigs, helping with the harvest and planting, and carrying messages. They were even recruited to guard prisoners. They were "the odd-job men, the rural proletariat." In addition, until the 13th century, there were also some slaves, who had no rights, though for the most part, slavery was largely gone from England and Western Europe.

In sum, nearly all the villagers on a manor – including villains, cotters, and free tenants – spent all their days in the fields, handling the plow, scythe, or sickle, and loading the cart, plus a few workers had specialized tasks, such as the baker, smith, carpenter, and miller, with the bailiff supervising the mills. Plus there were some part-time and itinerant craftsmen who plied their wares, such as tinkers who repaired brass jars and pans; carters, who brought dung carts at mowing time; men to brand animals; and women to milk sheep.

It was an extremely hard life, far different from the increasingly luxurious life of the lords of the manor and the royalty, which the peasants, craftsmen, and tradesmen supported by their work.

Peasant Rebellions and Revolts

Given their miserable conditions, occasionally the peasants engaged in some strikes to protest their conditions. For example, the Peasants Revolt of 1381 occurred at a time when the sufferings of the peasants was even greater due to the high taxes of the Hundred Years War and the ravages of the plague, which led to a shortage of labor, though the lords weren't willing to increase the wages. In response, the serfs demanded their freedom and refused their feudal duties, and in June 1381, three armies of peasants led by John Ball, Wat Tyler, and Jack Straw, stormed into London and beheaded a number of high officials, including the archbishop of Canterbury and lord treasurer. Among their goals they wanted to seize the lands of the nobles and gentry, expel most of the clergy, except the friars, and execute all the government ministers, lawyers, and judges, though they claimed they were still loyal to the king, 14-year old Richard II. However, when one of the peasant leaders, Wat Tyler, met King Richard on horseback to discuss what the peasants wanted, he was so insolent and insulting, treating King Richard as an equal by shaking his hand, calling him "comrade," and asking for beer, that the king's knights attacked Tyler. After they dragged him from his horse, one of the royal squires stabbed him, and after that the king's party dispersed the peasant army. Meanwhile, in the country and towns, other peasants attacked manor houses and abbeys and beheaded many officials. But eventually, John Ball and the other leaders were executed, and their severed heads were put on display on London Bridge.

Likewise, in France, the peasants' hard life led them to rebel from time to time. For example, some peasants responded to an excessively harsh lord by breaking into a manor house, drinking his best wines, killing the bailiff, and burning the house with the rent rolls and records. But then the neighboring lords would muster their troops, and sometimes the king arrived with his own forces, leading to the defeat and slaughter of the rebels. The most notable of these uprisings was the *Jacquerie* in 1358, when many peasants launched a major attack against the nobility, until their revolution soon sputtered out, too, at the hands of the more powerful, better equipped army of nobles and the king.

Thus, while these peasant revolts over the centuries helped to point up the peasants' terrible working and living conditions, they did little to change the system. The long hard workdays and low wages continued to be the common lot of most peasants, though a few of the wealthier serfs and freemen were able to live a slightly more comfortable life than the rest.

Modern Day Peasants

A modern day equivalent for the medieval peasants might be the large number of low-paid workers in certain industries, notably fast-food operations, huge discount chains like Walmart, and some factories, though much of today's low-paid factory work is outsourced to sweatshops, especially in Asia, Mexico, and South America. Obviously, people today aren't doing the same kind of work, and new technologies have automated much of the grunt labor that used to be done in the fields in the Middle Ages. However, what is similar is the highly regulated, routinized work, with a large workforce that works a long day, with regular oversight by sales, operations, or factory supervisors who are like the medieval bailiffs and seneschals. Another parallel is that a large percentage of modern day employees are struggling and barely making it, much like the peasants, and their low-paid labor helps support the luxurious lifestyle of the upper classes, who have the wealth and power, then as now.

They may not work on farms today, but they have equivalent repetitious, routine jobs. In fact, like the farmers of the Middle Ages, many work with food, such as fast-food workers, dishwashers, cashiers in restaurants, and farmers, and these low-level jobs are expanding, creating a growing peasant/serf class in America. And now much has changed in the last decade, except conditions have been getting worse for low-income employees, especially with the pandemic, since they are more likely to be laid off from these jobs, and they make up the bulk of the many millions filing unemployment claims, and some cannot even do that since they are undocumented workers.

For example, to illustrate what things were like a decade ago, in a 2013 article on "The 8 Lowest-Paying Jobs in America," Eve Tahmincioglu, an MSBNC.Com Contributor writes that "The United States may soon have to replace the expression, 'the land of opportunity' with 'the land of low wages.'" As she describes it, the greatest growth of jobs in the last decade has been in jobs paying less than $10 an hour, due to the "down-waging" of American jobs, according to Peter Creticos, president and executive director for the Institute for Work and the Economy. A key reason for this development is the bad economy, leading many members of the huge baby boomer market to continue to remain in the job market, many beyond their retirement age. Moreover, many midcareer people who were downsized have been taking such low-paying jobs for survival, so that younger workers just beginning to work have increasingly been unable to find such jobs, and often they have continued to live with their parents as a result.[135]

The result today is that almost half of U.S. workers in the prime work years of 18 to 64 are employed in low wage jobs, according to research by the Brookings Institute. And the vast majority of these employees — 53 million of them — are between 25 to 54, so they are not just starting out in their careers. Their median hourly wage is $10.22 an hour, only a few dollars more than the federal minimum wage of $7.25 an hour, but far below what is regarded as a living wage in many areas of the country,[136] since their median annual earnings are about $18,000.[137] And in general, the types of individuals who are most likely to be stuck in low-wage jobs are women, people of color, and those with a low educational level.[138]

In turn, such low-paid work is much like what the peasants experienced in the Middle Ages, though the type of work was quite different, except for the farm laborers who toiled in the fields, both now and then. Today, besides farm workers, the 8 lowest paid jobs, according to the Department of Labor's Bureau of Labor Statistics, include food preparation and serving workers, commonly in the fast food industry; dishwashers, cashiers, hosts and hostesses, amusement park attendants, movie theater ushers and ticket takers, and personal and home care aides. Many of these jobs, including working with food preparation and service, are often dead-end and/or part-time jobs. But despite the low wages (about $8.71 an hour, long hours, and hard work, the occupation has become the fourth largest in the country with 2.7 million workers. Consider these employees much like the serfs and freemen, who had to work long-hours with little to show for it after deducting all their costs for their rent and taxes, or the cotters, who helped out on a part-time basis for long-hours when needed, such as during the planting and harvest season.

Likewise, the other lowest-paid employees might similarly be compared to these low-wage, hard-working medieval workers, especially given the irregular hours and high-turnover characteristics of the work of dishwashers (about 1 million in the U.S.), cashiers (about 3.3 million), amusement park attendees, and farm workers (about 250,000). As for personal and home care aides (about 630,000) and hosts and hostesses, these might be compared to the household servants in the retinue of the king and nobility, also at the bottom of the status pyramid, though they might work closely with those living the luxury life.

These low wages generally translate into earnings of about $23,000 to $26,000 a year. For example, based on an employment survey by the U.S. Department of Labor in May 2019, the top 25 worst paying jobs in America include these[139]:

-   Fast food and counter workers ($23,250)
-   Cooks in fast food restaurants ($23,530) and in restaurants generally ($27,500)
-   Amusement and recreation attendants ($24,330)
-   Cashiers ($24,370)
-   Dishwashers ($24,410)
-   Ushers, lobby attendants, and ticket takers ($24,870)
-   Dining room and cafeteria attendants and bartender helpers ($25,020)
-   Laundry and dry-cleaning workers ($25,420)
-   Childcare workers ($25,510)
-   Hotel, motel, and resort desk clerks ($25,950)
-   Home health and personal care aides ($26,440)
-   Waiters and waitresses ($26,800)
-   Maids and housekeeping cleaners ($26,810)
-   Automotive and watercraft service attendants ($26,860)

As you can see from this list, these workers are also the most likely to be laid off during the pandemic, given the devastation of the hospitality, travel, and restaurant industries.

GINI GRAHAM SCOTT, PHD

The companies that pay the lowest wages might also be compared to the lords with the harshest work conditions for the peasants, freemen, and cotters. For example, in a 2013 article describing the "10 Companies Paying Americans the Least," Mark Sauter, Alexander E.M. Hess, and Thomas Frohlich describe how low – and minimum-wage workers are growing faster than any other group of workers, while the profits at many of the corporations employing the most poorly paid workers have risen, such as at McDonald's, Walmart, and Target, who together employ several million Americans. [140] As Sauter, Hess, and Frohlich note, the companies with the poorest pay fall into three major industries, retailers such as Walmart and Sears, restaurant chains such as McDonalds, and grocery stores, such as Kroger. Such industries require a large number of low-paid workers to deal with customers by taking orders, stocking clothing and goods, and waiting on tables. At the same time, the CEOs at these companies receive a very large compensation. For example, the CEOs of 9 of the 10 companies that pay the lowest wages make more than $10 million a year, while the CEOs of Walmart, Michael Duke, and Starbucks, Howard Schultz, make over $20 million a year.

The parallel with the peasants, freeholders, and cotters working for the lavish-living lords to whom they pay rents and taxes is clear. While the lords and CEOs obtain income from the low-paid workers so they can live in style, the employees have to struggle to survive on their very low pay. These 10 companies that pay the least are but an example of the disparity of pay throughout corporate America between the lowest paid workers who do the heavy lifting and the highly paid top officers, especially the CEO who are at the top of the earnings pyramid.

For example, when you consider that the lowest paid workers averaged about $23,000-27,000 a year, the difference between their pay and the highest paid CEOs and executives is astronomical, especially for the high-tech titans who are like the royalty of today. As a July 2020 Bloomberg article indicates, these are the annual earnings of these high paid CEOs and executives.[141]

- Elon Musk, Tesla - $595 million
- Tim Cook, Apple - $134 million
- Joseph Ianniello, Viacom CBS - $116 million
- Sumit Singh, Chewy - $108 million
- Jonathan Gray (COO), Blackstone Group - $108 million
- Robert Swan, Intel - $99 million
- Sundar Pichal, Alphabet - $86 million
- Satya Nadella, Microsoft - $77 million

These earnings include income in a variety of forms from compensation to stock ownership. And during the pandemic, while low-income earners have suffered the most from lost jobs, the income of many of those in the highest brackets have gone up, due to rising stock prices. Or as Anders Melin and Cedric Sam put it: "The astronomical executive pay…is a reminder of how inequitably the riches are shared — an imbalance that has become even more pronounced as millions of Americans, but few executives, have lost their jobs during the pandemic, while stocks have soared."[142]

This huge imbalance represents a continuation of a trend over the last decade, highlight the divergence between the very rich who are like modern-day royalty and the very poor who are like the peasants who are losing even more money to their lords and kings. For example, a breakdown of the 2013 profits and earnings of the workers and CEO at the three companies paying the least wages illustrates this disparity.

- At Walmart, the company ranked first in paying employees the least, 1.4 million associates work at 4800 stores. While the hourly wages for sales associates are less than $9, Walmart pays its CEO $20.7 million, and has a net income of $17 billion on revenues of $469 billion.
- At McDonald's, ranked number 2, about 740,000 workers are employed in 14,200 stores. The hourly median wage was just over $9 in 2012, but many employees, such as cashiers and crew members, earn much less, commonly just the

minimum wage. By contrast, McDonald's paid its CEO $13.9 million and had a net income of $5.5 billion on a net income of $5.5 billion.

- At Target, ranked number 3,361,000 workers are employed at 1800 stores. The hourly wage for a cashier or sales employee is under $9 an hour, while the CEO compensation is $20.6 million, and the company had a net income of $3 billion on revenues of $73.3 billion in 2012.

A similar disparity between the lower-paid employees and the CEO can be shown at the other top ten companies paying the least which include the following CEO compensation in the retail and restaurant space:

- Kroger: $11.1 million,
- Yumi Brands, $14.2 million,
- Sears Holdings, $1.3 million,
- Darden Restaurants, $6.4 million,
- Macy's, $13.8 million,
- TJX Companies, $21.8 million,
- Starbucks, $28.9 million.[143]

Given these low wage earnings, many of these workers are living in poverty, especially if they are the only wage-earner in the family and have children to feed. As a result, many have to depend on welfare programs, such as food stamps and Medicaid, though many slip through the cracks and are unable to get such funding, leading them to look to relatives or end up homeless. The situation might be comparable to peasants and freeholders struggling to survive in medieval times, throwing themselves on the mercy of the lords of the manor, and in some cases losing their homes and becoming landless cotters.

It's a trend that has continued in the last decade. For example, a 2013 study by the U.S. Berkeley Labor Center and the Department of Urban and Regional Planning at the University of Illinois at

Urbana-Champaign illustrate the plight of the lowest paid of these low-paid workers – the fast food workers, in its report: "Fast Food, Poverty Wages: The Public Cost of Low-Wage Jobs in the Fast Food Industry." As the report describes, full-time workers at McDonald's, Burger King, and other fast food restaurants "don't make enough to support themselves," forcing many of them to turn to food stamps and Medicaid. In fact, as the report notes, according to Stacy Finz's article, "Low Pay is Costing Billions, Study Says," "People work-ing in fast-food jobs are more likely to live in or near poverty than any other job sector, with 43% having an income two times below the federal poverty level or less." Though most people think that employees at fast-food drive-throughs are generally in high-school or college, in fact 26% of these employees are single and married adults with children, and many of them have to turn to public assis-tance programs for help. As the study found, 52% of the families of fast-food workers were enrolled in one or more public assistance programs, compared to 25% in the workforce as a whole. [144]

The low wages of retail workers have similarly led employees to look to others for help. For example, one Walmart store in Canton, Ohio, held a food drive for co-workers to help other employees in need, leading some customers and community members to ques-tion the low wages paid to workers. For instance, one Walmart shopper told the *Cleveland Plain Dealer* that she thought the need for workers to seek support from others due to their low pay was a "moral outrage." As she stated: "That Walmart would have the audacity to ask low-wage workers to donate food to other low-wage workers – to me, it is a moral outrage."[145] In turn, this effort to seek aid from others is like the peasants turning to one another or the Church for alms in the Middle Ages.

Modern Day Rebellions and Revolts

Just like the peasants occasionally organized revolts during the Middle Ages, so the poorly paid workers at some of these companies have organized their own protests today. And just as the peasant revolts were generally snuffed out in medieval times, so were many of the modern protests, after making a brief splash in the news media, although in a few cases, a strike did lead to a victory resulting in a small increase in wages and improved working schedules.

For example, in July 2013, hundreds of fast food workers began a strike over minimum wages by walking off their jobs to gain support for getting paid $15 an hour, rather than the $7.25 minimum wage. As Tiffany Hsu described in an *L.A. Times* article: "Hundreds of Fast Food Workers Strike Over Minimum Wage," these strikes were organized by a number of advocacy groups, such as Fast Food Forward, in cities around the country, including New York City, Chicago, St. Louis, Detroit, Milwaukee, Kansas City, Mo., and Flint, Mich., to protest the $7.25 federal minimum wage. In addition, some demonstrators from mega-chains, such as McDonald's and KFC, protested that they should have a right to form unions without retaliation. A medieval comparison might be with the peasants in a number of communities coming together to show their unity in protesting conditions on the manors of the lords they worked for. [146]

But whether modern-day or medieval protests, the strikes led to efforts to put them down. While the strikes in the Middle Ages were ultimately put down by the nobles' superior power, sometimes supported by the kings armies and often resulting in the execution of the strike leaders, today the efforts to undermine a strike takes a more political or technological form. For instance, in response to the July walkouts by fast food workers, conservative critics, such as the Employment Policies Institute, argued that paying workers a $15 minimum wage would actually be harmful for employees, especially in the low-margin restaurant industry, since companies forced to pay higher wages might be likely to shift from human labor to automated technology, such as by using mobile apps to permit ordering or paying on a Smart phone or other touch-screen device. [147]

Yet, in spite of such resistance, these strikes by low wage workers have continued, much as the medieval peasants continued to organize further protests against their poor conditions. For example, in

August 2013, the fast food workers' movement to protest low wages and earn more spread to 35 cities. As described by Victor Luckerson in a *Time* article: "Fast Food Strikes Go Viral: Workers Expected to Protest Low Wages in 35 Cities Thursday," the growing movement among fast food workers to demand higher wages gained momentum by spreading to the South and West Coast, and was expected to grow even more. As Luckerson noted:

> The rumblings against the long-standing economics of fast-food began last November in New York, when about 200 restaurant workers went on strike in a one-day protest. By July the movement had ballooned to include thousands of workers across seven other cities, including Chicago, Detroit, and Kansas City. Now, with workers in places like Los Angeles, Memphis, and Raleigh getting involved – with extensive financial backing from the Service Employees International Union – organizers and labor experts expect this week's strike to dwarf previous protests.[148]

Since then, this spirit of striking has spread to low-wage workers in other industries, much like the medieval peasant revolts spread to numerous manors in nearby counties and occurred in a number of countries, before they were ultimately shut down. A modern-day example is the growing strikes by workers of Walmart, the company with the distinction of paying the least to its workers. These strikes began in October 2012, when Walmart workers launched labor protests and strikes in 28 stores and 12 states, "the first retail worker strike in the company's 50-year history," according to a report in *Democracy Now.* [149] According to the organizers, the employees were protesting the company's efforts to "silence and retaliate against workers for speaking out for improvements on the job," much like the lords in the Middle Ages retaliated by cracking down and sometimes executing the leaders of the protests.

As described by Josh Eidelson, a contributing writer for *Salon* and *In These Times*, who first wrote about the Walmart store strikes and followed the story over the next year, this strike marked a "new wave" in a fight against U.S. labor and the world's largest private employer. As Eidelson stated in an October 10, 2012 *Democracy Now* interview:

> Yesterday, when Wal-Mart store workers at multiple stores walked off the job, this was the first – the second time in five days. It was also the second time in 50 years of Wal-Mart that we've seen multiple U.S. store workers going out on strike together ... It's a wave that started, in many ways, this summer in June, when we saw eight workers go out on strike at a Wal-Mart supplier, CJ's Seafood. It continued last month when workers in Wal-Mart's supply chain ... went out on strike in California and then in Illinois. And it escalated last week and again yesterday with a combined 150 Wal-Mart store workers taking this unprecedented action.

Not surprisingly, Walmart sought to fight back, including filing a complaint with a federal agency, claiming the worker's actions through OurWalmart, a subsidiary of the United Food and Commercial Workers Union (UFCW), were illegal actions violating the National Labor Relations Act, which prohibits picketing for over 30 days without filing a representation petition. And that's what the strikers had done, since OurWalmart had been unlawfully organizing picket lines, in-store 'flash mobs,' and other demonstrations over the past six months, according to Emily Jane Fox in a *CNN Money* article: "Wal-Mart Warns Workers on Black Friday Strike."[150] A medieval equivalent might be appealing to the king to bring in his troops to quell the revolt.

But 500 Walmart workers struck anyway on Black Friday by walking off the job, an action hailed by the original eight workers who struck against Walmart's seafood supplier who threatened to beat the workers with shovels and attack their families.[151] Afterwards, even more protests, rallies, and strikes continued the following year, including a walkout in June 2013, after which Walmart fired

20 workers who joined this walk-out; a rally outside company head-quarters in August for better hours and wages, and protests in September in 15 different cities to protest the company firing the workers in the June protest. While these actions were organized by OURWalmart, another protest in October was organized independently by about 80 workers in Miami, who walked off the job seeking higher wages and better hours, according to Bryce Covert in a *Think Progress* article: "Dozens of Walmart Workers Walk Out on Strike in Miami".[152] And according to OURWalmart, this strike did result in some victories: workers who wanted 40 hour work schedules got them; employees scheduled to receive wages gained 50 cent instead of 40 cent raises; a disliked manager got transferred; and Walmart paid the workers for the hours they were on strike.[153]

In November 2013, still more strikes erupted, this time by Southern California Walmart workers, who walked off the job on November 6 seeking a minimum of $25,000 a year, resulting in the arrest of more than 50 workers and supporters. A week later, on November 12, Walmart workers in Seattle launched a one-day walk-out strike.[154] Still another strike occurred November 18, when the truckers who haul goods for Walmart at the Port of Los Angeles went on strike in support of the workers at Walmart and other low-pay companies, such as Costco and Sketchers, sporting signs such as "Stop the unlawful war on workers." The port drivers had the support of the Teamsters Union, too.[155]

Meanwhile, to build momentum, on November 12, 2013 the Our Walmart Campaign launched a website where Walmart workers could share their stories and request protests anonymously or by name. One Chicago employee, Charmaine Givens-Thomas, even prepared a petition to President Obama, much like an organization of peasants might send a petition to the king, in which she asked for his support by "meeting with the courageous workers who are risking termination or other disciplinary action by joining together as the Organization United for Respect at Walmart."[156]

A series of strikes and protests were planned for Black Friday, the big day for sales after Thanksgiving, at stores all over the country.

In short, just like the peasants strikes erupted and spread at times during the Middle Ages to protest the terrible conditions under which they struggled to survive, so have modern low-wage workers been organizing to improve their conditions and gain further support for their plight. And just like the lords acted to quell the protests, so have the low-wage companies taken steps to counteract the protests, such making some concessions in individual stores, firing and suspending strikers, and seeking legal action in court to stop the protests. Even so the protests have continued, though it is unclear who will ultimately prevail.

Still, to promote their cause, besides protests, the workers turned to the traditional and social media to publicize their plight, such as by showing the callousness of a company. For example, one McDonald's employee who worked there for 10 years and struggled to support her 7-year old daughter and 2-year old son on her $8.25 wages called the fast food chain's employee McResources hotline to see if the company could improve her situation. But instead of the company doing anything to help, say by contributing to her heating bills, their advice was to seek government assistance, such as food stamps, Medicaid, or the Low Income Home Energy Assistance Program, to add to her low wages. She then turned the recording of the call over to the fair labor advocacy group Low Pay Is Not Okay, which posted parts of it as an online video and shared it with the *Business Insider*.[157] The employee's experience might be a little like that of a medieval peasant with a family who is struggling to pay the rent and support his family with the large share of his crops due to the lord. But then the lord, instead of providing some direct relief, such as seeking less rent or a lesser share of the crops, tells the peasant to seek some relief from the king, which might be difficult to get, much like the employee found the process of getting government assistance in the past too complicated.

In sum, there was a growing discontent by lower-income workers, much like the peasants in the Middle Ages, and today, the workers can use the social media as well as the traditional media to spread their cause. Yet, even though the workers may be gaining growing support and sympathy, leading to expanding protests and more awareness of their situation, they still face very long odds, because of the wealth and power of the ruling classes. For not only are the workers up against the power of the CEOs and targeted companies, but they are posing a threat to others in the higher reaches of society – from bankers to politicians, who are making millions of dollars, as well as to middle-income individuals who would have to pay more for consumer products, if the low-wage workers are paid more. This resistance is much like what happened when the nobles and kings in the Middle Ages joined together to beat down any peasant uprisings and keep down their earnings by keeping their taxes and contributions from their crops as high as possible.

Yet, while these protests gradually wound down after 2013, they did inspire some changes, as some states began to pass laws to increase the minimum wage, making things a little better, but not by much. For example, in 2014 and 2015, 12 states passed legislation to raise the minimum wage, and by 2017, 19 states began the year with higher minimum wages, and by 2020, 21 states had higher minimum wages, a number of them increasing the rate to $15 over the next three to five years.[158]

Work and Income for the Top 1% Today

Besides the highly paid company CEOs, other high-income individuals who live like royalty are the finance barons, who not only get salaries, but also extra payments through bonuses, stock options, and other financial instruments. The owners of large successful companies would also fall into this category.

To take the 20 richest Americans, according to the *Forbes'* list for 2020, the net worth of these individuals is at least 10,000 times the earnings of the average annual pay of $56,516, according to *CNN Money*, a division of CNN, *Fortune*, and *Money*. And the wages for the most popular professions are about $25,000 or less. The lowest paid workers in the United Sates are Laundry and Dry-Cleaning workers, who average about $22,000 per year. 147,000 Americans work in Food Service, and average about $22,600 per year in wages.[159]

At the top of the list is Jeff Bezos of Amazon, with $113 billion in net worth.[160] These differences are so great, that those with this kind of income and their families live in a different reality than the average working American, and even more so than the vast millions of workers in one of the low income jobs earning $30,000 or less.

The Forbes list also shows that the source of income of these high net worth individuals largely comes from founding very successful companies or attaining great success in real estate and other investments, whereas individuals and their families at the bottom have little capital to even begin getting to the top by starting a company or becoming an investor. Like the peasants and cotters in the Middle Ages, they are effectively shut out from becoming part of the American nobility, with rare exceptions, although some lower income workers can gain access to the now declining middle class, such as by having a special skill or getting an education which opens doors, much as some peasants were able to find opportunity in the cities and become part of a growing bourgeoisie in the middle and late Middle Ages. For example, the individuals with the most net worth on the list include:

Bill Gates – Founder of Microsoft, $98 billion
Warren Buffett – Founder of Berkshire, Hathaway, $67.5 billion
Larry Ellison – Founder of Oracle, $59 billion
Mark Zuckerberg – Founder of Facebook, $54.7 billion
Jim Walton – part of the Walmart family, $54.6 billion
Alice Walton – part of the Walmart family, $54.4 billion
S. Robson Walton, part of the Walmart family, $54.1billion
Steve Ballmer – Microsoft, $25.7 billion
Larry Page, Google, $50.9 billion

What is notable about these top 10 net worth individuals, as well as others on the 400 richest Americans list, is that many of them were founders of companies taking advantage of new technologies and retail models, such as Bill Gates, Larry Ellison, Jeff

Bezos, Larry Page, Sergey Brin, and Mark Zuckerberg; were wise investors, such as Warren Buffett, Charles and David Koch, Carl Icahn, and George Soros; or were part of a successful manufacturing or retail company, such as the Waltons of Walmart, and Mars of the Mars Candy Company. Others on the list are associated with the ownership of large corporations and financial positions, such as being involved with investments, banks, hedge funds, private equity, money management, venture capital, leveraged buyouts, and real estate. The oil and gas industries, pipelines, media, software, pharmaceuticals, medical equipment, hotels, and retail are also represented as sources of high earnings. However, what is most notable is the dominance of financial connections as the path to wealth, reflected in the contrast made in the media between Wall Street and Main Street. As described in the next chapters, this huge wealth of those on top enables them to live in the royal style characteristic of the nobles and kings of medieval times. And aside from running companies or managing investments, they have no need to engage in the typical daily work of the average wage earner, much like the nobility of the Middle Ages had the time to cultivate a life of leisure, culture, political and social battles, and war; and had no need to work at routine tasks like the peasants and cotters.

The Growing of Specialized Professions and a Middle Class in the Towns

Outside the rural areas, a small growing middle class emerged in the middle and late Middle Ages with the development of specialized trades, the formation of guilds to protect those in many of the trades, and the growth of shop owners and traders in the towns. While the size and complexity of this middle class group was much smaller in the Middle Ages, it might be comparable to the middle class in America which is made up of middle and upper middle working class, business people, and professionals today, although this class has been shrinking due to the Great Recession, which has led to lost jobs and reduced incomes for many in this group, resulting in the increasing divide between the upper reaches of society and those in the lower classes today.

As Dorothy Mills describes it, these towns began to emerge in the 11th century and grew in size and importance, as knights sought better armor and weapons and the Crusades introduced the many products from the East, such as fruits, spices, dyes, perfumes, and jewels. Sometimes they developed out of the traditional manorial village; sometimes a great lord founded a town on his land; and sometimes they developed on the site of an old Roman town, since it was well situated on a river or had easy access to the neighboring countryside. Plus some emerged around a monastery, church, or popular shrine. This growth of towns also led Italy to become a center for trade from the East to central and northern Europe [161]

Initially these towns were under the control of an overlord, such a king, noble, or the Church, and they owed feudal services in the form of taxes, tolls, or agricultural services to the lord. In addition, they were subjected to the regulation of feudal officials, such as sheriffs and bailiffs appointed by the lords who controlled these towns. Then, gradually beginning in the 12th century, the towns began to gain their independence from paying feudal taxes, became free to carry on trade without interference from anyone outside the town, and gained the ability to govern themselves, commonly by getting a charter granted by the kings and nobles, commonly in return for money and supplies to help fund the Crusades. So soon the townspeople could elect their own officials, gained control over their own courts, and had the right to regulate trade.

At first, these medieval towns, like the manors, were walled and could only be entered through gates which were usually closed at night until dawn. Then, as some merchants gained greater success in the later Middle Ages, they began to form a class of merchant nobility and live in large luxurious houses, like the landed aristocrats.

It was in this context that the middle classes began to emerge in the towns. As Morris Bishop describes, the "merchants made the towns," and they created a new economy based on money rather than land. At first, these merchants were outsiders on the edges of feudal society, much like the new companies of today have begun as small start-ups founded by individuals outside the mainstream. Some high profile examples include the founders of new transportation companies like Lyft and Uber, which are challenging the entrenched taxi companies by offering apps for rides on smart phones by local drivers, and the shared housing companies like Airbnb, which are challenging the established hotel industry by inviting local homeowners and apartment dwellers to rent out their homes and apartments for a few days. As Bishop describes the roots of the new merchant class:

> A new class appeared on the edge of feudal society: the merchants. Probably they originated among the landless men, escaped serfs, casual harvest laborers, beggars, and outlaws. The bold and resourceful among them, the fair talkers, quick with languages, ready to fight or cheat, became chapmen or peddlers, carrying their wares to remote hamlets. They were paid in pennies and farthings and in portable local products, such as beeswax, rabbit fur, goose quills, and sheepskins for making parchment. If they prospered, they could hire others to tramp the forest paths.[162]

As the number of merchants grew, they created towns, and they needed a variety of workers to help build and protect these towns, as well as provide food for them. As Bishop points out:

> They needed walls and wall builders, warehouses and guards, artisans to manufacture their trade goods, cask makers, cart builders, smiths, shipwrights and sailors, soldiers and muleteers. They needed farmers and herdsmen outside the walls to feed them; and bakers, brewers, and butchers, within.[163]

The merchants also began to change the politics of medieval society, since they created self-governing units for the towns, and they contributed to the centralization of power in the king, since they often opposed the local nobles in favor of supporting the king. They also increased their ranks by giving serfs an opportunity to win their freedom by living in their walls for a time, commonly a year and a day.

Then, as these towns grew, the merchants formed the Guild Merchant to protect and regulate trade in each town. The guilds were organized to keep a monopoly of trade for the merchants in that town, and most guilds were organized under the rule of a town alderman and two stewards, assisted by a council. The established the rules for trade in town to both protect the members and strengthen the guild in that no townsman who didn't belong to the Guild Merchant could buy or sell in the town except under the guild's conditions. For example, traders from other towns or foreigners from other countries were not allowed to buy or sell in any way that interfered with the interests of the townsmen who owned a house or land in the town, and the traders had to pay all the tolls and taxes from which the townspeople might be exempted. These guilds were also protection societies, so that if one member fell on hard times, others would help, much like modern insurance companies, charities, and professional services help individuals today. As Brian Tierney describes it:

> They were … organizations created by the burghers to serve their common interests. On one hand, they were organized for security of all sorts. When merchants lost their stock in a wreck or at the hands of a robber baron, other guild members aided them to start again … Often the guild maintained a school to train the members' sons … On the economic side, the guild secured a monopoly of the town's business for its members. No nonmember could sell at retail in the town. If foreign merchants brought goods to the town, they had to sell them to a member of the guild or at least pay a very heavy sales tax.[164]

At first, in most towns, there was a single guild for both artisans and merchants. But over time, the two groups began to split
up, since the merchant could earn much more than the artisan.
Moreover, the merchants who brought goods into the town wanted
higher prices so they would make more in profits, while the artisans
who bought the goods wanted lower prices, just like manufacturers and retailers today want to increase their profits by charging
more, while consumers hope to pay less and look for deals, such as
on Black Friday, the day after Thanksgiving or after the Christmas
holiday season, when prices are low to entice customers to buy now
in order to get rid of unsold goods.

Increasingly, through the 13th century, driven by the merchants,
trade spread, as the merchants transported and sold anything that
made a profit. Initially, these traders dealt in basic raw materials,
such as iron from France, Spain, and Germany, tin from England,
and lead and copper from Germany and Italy. Still other basic
products that were part of this trade included coal, salt, and fish,
and as transportation became cheaper and more efficient, according to Bishop, "foods began to travel," and there were even factories
for making sugar, syrups, and preserved food in France and Spain,
while Italy produced pies and sea biscuits, wine became a big business, and textiles became a big international commerce. The wool
trade proved especially profitable for England, while Italy became
the center of a thriving garment trade. By 1306, Florence had 300
workshops turning out robes and gowns. Also, then, like now, new
technologies contributed to putting many workers out of work, such
as when a manufacturer in Bologna built a silk spinning mill that
was powered by water which put 4000 workers out of work, much
like new methods of automation through the use of robots has led
to millions losing their jobs and joining the unemployment rolls
today.

Along with trade, manufacturing grew and new technologies
expanded old industries. For-example, in the 12th century, stain
glassed windows began appearing in churches; in the 13th century,
glass makers created glass drinking vessels, and spectacles were

introduced in Europe, drawing on the influence of the Arabs who made lenses in the 11th century; and in the 14th century, glass windows became common in houses. Still other industrial shops in the late Middle Ages included the production of tiles, bricks, church bells, tanned leather, weapons, soap, paper, ink, paints, and pottery. Also new technologies and methods developed to make operations even more efficient, such as the use of the steel for making tools and other devices for hauling stones and cement and loading and unloading ships. Still other technologies contributed to commerce on the seas, such as the sternpost rudder, the compass, which originated in China, and the quadrant.

As a result of this growth of trade and manufacturing, some merchants became wealthy from these developments by the 13th century, and they not only used their money to live in luxurious homes, but used it to found institutions, build churches, and engage in various civic duties, including participating in the government. For instance, in England, after 1295, a Model Parliament was formed, and representatives from the towns joined the knights from the shires in sitting in Parliament.

Meanwhile, workers involved in special crafts began to form guilds to regulate and protect trade in each of these crafts. Commonly, the workers left the original merchant guild to create their own craft guilds, and by the end of the 12th century, there were craft guilds for the most important industries in most towns, and they grew even more rapidly in the 13th century. Among the crafts formed were those of spinners, weavers, tailors, furriers, bakers, brewers, silversmiths, goldsmiths, and by the 15th century, many dozens of these craft guilds existed in each city for every occupation. For instance, according to Mills, York in England had about 60 craft guilds. And as Tierney points out, even prostitutes had their own guild, much like sex workers have formed their own union today.

Initially, these craft guilds were formed to provide some control over the work produced, and a man had to show he had the ability to engage in a trade before he could join a guild. Also, the craft guild sought to set the wages and prices to be fair for both the worker and consumer, as well as providing for the quality and method of manufacture.

The guilds also established a system of apprenticeship, whereby a master had to provide an apprentice with bed, board, and training, and sometimes provide some clothing and a small salary. Sometimes a master was required to teach the apprentice to read and write, too. Commonly the length of an apprenticeship was four to seven years, with seven years being the most common. Once the apprenticeship concluded, the individual became a journeyman, which sometimes meant traveling around working for masters in different places. Finally, at the end of the training period, the craftsman could designate himself as a master, and commonly had to show some evidence of his ability, such as passing an exam by the masters of the guild or providing an example of his work.

The guilds also limited the number of people who could ply a trade to help regulate the competition, so the supply of goods was not much greater than the demand, which would reduce the price. Such policies might be viewed as equivalent to the way the labor unions and professional organizations of today regulate the norms, standards, and customs of the members of each trade. In fact, this is a comparison that others have made today. As Mills notes:

> Comparisons have sometimes been made between the medieval craft guild and the modern trade union. Both associations were concerned with industry and with the standards of living, but the trade union is an association of workers in the same industry all over a country, whereas the members of a craft guild were the workers in one town, and each industry had its own guild in each town.[165]

Yet, while the craft guild included employers and masters as well as workers, and it was designed to protect the interests of the consumers, too, the guild served to raise the standards for the workers, along with the standards of the goods, which helped propel these workers into a new middle income group in the towns. Certainly, a big difference between the guilds and the unions is that during the Middle Ages all the work was done by hand, whereas now each year brings new technologies and often routine jobs have become automated. Even so, the organizing principle of bringing together workers in a certain industry to better their conditions and their pay is true of both medieval and modern times.

For the most part, all of these workers – merchants and artisans – were men, though women sometimes worked with their husbands, and occasionally a woman practiced a craft herself and became a member of the appropriate guild, most commonly when a man died and his widow continued his business. Still, there were some guilds with a high percentage of female workers, such as making textiles, much like many women play a leading role in the fashion industry today, such as Stella McCartney and Betsey Johnson though most of the famous designers and fashion company owners, like Tommy Hilfiger, Versace, and Armani, are all men. But mostly, though women did much of the work, they had little power over their lives, even in the thriving economy of the towns, since women were expected to either marry or join a convent. If a woman did marry, the man ruled the family, and marriages were usually arranged to gain land or property. Some women were pledged in matrimony as early as four or five years old to secure these deals. [166]

This role of women is one of the biggest differences between the Middle Ages and today, in that romantic love is generally considered the ideal basis for a modern marriage and woman have many freedoms not available to the medieval woman, such as the ability to not marry, get an education, and seek fulfillment in work and business opportunities. Yet the disparity in income and work opportunities for men and women remains, in that women only earn about 81% of what men do. In a report drawn from U.S. Census and Bureau of Labor Statistics by the Catalyst Center, the median annual earnings for full-time, year-round women workers in 2018 was $45,097 compared to $55,291 for men, whereby women were only earning 76% what men did. When the median weekly earnings of women and men was compared, the women only earned $821 or 81% of the men's median earnings of $1,007. The comparative earnings for women in full-time management, professional, and related occupations were even worse – only 73% of men's income, since the women earned 0.62 cents for every dollar the men did.[167]

Summing Up

In sum, despite the differences in technology and lifestyles, society today reflects the ordering of society in the Middle Ages in many ways. A major similarity is the great disparity in wealth between those on the top of the economic heap – the king, nobles, and very successful merchants in medieval times; the CEOs, company founders, investors, and the other wealthy individuals today — compared to those on the bottom rungs — the peasants, artisans, and other everyday workers in medieval times; the low-wage employees of today. In fact, as the disparity of income between the top tiers of society and those on the bottom increases today, the modern organization of society is increasingly like that of medieval times.

While in the early Middle Ages, the basis of wealth was in land and the conquest of territories, in the middle and late Middle Ages, a growing merchant class created towns and a money economy, leading to another basis for a growing disparity of wealth, as some merchants became increasingly wealthy and successful, while the artisans and other workers in the towns became much like the peasants and cotters in the country in their low pay. While the crafts guilds helped to prop up the earnings of guild members somewhat, the growth of trade and the towns made the rich merchants even richer, much like today's global economy has contributed to the growing inequality between the very very rich – and most of the other employees and small business owners today.

Chapter 7: Enduring Institutions: The Power and Influence of the Military and Family

Several institutions have formed the bulwark of society, both in the Middle Ages and today. Although they have been influenced by new technologies and changes in how they have been constituted and run, their central place in supporting society has remained. Two of these institutions are the military and family, as illustrated in this chapter.

The Power of the Military

The role of the military was critical in creating and supporting the medieval kingdoms, since these kingdoms were continually fighting wars, such as the 100 Years War between England and France, and supporting these wars through heavy taxes on the peasants and small middle class of primarily shop-keepers and artisans. Today, continuing wars are similarly proving very costly, and they threaten still more popular resistance in the form of political action and voting against such expenses. Yet, even with such resistance, the military-industrial complex forms a major part of the modern government budget, and numerous contractors, from paid mercenaries to equipment manufacturers, contribute manpower and supplies to support the U.S.'s wars to contain threats around the war, a little like the Crusades in the Middle Ages brought warriors from England and Europe to the Middle East to fight the infidels.

Another parallel is the continuing evolution of weaponry, despite vast differences in technology, which has created a more extensive and deadly modern war. This modern weaponry escalation reflects a similar pattern in the conflicts of the Middle Ages, which led to the advancements in the technology of war over the centuries. Even today's military-industrial complex has roots in the military societies of the Middle Ages, as does the use of paid mercenaries and the increasing privatization of much of the U.S. military and intelligence operations by using private contractors, much like the medieval lords called up local peasants and townsmen to fight their battles against other lords or in the Crusades. The big difference is the scale of these modern wars and the level of profits of corporations involved in the war effort, such as Halliburton and U.S. oil companies, who have upped their earnings through the wars where the U.S. has taken an active role, such as in Iraq and Afghanistan. But in the Middle Ages, merchant profiteers flourished, too, since they profited handsomely from the weapons, armor, and other materials they made to supply the warriors fighting these wars.

Since the Middle Ages was a time of continual fighting, both to acquire land, protect one's own land, and conquer or convert other people in the name of religion, the role of the military became especially important, and the knights became revered for their role. Even after the wars ended, the battles between knights were turned into mock battles through tourneys and jousts, which has parallels in the battles between knights and other rivals today in video games and films glorifying the military. Although knighthood was born out of the tradition of vassalage in feudal times, when the vassal owed a duty to his lord and the nobles owed a duty to their king to fight on their behalf, the knights developed their own code of honor and chivalry to reinforce the military tradition of strictly adhering to a military hierarchy of command – a tradition still in place in today's military service, even though the choice to serve is voluntary.

The Ideal of the Knight

As Bishop describes it, the ideal of the knight, according to 12th-century English philosopher John of Salisbury was this: "To protect the Church, to fight against treachery, to reverence the priesthood, to fend off injustice from the poor, to make peace in your own province, to shed blood for your brethren, and if needs must, to lay down your life." Given this ideal, in the Middle Ages, knighthood was "more than a career; it was a spiritual and emotional substructure for an entire way of life." [168] Some of these ideals have, in turn, been incorporated into the current code of the military officer, such as ideals of honor, honesty, bravery, loyalty, and courage.

Back in the Middle Ages, gentlemen were raised from babyhood to develop a tough body and spirit and be prepared to fight in various kinds of wars, from those involving lords against lords to a war instituted by the king. In turn, the soldier was commonly paid for his services by goods plundered from merchants on the roads or by booty gained by capturing an enemy, while the kings eagerly engaged in these wars with the help of their nobles to gain new territories or fill up the royal treasury.

As Bishop points out, nobles found a joy in war, since peacetime life could be very dull, since "the typical noble had almost new cultural resources besides hunting. Battle was climax of his career as it was often the end." In turn, the knight had high status, as the companion of his own lord or king. Around the year 1200, even the church helped to build up the role of the knight as a kind of spiritual calling. As Bishop notes:

> The church took over the dubbing of the knight and imposed its ritual and obligation on the ceremony, making it almost a sacrament. The candidate took a symbolic bath, donned clean white clothes and a red robe, and stood or knelt for ten hours in a nightlong silence on the altar, on which his weapons and armor lay. At dawn mass was said in front of an audience of knights and ladies. His sponsors presented

him to his feudal lord and gave him arms, with a prayer and a blessing said over each piece of equipment...The initiate took an oath to devote his sword to good causes, to defend the church against its enemies, to protect widows, orphans, and the poor, and to pursue evildoers. The ceremony ended with a display of horsemanship, martial games, and mock duels. It was all very impressive; the more earnest knights never forgot their vigils or belied their vows.[169]

At the same time, it was quite expensive to take on this role of being a knight, so by the 14th century, some gentlemen who were eligible to become knights, opted out and remained squires, who assisted the knights. The modern-day equivalent might be the individuals who opt for high-level military careers and seek an education befitting an officer at the top military schools like West Point for the Army and Annapolis for the Navy. The modern-day military has also continued the ideal of honor and service to those higher ups, expressed in various ceremonies, from drills and badges of honor to the military salute to acknowledge the superior officer.

The Caste System of the Military

Another major parallel between the military today and during the Middle Ages is the caste system which creates a wide gap between the high-status officers and everyone else, despite the modern additions of a navy, marines, and air force. The king might correspond to the U.S. President as the Commander in chief and the top general in each service division, much like the military in other countries. The nobles and knights on horseback who headed up military units could be comparable to the top commanding officers, such as majors, colonels, and lieutenants, and the peasants and others recruited to fight in the infantry or as seamen would be akin to everyday soldiers in today's armed forces and navy.

An apt discussion about the modern American military caste system is an "Overdue Critique of the American Military Caste System," posted by a commentator who received an honorable discharge after 7 years of enlisted service in the U.S. Air Force and calls himself "Wise Sloth." While his article critiques the system and suggests it is due for an overhaul in today's modern enlightened age, it points up the characteristics of the military based in old traditions that go back to medieval times and even before. For example, he points out that the military developed in a time when "the upper class was extremely well educated, and the poor and mostly illiterate. The job of designing and implementing military strategy naturally fell to the upper educated upper class, and the job of dying in the mud naturally fell to the illiterate lower class. This division of labor also served as a way to further institutionalize the caste system that separated the upper class from the lower class."[170]

Then, as Wise Sloth points out, though the industrial revolution and information age created a middle class (though a small middle class did emerge in the towns and cities of the late Middle Ages) and the U.S. Constitution, Bill of Rights, and Universal Declaration of Human Rights reduced the caste system with new social contracts, the military sidestepped most of these social changes by creating the Uniform Code of Military Justice (UCMJ) and the officer corps, which has led to abuses by the officers on other soldiers. Though this once closed caste system has been modified somewhat by the ability of talented individuals of all classes to get training through the U.S. Army War College and scholarships to other military academies,[171] at its heart, the great difference between the status of officers and enlisted men, and now women, in the military, hark back to the disparity in medieval times, when the king and nobles called up an army of peasants and other lower-class recruits to fight for them to subdue other lords or conquer territories in other lands.

One of the signs of this distinction is the use of the salute, whereby an enlistee who sees an officer or a general's staff car has to put their hand on their head until the officer returns the salute, giving the enlistee permission to lower his or her hand. Although this salute may appear a simple sign of respect, the enforcement of the salute reflects the way it maintains the class division between officers and enlistees. As Wise Sloth describes it:

> If an enlisted troop refuses to salute an officer they'll get a letter of counseling. If they still refuse to salute an officer, they'll get a letter of reprimand. Then an Article 15. Then a court martial. Then they will lose rank, pay, privilege and ultimately their freedom when they're sent to jail. When they're released from military prison they'll be given a dishonorable discharge that will prevent them from getting a good job for the rest of their life... Enlisted troops are taught to salute officers out of respect, but failing that, they're forced to salute officers out of fear... So make no mistake, the salute isn't designed to exchange gestures of respect. It's designed to systematically indoctrinate lower ranking troops to accept their place in the lower social caste that robs them of the dignity supposedly guaranteed to all men.[172]

Still another example of this rigid class distinction then and now is the power of orders and the punishments for not following them. For example, just as the king and nobles could order their armies to do anything in battle, such as charging in the face of slings of arrows and galloping horses, an officer today can order enlisted troops to "do anything within the limits of the Geneva Convention," including kill other human beings and face the possibility of being killed oneself. Should the lower caste member refuse, he or she can be court martialed and go to jail.

Moreover, the salute is just a symbol of the rigid military caste system that governs all personal relationships, much as social relationships were governed by one's place in society in the Middle Ages. For example, a Tour of Duty Advisor's Notebook created for fan-fiction writers points out that there are three levels in this caste system – officers, non-commissioned officers (sergeants), and enlisted personnel; and even when these individuals are off-duty or out on the field, none of these groups normally has any contact with the others. A reason for this is that at some point an officer may have to order a subordinate to do something that might get them killed, and the subordinate is less likely to obey the order of the individuals regard themselves as friends or equals. As a result, officers can get in trouble if they socialize with NCOs or enlisted personnel off-duty, and each group has its own clubs, quarters, and recreation areas, which helps to keep them apart. [173]

Then, too, officers are further ranked based on their source of training. At the top are the officers who received their training at West Point for the army or at Annapolis for the navy. Next come the ROTC officers, who are all college graduates, and at the bottom are the OCS officers, who are former Army enlisted personnel who went through a hard six-month training program before being commissioned as second lieutenants.

The housing and eating arrangements in the field likewise reflect these separations by rank, much like the kings and nobles were clearly separated from the infantry not only by their horses and symbols of heraldry, but by their positions and accommodations during battle. For example, a medieval military commander might sit on his horse on the top of a hill watching the battle, while the infantry members slogged ahead with their swords, shields, and crossbows or longbows to attack or defend themselves when the knights on horseback charged in.

The TOD Advisor's Notebook further illustrates these stark differences. Out in the field, such as in Vietnam, unmarried or unaccompanied officers had their own quarters, in which lieutenants shared a room, and captains and majors shared a room. The senior officers, lieutenant colonels and above had air-conditioned trailers, and the generals had their own prefab houses. The officers also had their own latrines and showers, which were cleaned by the enlisted men. When off-duty, the officers had their own officers' club to go to, and on larger bases, there might be separate clubs for officers of different units or of different ranks. Normally, the officers ate together too. In the field, the officers would normally eat with their own command group, and in the event they had to eat in the mess hall with the enlisted men, they would have their own table, usually in a corner, and separate from the NCO's.

In short, everything about the military system, from its ranks to its salutes to accommodations and eating arrangements, helped to reinforce the class distinctions between the high officers on top and the enlisted men below, much as in medieval times, when the kings and nobles distinguished themselves from the everyday soldiers with their horses, different types of weapons, such as the lance and armor, which the ordinary soldiers didn't use, and symbols of heraldry, showing their superior class.

The Importance of Family Connections

Just as the military status structure reflected and reinforced the distinctions between those at the top of the class hierarchy then and now, so did family status, which was extremely important in contributing to power and wealth in both medieval and modern society. Family connections played a major part in helping the kings and nobles increase their power, by helping them acquire land and wealth through wars against other nobles or wars of conquest elsewhere, and by cementing alliances with other wealthy nobles. At the same time, families were important in helping the peasants work their land or acquire income through other sources, and they contributed to the wealthier peasants maintaining or extending their holdings, while providing the funds through taxes, produce, or goods for the kings and nobles to live in their lavish lifestyle. Likewise, today, families play a similar role for the wealthy elite and the struggling lower and middle classes. The following then and now comparisons show how.

The Role of the Family in the Life of the Peasants and Lower to Middle Income Individuals Today

To read about the lifestyles of the peasants and villagers of the Middle Ages is to recognize the many parallels with the lower and lower middle-income individuals of today. There are the same daily struggles to survive, to get ahead within the limits of achievement available for most lower and middle class members, and to pay what one owes to the government – now the state and Federal tax authorities; then the nobles and the king.

In the beginning through the middle of the Middle Ages, from about 400-1200 AD, times were especially difficult for the peasants, because they had little alternate to working the land and being recruited to fight in battles as vassals to the lord. Then, as described by Barbara A. Hanawalt in *The Ties that Bound: Peasant Families in Medieval England*, there were many more opportunities with the development of towns and specialized crafts that provided extra sources of income.[174] The great distinction between the nobility and the other classes remained solidly in place, but at least the peasants, craftsmen, and small shopkeepers had some opportunities to increase their wealth and status, much like the lower, working, and middle classes, including small businesspeople and professionals, do today. While Hanawalt's study is focused on England, a comparable relationship between peasants and nobility existed in France and other countries in Europe at that time.

As Hanawalt describes it, the peasant family was the "basic economic unit for working the land, producing and socializing the younger generation, and finally passing on wealth from one generation to another. Even a sweep of plague through a community did not destroy these familial capacities. People remarried if they lost a spouse, and relatives came to claim a family holding left vacant....Using a range of economic strategies, the peasant family continued to function effectively and often expanded in wealth and options as new economic opportunities opened up in the fifteenth century."[175] Drawing on manorial records, letters, and literary sources, such as medieval folk carols and records, Hanawalt presents a rounded portrait of what life was like for a peasant family in medieval times.

As previously described, the village lands were divided into three distinct areas. In the center were the peasants' houses, outbuildings, and gardens. Then came an agricultural area which consisted of fields and meadows surrounding the village, which was mostly devoted to crops through most of the Middle Ages. Then, after the Black Death wiped out about a third of the population in the middle of the 14th century, more lands were given over to livestock, which required less labor. Finally, there was an area of woods around the village. Commonly, the peasants had contacts with nearby villages and market towns within a five-mile radius of the village.

The fields were divided into strips worked by the peasants, traditionally about one virgate, equal to about 30 acres, although the original land distribution might have been unequal, so some individuals had only a few acres or a half-virgate. But while a half-virgate was common by the 14th century, there were some inequalities in landholding, which became even greater during the 15th century, due to some peasants abandoning their land while others increased their holdings from the vacated lands, so that more and more peasants held more than a virgate. As Hanawalt describes:

> The villages were not occupied by peasant families of equal wealth and status. The village population included virgaters with sufficient land to easily support a family and produce for the market; half-virgaters, who could assume to support a family; and cottages, who would have only a small croft and a few acres in the open fields. Those with little land supplemented their livelihood by hiring out their labor or practicing a craft.[176]

The manorial system administered by the nobility was placed over this agricultural system, since the land was owned by the lord of the manor to whom the peasant owed taxes or a share of the produce. Or in some cases, an agricultural area might be split between two manors, so the peasant owed money to both. Given this distinction between the lords and peasants, in effect two systems existed side by side – the manor where the nobility pursued their lifestyle of luxury and wars built on the work of the peasants and villagers, and the village with its agricultural lands, where the peasants and other workers toiled to support both their lifestyle and that of the nobles.

In contrast to the nobles, the peasants had a much smaller family structure, since they had much less land, property, and power to pass on to their relatives and the next generation. Moreover, they faced the question of legality of ownership, since the lord owned all of the land occupied by the villeins or tenant farmers and in theory the lord could take it back and pass it on to someone else at any time. However, in practice, according to Hanawalt, "the family claimed the right to keep the land from generation to generation, to cultivate it, and to pay such rents as the lord demanded." As a result, the peasants could use whatever inheritance rules they wished, if the change in holding the land was recorded on the manorial court rolls.[177]

In other words, the process worked a little bit like assigning a copyright or a franchise operation today. The copyright owner or franchisor holds the right to the property and is merely letting another individual or company handle the publication or operation permitted by the licensing contract in return for a royalty or franchise fee. But the assignment time is limited, since the original owner can, subject to certain legal restrictions, take back the license agreement at any time, if the publisher or franchisee fails to make the necessary payments or otherwise live up to the licensing requirement.

For a time, peasant families followed the practice of dividing up the land using a system of partible inheritance, which divided the land between the surviving sons, who worked the land jointly or divided it into smaller parcels. But as the population grew and land became limited, the impartible inheritance approach became more common for peasants, as well as the nobility, which meant favoring one son, usually the eldest. For the peasants, this meant the sons who did not get the land sought other land, such as property that had become vacant, sought apprenticeships, or hired themselves out as laborers. Meanwhile, the lords liked this unigeniture system, since it kept the family's tenancy intact, which guaranteed that it would remain a unit of cultivation. In the event that any land became vacant after a death, lords encouraged relatives with a blood tie to the land, such as nieces and nephews, to purchase the right to it at a lower price than anyone with no such tie. Yet, even if the land stayed in the family, the lords still owned it; the peasants were simply buying the right to hold and work on it, thereby contributing to maintaining the disparate class system.

Another trend that developed in the 13th century was peasants going to the English courts to prove they were "free peasants" as opposed to "villeins," and they used their family histories to show they had freeborn relatives, while the lord sought to show they had unfree ancestors in their family tree. Yet, while, the peasants could show a mix of free and unfree relatives to the inquest jury, drawn from members of the community, mostly the lords won, again reflecting their much greater power and influence.

However, for the peasants, the connections to family only went so far, in contrast to the much greater importance on family lineage for the king and nobility that was used to lay claims to position and vast estates. As Hanawalt points out, for the peasants: "Lineage did not have the great importance that it did to the nobility." And certainly, the limited control of land and financial resources contributed to lesser importance, much as is true for lower income families today, since they have less ability to help one another. As a result, as Hanawalt notes, medieval peasants "did not routinely live in extended families and seem not to have relied extensively on kin." Rather, according to the medieval records, the peasants did not exchange work with kin or rely on their extended to help in hard times. Instead, they largely relied on the work of their nuclear family and supplemented that by hiring services or engaging in some reciprocity with their neighbors.[178]

In short, for the medieval peasants by the 14th and 15th century, kinship networks tended to be loose and played only a small part in the social structure of a village. Most important was the family's community status based on the property they owned. In the lower economic group, the basic social unit was a small nuclear family, in which the children left home to work as servants and laborers, and since the family had little property to distribute, they made few claims on the family. But even for middle and higher income peasants with more property, where sons and daughters might marry while the father was still alive and live on the same property, thereby providing some mutual help in the fields, neighbors were still more important than kin for helping out with the work.

In turn, the size of the landholdings and the amount of labor available was the basis for the peasant family's economic status. Those with more land and labor did much better than those who only owned two or three acres, while the poorest in the community had to depend on wage labor, begging, and gleaning, which meant collecting leftover crops from the farmer's field after the harvest. However, having more land meant more rent was due to the lord in the form of money or produce. Additionally, each family had to pay assorted fees and fines, such as a fee for taking a case to the lord's court or a fine for engaging in certain prohibited economic activities, such as brewing and cutting wood or failing to meet the terms of the lease for their property. A key reason for paying all these fees and fines was to support the noble class. As Hanawalt puts it:

> The cost of maintaining the noble class was a great and inescapable drain on peasant family resources and was ameliorated only slightly by the feasts that the lord owed his villeins for boon work and his generosity (often stingy) in forgiving fines of those too poor to pay.[179]

The equivalent today might be the high rents and taxes individuals and families pay to landlords, mortgage holders, and various levels of government, which contribute to the wealth of the upper classes; the political class comprised of mostly wealthy office holders; and the laws which favor the wealthy in many ways, including tax exemptions and lower tax rates for capital gains.

Peasant households also had to contribute to ceremonial expenses, such as paying annual tithes to the church, giving to charity for the local poor, and paying for community and religious ceremonies, such as celebrations of saints days, and for family ceremonies, such as baptisms, marriages, and funerals. Otherwise, the household would face the loss of status, ridicule, and even physical violence for not participating. Such ceremonies were considered so important that families might even go into debt or ruin themselves with heavy investments of funds to save face. It's the medieval equivalent of "Keeping up with the Jones" that reflects the emphasis on success and achievement for the individual and family today, though within the limits of being part of the lower to upper middle classes, since few can hope to rise to the stratosphere of the superrich.

In any case, like middle income families today, the medieval families sought to better themselves by engaging in a variety of economic activities. For example, a family with sufficient land and money could increase their land holdings by renting or buying parcels of land, acquiring them as dowry, or by clearing and claiming them, which could also be a way to set up their sons in separate households. And wealthy villagers could employ others, such as laborers to help with the harvest and servants to help their wives with brewing, housework, and other side economic activities. At the time, acquiring additional land was the most common way that the peasants gained greater prosperity and status in the community, though the more successful peasants also used advantageous marriages to increase their landholdings and status, much like the nobility then and now. For example, if a father had no sons, the daughter could inherit the family holding, making her a desirable marriage partner, as could a widow who took over the land held by her late husband. In turn, a wealthy widow or heiress might be likely to marry into one of the prominent village families, who could provide her with a substantial dowry to match her inheritance.

Still another way a family might increase its economic status was through gaining skills or influential offices. For example, the family might arrange to educate one son, commonly the oldest, so he could be hired into a management position as a manorial official.

Or a family member might seek to become a bailiff or obtain a village office, such as a juror. In fact, these positions were so important that the primary village families "jealously guarded access to these village offices and became village oligarchs."[180]

In sum, among the peasant families, there was a class structure into three basic status positions. The wealthy families had more prosperous landholdings, which they passed down to their children, and because of better diets, they had more children to help in farming the land, or they hired labor. These wealthy families also had the capital to purchase additional land and the labor to work it, and they entered advantageous marriages that increased their wealth and status. Next on the status hierarchy were the middle status villagers, who had sufficient lands and family labor to make a living, but it was difficult to pass on the family holdings to all children, so that some of the younger ones might not receive their full share and would have to find alternative ways to make a living. These families also relied the most on reciprocal arrangements with neighbors and friends for help in hard times. Finally, the cottagers had only a few acres of land, but they could better their position by pursuing a trade or craft on the side, particularly after the population declined due to the Black Death in the middle of the 14th century.

In turn, there are parallels with the social and economic structures of today, where lower and middle income families tend to be much smaller nuclear units, whereas combining together as a family unit can contribute to the success of the business, as well as to the fortunes and status of the family. There is even a *Family Business Magazine*, which has been publishing for over 30 years as of November 2020.

This success of the family business has long been recognized. A decade ago, according to a 2011 *Business Insider* article by Karlee Weinmann and Aimee Groth, around one-third of the top 500 companies on the Standard and Poor Index are family-controlled, and many of these are more successful than other firms in revenue and employment growth. Why? Because, they "have a longer-term view of investment, they're more stable, and inspire more trust and commitment in their employees." Some of the biggest companies have propelled their owners into the high ranks of today's modern nobility, such as Walmart, owned by the Walton family, with annual revenues of $422 billion; the Ford Motor Company, owned by the Ford family, with annual revenues of $129 billion; Cargill, the agri-business supergiant, owned by the Cargill and Macmillan families, with annual revenues of $108 billion; and Koch Industries, which started out as an oil and gas business, with $100 billion in annual revenues. [181]

More recently, The Family Capital 750 has been ranking the top 750 family businesses and points out that "family businesses stand at the center of the global economy," noting that these 750 business generated $9.1 trillion in revenue in 2018 and had 30.5 employees, as a major driver of economic growth around the world. In their view, the advantages of being a family business include "strong values, patience capital, long-term goals, and fast decision-making.[182] These companies also have a long history, several dating back to the mid-19th century; others to the beginning or middle of the 20th century.

Many of the companies listed were on the top of the top 500 list in 2011, and now their revenues are even more. To qualify for their list as a family business, the family members must control at least 50% of the voting shares in a privately held company or 32% of the voting rights in a publicly listed company. The top ten companies on their list are these:

- Walmart, Inc, in the retail and consumer market, owned by the Walton family, founded in 1945, with $500 billion in revenues; up from $422 in 2011.
- Volkswagen AG, in the automotive sector in Germany, owned by the Porsche and Piech families, founded in 1937, $270 billion in revenues.
- Berkshire Hathaway, Inc., in the financial services sector, owned by the Buffet family, founded in 1889, $248 billion in revenues.

- Exor N.V., in the financial services sector in the Netherlands, owned by the Agnelli family, founded in 1927, $163 billion in revenues.
- Ford Motor Company, in the automotive sector, owned by the Ford family, founded in 1903, $248 billion in revenues; up from $118 billion in 2011.
- Schwarz-Group, in the retail and consumer markets in Germany, owned by the Schwarz family, founded in 1930, $118 billion in revenues.
- Cargill, Incorporated, in the retail and consumer markets, owned by the Cargill family, founded in 1865; $115 billion in revenue; up from $108 billion in 2011.
- Bayerische Motoren Werke AG, in the automotive sector in Germany, owned by the Quarndt and Klatten families, founded in 1916; $112 billion in revenues.
- Tata Sons Private Ltd, in the diversified industries sector in India, owned by the Tata family, founded in 1868; $111 billion in revenues.
- Koch Industries, in the diversified industries sector, owned by the Koch and Marshall families, founded in 1940; $110 billion in revenues, up from $100 billion in 2011.[183]

Given their long history, these huge family businesses are like the royal dynasties, which have lasted for generations, in medieval times.

While some family businesses have become mega-industries, for the most part, these small family businesses have remained small business, operated by family members, and sometimes with the help of friends, much like some peasant families were able to become wealthy and acquire local village status and political influence. Still their success came on the lands and in the villages owned by the lord of the manor; and normally they were unable to catapult themselves into the rarified stratosphere of the nobles, though some family members with sufficient education might gain some lower level manorial positions, such as manager of a manor. Today the main levers for entering the modern day nobility include attaining huge wealth in business, such as in investment banking, Wall Street, founding a mega-million company, or joining the celebrity class at the top of the entertainment A-list roster.

But for most individuals starting out in the lower, middle income, and lower upper classes – comparable to the three tiers in the peasant economy, that kind of leap is impossible. Numerous researchers and writers point to the limited class mobility in America, which is even less than in other Western Europe and English-speaking nations. So, individuals are largely stuck in the same social and economic class as their parents – an awareness that has been growing and leading to increased street protests, much like the peasant protests that gained force in the mid-14th century. As Jason DeParle writes in a *New York Times* article, though American life is built on the belief that one can rise from humble origins to economic heights, many researchers have reached the opposite conclusion. That is because:

> Americans enjoy less economic mobility than their peers in Canada and much of Western Europe ...
>
> One reason for the mobility gap may be the depth of American poverty, which leaves poor children starting especially far behind. Another may be the unusually large premiums that American employers pay for college degrees. Since children generally follow their parents' educational trajectory, that premium increases the importance of family background and stymies people with less schooling ...
>
> At least five large studies in recent years have found the United States to be less mobile than comparable nations ... Just 8 percent of American men at the bottom rose to the top fifth ... Despite frequent references to the United States as a classless society, about 62% of Americans (male and female) raised in the top fifth of incomes stay in the top fifths, according to research by the Economic Mobility

Project of the Pew Charitable Trusts. Similarly, 65 percent born in the bottom fifth stay in the bottom two-fifths.[184]

A key reason for this lack of mobility is family background. Though most Americans may have higher incomes than their parents because the country has grown richer, they are still limited by their family's economic status in what they can do. Among other things, "poor Americans have to work their way up from a lower floor," and the high pay opportunities for more educated workers give the children of educated and affluent families an advantage, since they "have access to better schools and arrive in them more prepared to learn," because upper-income families have more money to invest in their children's education and better understand what is necessary to get a good education. Then, too, another limitation to mobility is "the sheer magnitude of the gaps between rich and the rest," giving the privileged even more power to protect their own interests.

This observation is echoed by Columbia University statistician and economist Howard Steven Friedman in an article on "The American Myth of Social Mobility." As he notes, the belief in the "American dream" is shown by numerous surveys which indicate that "Americans have a greater faith in their country being a meritocracy than citizens of nearly every other country on earth." But this belief is a myth, since there is "far less social mobility in the United States than in other countries and other studies have shown clearly that this mobility is declining." Moreover, the educational system plays a role in supporting this economic divide, since the amount of money one's parents have is much more influential than academic potential in getting a higher education, which is a key to socioeconomic mobility. Thus, as Friedman concludes, the data about family status and mobility "point to a rigid and entrenched structure of wealth at odds with our American sense of this being the land of opportunity."[185]

In short, in medieval times and today, family status is a key factor influencing one's success. While one's family can provide some help in getting ahead, its position in society limits the level of success the individual can achieve. Yes, the family business can be a route for advancing the interests of a family and the individuals within it; but only a small number of family businesses achieve the super success that can propel them into the realm of the superrich. Moreover, most of these modern lower and middle class families tend to be smaller nuclear families like the peasant families, and members don't have the extended family networks where lineage, property, and power help to maintain that status and power from generation to generation – in both the Middle Ages and today.

The Power and Influence of the Families of the Nobility and Superrich

The power and influence of the families of the nobles and king during the Middle Ages are widely known, and in many cases, they can be traced back to the battles to establish and maintain a kingdom dating back to the fall of the Roman Empire, when tribes battled it out for power and warrior kings and nobles emerged as the victors. Then, as the victors consolidated their power, family lineages were born, and the assistance of other family members was drawn upon to maintain or expand one's power over a kingdom or noble's manor. In much the same fashion, the families of the superrich today have contributed to gaining both wealth and political power.

For example, in England, the first line of kings were the Saxon rulers, beginning with Alfred the Great, King of Wessex, who united most of England in 871 and continued the line through his sons and their sons, until briefly, a Danish king Harthacnut, took the throne in 1016 to 1035 as a result of Danish conquests. But Harthacnut was soon thrown out, when Edward the Confessor, in the Saxon lineage, regained the throne until William the Conquerer's conquest in 1066 set the stage for a series of Norman Kings, until the Angevin or Plantagenet kings gained the throne under Henry II, who became king in 1189. He reigned for about 200 years, through the reign of Richard II, who was king of England until 1399, when he was killed during the Crusades. Thereafter, the next family lineages to gain control of the throne were the Lancastrian and Yorkist kings, beginning with Henry IV in 1399, through Richard III, who ruled until 1485, setting the stage for the reign of the Tudors beginning with Henry VII in 1485, at the end of the Middle Ages.[186]

As described in Chapters 3 to 5, the political history of England and France, as well as the other European nations that emerged by the High Middle Ages around 1000 AD, is marked by these family units banding together to fight to put one of their own on the throne and keep the throne in the family after the death of the king. For example, this occurred in England, in Scotland, and in France, where the Carolingian dynasty was followed by the rule of the Capet family and its near relatives for nearly 1000 years.

The typical way to keep the throne in the family was through the system of primogeniture, whereby the throne was normally passed on to the eldest son, or if he wasn't old enough, he received the title, while a regent handled the actual running of the government, until the king came of age. But sometimes the rivalry between sons for the throne led to betrayal and murder within the royal family, or sometimes by other noble usurpers seeking to gain the throne. In some cases, a younger son gained the throne when an older son died of an illness or in a battle, such as to fight off invaders or to conquer territory during the Crusades. In other cases, when the king had no sons, commonly the throne would pass to a close relative to keep the throne in the family, though often battles erupted between the relatives, with the support of other family members, to gain control.

The great lords followed a similar pattern of keeping the manor in the family, primarily through the system of primogeniture, whereby the right to the manor, like the right to the throne, normally went to the eldest son. What of the sons who didn't become king or lord of a manor? Commonly, they joined the priesthood or fought for the king or lord as knights in battle.

Later, once a class of rich and powerful bourgeoisie developed in the late Middle Ages with the expansion of trade in the 14th and

15th century, they aped the nobility by keeping their business and wealth within the family.

Meanwhile, the women played a role in strengthening the family's power by being pledged in marriages to benefit the family, at a time when arranged marriages among the nobility were the norm, and romantic love was an ideal off in the future. Despite the ideal of courtly love whereby knights battled it out to impress a lady of the nobility, when it came to marriage, the head of the family would weight all sorts of strategic considerations, where skill in battle was just one component and creating alliances through marriage between powerful families was a key goal. For example, in 1135, Henry I's daughter Mathilda was married to the count of Anjour in France, and in 1154, King Henry II, the son of Mathilda came to the throne, which marked the beginning of the Plantagenet dynasty in England. Having been the Count of Anjou, Henry now gained many lands in France, including Normandy, Brittany, and Anjou. Then, to gain even more lands in France, Henry II married Eleanor of Aquitaine, who had once been the wife of Louis VII of France. Though England lost most of the French territory during the 1202-1203 war with France, and Eleanor entered a convent at 79, the attempt to secure more territory through an auspicious marriage worked for a time.[187]

As another example, the kingdom of Portugal was founded as a result of the alliance formed after Alfonso VI, the king of Castille from 1073 to 1086, gave his daughter Theresa in marriage to Henry of Burgundy, who had been one of the knights helping Alfonso fight the Muslims. As part of her dowry, Alfonso VI gave Theresa and Henry the counties of Portucali and Coimbra, that later became the foundation for the kingdom of Portugal.

Still later in 1420, after Henry V reconquered Normandy for the English in the Battle of Agincourt and forced King Charles VI of France to sign the Treaty of Troyes, recognizing the English conquest, he also married Charles VI daughter, making him heir to the French throne, while Charles VI disinherited his own son. Eventually, these plans never worked out, since Henry V died of dysentery, leaving an infant son, who later became King Henry VI of England, more fighting, with some help from Joan of Arc, led the French to drive the English out of Normandy and Acquitaine, leaving only Calais under English control when the Hundred Years' War ended in 1453. But these plans for strategic marriages show how marriage was used like a chess piece to create political alliances and gain territory.

In like fashion, as a wealthy merchant class developed in the cities in the late Middle Ages, the family played a key role in creating the superwealthy banking dynasties, especially in the city-states of Italy, which were the center of the banking business. One of the most notable of these family was the Medici family of Florence, who initially gained their wealth through the textile trade and dominated the city government. First to hold high public office was Ardingo de Medici in 1296, and over the next 30 years, two other family members held office. Subsequently, after a period of decline, Giovanni Medici increased the family's economic status which translated into political power, and he took on the same high political office in 1421, and following his death in 1429, Cosimo de Medici took over the leadership of the family offices. [188] A key to the Medici's financial and political success was their creation of independent banks throughout Europe, where each bank manager was responsible for any loans made by his bank, so another bank or the parent bank had no responsibility for any losses. The result was the family became extremely wealthy, leading them to dominate the government of Florence, gain control over the church, and marry into the royal families of Europe.

Similarly, the Fugger family in German gained their wealth through banking. Initially, Jacob Fugger, a descendant of the Fugger merchant family in Augsburg, became a major merchant, mining entrepreneur, and banker between 1487 and 1525. At first, the family gained its wealth through the textile trade with Italy, and then the company expanded quickly after Jacob and his brothers Ulrich and George began engaging in banking transactions with the House of Hapsburg and mining operations. By 1487,

Jacob had become the head of the Fugger business operations, and he worked closely with the Hapsburg dynasty. He even used his wealth to influence European politics, including paying bribes to gain the election of the Spanish king Charles V to become Holy Roman Emperor, and he funded the marriages which enabled the House of Hapsburg to gain kingdoms in Bohemia and Hungary. At his death in 1525, he bequeathed the company assets to his nephew Anton Fugger, who continued the family tradition.[189]

Likewise, today, the superrich families have created economic and political dynasties. While arranged marriages are no longer the norm, romance has still led to marriages among the very wealthy, which has contributed to the increasing power of these families. Many of these families in the U.S. trace their fortunes back to the early 20th century or even to the late 1800s, the age of the Robber Barons, and they have used those resources to maintain their position, while others have acquired their wealth since the 1950s. Whatever the original source of wealth, once the founder has established the family fortune, successful families have used that wealth to pass their good fortune on to their children, grow even richer through successful business ventures and investments, and often marriages between the children of wealth families, though not arranged as during the Middle Ages, have contributed to even further success and power.

For example, in 1937, Ferdinand Lundberg created a list of dynasties in *America's 60 Families* by using tax records to uncover their financial and political dealings and estimate their family fortunes. As he wrote back then, and is still true today, although some names have been changed, is the following:

> The United States is owned and dominated today by a hierarchy of its sixty richest families, buttressed by no more than ninety families of lesser wealth ... These families are the living center of the modern industrial oligarchy which dominates the United States, functioning discreetly under a *de jure* democratic form of government behind which a *de*

facto government, absolutist and plutocratic in its lineaments, has gradually taken form since the Civil War. This *de facto* government is actually the government of the United States — informal, invisible, shadowy. It is the government of money in a dollar democracy.[190]

The major families, listed according to their 1924 tax records with their primary source of wealth, include the following among the top 21 families, which are still widely known today:

- Rockefeller family – Standard Oil
- Morgan family – J.P. Morgan & Company
- Ford family – Ford Motors
- Mellon Family – Aluminum Company
- Vanderbilt family – NY Central Railroad
- Whitney Family – Standard Oil
- Du Pont Family – DuPont
- Guggenheim Family – American Smelting & Refining Family
- Duke Family – American Tobacco Company
- Lehman Family – Lehman Brothers (at least until the company collapsed, contributing to the Great Recession in 2008)
- Reynolds Family – R.J. Reynolds
- Astor family – Real estate

In fact, a list of the most enduring families today in the *Town and Country Survey* includes many of the families on this 1924 list.

1. Du Pont – founder of the chemical company by the same name
2. Vanderbilt – built his wealth through railroads and shipping
3. Rockefeller – includes John D. Sr., the founder of Standard Oil
4. Mellon – founders of Alco Gulf and Oil
5. Fanjul – founders of the sugar and real estate conglomerate, the Fanjul Corporation

6. Hearst – includes newspaper baron William Randolph
7. Flagler – one of the founders of Standard Oil
8. Sulzberger – publishing family of the New York Times
9. Getty – founder of Getty oil, Getty Images and the J. Paul Getty Museum
10. Wainwright – includes a Life magazine editor and three successful musicians: Rufus, Martha and Lucy[191]

The 50 most prominent families in America were featured in a 2013 issue of *Town and Country*,[192] and at the top of the list is the Bush family, which includes "two former presidents, a senator, and two governors, according to Mayley Peterson, reporting in a UK publication: *Mail Online*. In second place is the Kerry family, which includes Secretary of State John Kerry, followed by the Murdochs, led by Rupert Murdoch, the billionaire chairman and CEO of News Corps, and the Emanuels, which includes Chicago's mayor Rahm Emanuel Ezekiel, a health care consultant, and Ari, a Hollywood superagent. More specifically, the top ten of these most powerful wealthy families which have members in top political positions are these:

1. Bush – includes two former presidents, a senator, and two governors
2. Kerry – includes the current secretary of state and former senator John Kerry
3. Murdoch – includes billionaire chairman and CEO of News Corporation, Rupert Murdoch
4. Emanuel – includes brothers: Chicago Mayor Rahm, healthcare consultant Ezekiel, and Hollywood superagent Ari
5. Kennedy – includes a former president, two senators, and a U.S. ambassador
6. McCain – includes powerful Republican Sen. John McCain, also a former presidential nominee
7. Powell – includes former secretary of state, Colin Powell, who also served as chairman of the Joint Chiefs of Staff and national security adviser

8. Pritzker – one of the wealthiest families in the U.S., which owns the Hyatt hotel chain and the Marmon Group
9. Jordan – includes Vernon E. Jordan Jr., leader in the civil rights movement and adviser to former President Bill Clinton
10. Barzun – includes Matthew Winthrop Barzun, a former CNET Networks executive who is also a U.S. ambassador[193]

Still others mentioned in an article on the "Top 10 American Political Dynasties," include the Cuomo dynasty, which includes Mario Cuomo, who became New York governor in 1983, and his oldest son Andrew, who ran for governor in 2010 and won the race. For a time, Andrew was connected to the powerful Kennedy family when he married Kerry Kennedy, although they divorced in 2003. Now Andrew is considering a White House run in 2015. Still another dynasty is the Rockefellers, who gained their political cloud as a result of John D. Rockefeller's fortune derived from the Standard Oil Company. John D. Rockefeller Jr.'s marriage to Abby Alrich, a daughter of a Rhode Island Senator, was regarded as a "politically savvy union," and it helped Nelson Rockefeller in his quest to become the Republican governor of New York as a result of well-funded campaign, and in 1974, he was the vice-president during Nixon's first term. More recently, John D. Rockefeller's great-grandson Jay Rockefeller continued the political legacy by becoming the governor of West Virginia for two terms, after which is was elected to the U.S. Senate four times, most recently in 2012.[194]

These 10 most enduring families on the 2013 *Town and Country* list are also included in a slide show on the *Town and Country* website, which points out that "generation after generation, these American dynasties have maintained their lofty position.[195] Some of the most recent success stories, like Mark Zuckerberg of Facebook fame or Sergey Brin and Larry Page of Google might not qualify, since they have become self-made billionaires, though they might begin their own dynasty. Rather, as in the Middle Ages, the modern families have built their dynasties through the same levers of dominance that led to prominence then, among them "money, power, philan-thropy, and taste."[196]

For many of these families, the foundations date back to the height of the Gilded Age in the late 1800s, when most of the founders made their money from the forces that fueled the Industrial Revolution, which included railways, shipping, oil, steel, and manufacturing. At that time, there were only several hundred prominent families in New York and around the country, and most tended to know each other, much like the superwealthy nobles and royalty of the Middle Ages tended to socialize with others in court society. As Richard McGill L. Murphy points out in "Making the Cut," "They intermar-ried, attended the same churches, graduated from the same schools, worked at the same firms, and joined the same clubs. And anyone who was anyone in society could be found in the Social Register."[197]

Since then, there has been a reshuffling, with many of the world's richest family been created more recently, as a result of the high-tech revolution. Then, too, these lists of wealthy families have gone global, whereby the Americans have only half of the wealthi-est families, while the other richest families, are in other countries, especially the oil rich Middle East.

For example, according to a LoveMoney listing in March 2020, the ten richest families globally were these — with six in the U.S. and the others Middle Eastern countries whose wealth came origi-nally from oil:[198]

1 - The Saud family, in Saudi Arabia, with a worth of $1.4 tril-lion; it has rule the country since 1744.

2 - The Al-Sabah family, in Kuwait, with a worth of $360 billion; which has reigned over the country for 247 years.

3 - The Al Thani Family, in Quatar, with a worth of $335 billion, which has been the ruling family there since the mid-19th century.

4 - The Walton family, in the U.S., with a worth of $195 billion, with a family fortune due to its Walmart chain founded in Arkansas back in 1962.

5 - The Bezos family, in the U.S., with a worth of $150 billion, based on the founding of Amazon in 1994.

6 - The Al Nayan family, in Abu Dhabi, with a worth of $150 billion, which has been the ruling family there since 1793.

7 - The Gates family, in the U.S., with a worth of $106 billion, based on the success of Microsoft, founded in 1975.

8 - The Koch family, in the U.S., with a worth of $84 billion, based on the success of an oil-refining company in 1940.

9 - The Buffett family, in the U.S., with a worth of $81 billion, based on the success of his very successful holding company, founded in 1970.

10 -The Mars family, in the U.S. with a worth of $78 billion, based on its founding as a candy and pets food company in 1911 and expansion into other popular brands.

The four other wealthiest U.S. families to round out the top ten are these:

12 -The Zuckerberg family of Facebook fame, with a worth of $70 billion.

14 -The Ellison family, whose wealth derives originally from the Oracle Corporation, with a worth of $65 billion.

17 -The Page family, whose wealth derives originally from Google, now part of Alphabet, with a worth of $56 billion.

18 -The Brin family, whose wealth also derives originally from Google, now part of Alphabet, with a worth of $54 billion.

Today, the top American families have become global in scope, given today's media and celebrity driven society, and many are in the entertainment industry, creating well-known family empires, who are often interconnected through marriages between super-stars who are part of family dynasties. Certainly, many superstars have rocketed to the stratosphere from low-income and middle-income families. But many others are propelled by their family connections, such as Donald Trump, who made his fortune in the real estate market, and has several children, most notably Ivanka and Eric, who have followed in the family's footsteps in both contributing to his expanding real estate and casino empire and in joining his *Celebrity Apprentice* franchise on TV. These connections eventually landed them in The White House, which President Trump turned into a family enterprise, with Ivanka Trump and her husband Jared Kushner becoming senior advisers, and his two sons Don Jr. and Erik running his various businesses, which President Trump remained connected to and used to reap rewards from government activities, such as by having events at his Mar-a-Lago estate in Florida and at his golf course where his secret service entourage and others had to pay for travel, rooms, and food.

Another example is the success of the Kardashians, who parlayed their connections to the O.J. Simpson case, since O.J. was represented by celebrity lawyer Robert Kardashian, into fame through their own reality show – *Keeping Up with the Kardashians*, which went on for 20 seasons until September 2020. They also created even more wealth and renown through a branded empire of fashion and beauty products linked to their name. At the same time, the Kardashian daughters continued the tradition of the superwealthy, in the Middle Ages and now, of marrying others with great wealth. For example, Kim married Kanye West, who has his own music empire and fashion line.

Plus, there are many other examples of modern-day superrich family dynasties with parallels to the medieval noble and royal families. And like their earlier counterparts, family members have parlayed their wealth into political power and social dominance, both then and now.

CHAPTER 8: THE LIFESTYLES OF THE SUPERRICH AND OTHERS – THEN AND NOW

A part from their political and economic clout, helped by family connections, the superrich royalty, nobility, and later the merchant class of the late Middle Ages share lifestyle similarities with the superrich of today, despite the vast differences in technology, while the peasants and artisans have much in common in their way of life with the lower-income classes of today. This chapter considers these parallels, from religion to art, culture, education, and leisure times. I'll describe each of one briefly to show general patterns; obviously each of these areas could be expanded with much more detail into a separate book.

The Power of Religion and the Media Today

It may not seem like the most likely comparison, but in many ways religion in the Middle Ages plays much the same role that the modern media does in providing legitimacy and credibility to those with other forms of power. Plus, both have use their support to build the awareness and power of those they support.

Clearly, during the Middle Ages in Western Europe, the Catholic Church was a dominant institution, and like the secular rulers, it had its own territories, where its abbeys and monasteries were akin to the manors of the nobles. The Church additionally provided a unifying force for the kingdoms of Europe and Britain.

While the Church was like an island of culture and learning in the first centuries after the fall of the Roman Empire, when England and Europe were engaged in heavy fighting to acquire territory and stave off invader, and it became its own wealthy empire, its ceremonies helped to sanctify the rule of the kings. In some cases, the support of the Church contributed to a ruler gaining the support of the people or helping other nobles to ascend to the throne. Then, in return for its support, often the new king would give the Church additional territory or funds to say thanks, a little like a political official today might promote legislation favorable to its big corporate contributors. While such political patronage helped to bind the loyalty of the lords to a king and lessor lords to the larger ones in the medieval feudal system that spread through England and Europe, a comparable system of contributions to the Church helped to bolster the Church's loyalty to that ruler, too, which in turn strengthened his rule. In turn, the rulers provided their own support to strengthen the church, especially in the early Middle Ages when the church suffered greatly from the invasions as well as from internal chaos and corruption.

For example, as Tierney notes of the period from the 9th through the 11th century:

> The strong pontificate of Nicholas I (from 858-867) provided only a temporary rally of papal power. After his death, the papacy and indeed the whole Western church were dragged down to a squalid state of corruption by the violence and anarchy of the times...The papacy was in a particularly vulnerable situation. Rome and the Papal States were continually threatened by Muslim incursions from Sicily, and there was no strong king or emperor to defend them...The popes of the early tenth century were merely chiefs of aristocratic factions...Meanwhile, all over Europe, the church was suffering grievously from the effects of Viking, Magyar, and Saracen invasions...Moreover, throughout the Frankish kingdom, lay lords took advantage

of the confusion to usurp church lands...In order to survive, the church was obliged to enter into close relations with the lay rulers, the only power able to offer protection.[199]

Then, in the tenth and eleventh centuries, a series of reforms transformed and strengthened the Church. As Tierney describes, the formation of the abbey of Cluny in France in 910 helped provide the foundation in which the abbot there became the head of an empire within the church, which included hundreds of monasteries spread throughout most of western Europe. Around the same time, an independent monastic reform movement was carried out in England by St. Dunstan that was supported by King Edgar who ruled from 959 to 975; and in Italy, a lay piety movement helped reform the church, too. The result is that these changes contributed to the Church gaining its great power and ability to influence the politics of England and Europe. As Tierney writes:

All these movements flowed together in a great international movement of reform led by the papacy from the mid-eleventh century onward. This papal reform movement can be called epoch-making...It transformed the structure of the medieval church and, in doing so, profoundly influenced the whole future history of Western institutions.[200]

One of the most important of these reformers was Leo IX, who ruled from 1049 to 1054. Among other things, he created a body of cardinals and he traveled around Europe, holding councils throughout the land to promote and implement the new reform decrees. Through his efforts, he effectively reestablished the leadership of the papacy of the Western church, and other reformers carried on his work after his death.

With its growing strength, the church entered lay politics. For example, in Germany, Pope Gregory VII encouraged the nobles to rise against their kings, and while the old order did continue, this Investiture Contest led to the creation of a kind of "duality in medieval government, a persistent tension between church and state ... Henceforth, there was never just one hierarchy of government, commanding obedience by divine right, but always two hierarchies, each limiting the power of the other." At the same time, after 1100, the papacy became more engaged in the world. Before then, devout Christians had sought to retreat from the world in an abbey against the barbarity outside. But now, as Tierney points out, the late 11th century reformers were inspired by the ideal of going out into the world to reshape it. They wanted to "make a harmonious Christian commonwealth out of the turbulent society of early medieval Europe."[201]

The result is well-known today. Essentially, a new wave of religious enthusiasm spread through England and Europe in the second half of the eleventh century and the first half of the twelfth century, most commonly within the established church, and especially through the creation of new religious orders. At the same time, as previously discussed, this spread of religious enthusiasm contributed to the impetus for the kings and knights to organize armies to go on religious crusades to recapture the Holy Lands for Christianity. Also, with the help of canon law, which was revived by the medieval intellectuals seeking order in response to the chaos and violence of the past centuries, the papacy established even more power over all the Western churches. As Tierney describes the process:

> Medieval intellectuals had a passion for order. It was a natural reaction against the chaos and violence from which their civilization was emerging ... Endemic warfare was taken for granted and ... the only known legal procedures were comparable to those of some savage and primitive tribal society in the modern world. Every fief had its own set of customs. There was no common law that was applied over a whole kingdom ... Moreover, the old rules of law were singularly ill-adapted to cope with problems arising out of the commercial life of the new cities.[202]

In response, to create order from this chaos, from about 1100 the medieval schools began to enthusiastically study classical Roman law, and the tenets of Roman law were incorporated to some extent in all the legal system of Western Europe, especially in the city-states of Italy, and to a lesser extent in England. The result was a codification of legal traditions both by the governments and the church, which not only strengthened the power of the king but of the papacy, so the pope now played a much more powerful role in advising and supporting the kings, in effect giving a divine sanction to their actions. As Tierney notes:

> This was an important stage in the growth of papal power. The theoretical claims of the twelfth century lawyer popes were not significantly different from those of their predecessors. What was new was that the peoples began to create an adequate administrative machine to give practical effect to those claims. From this time onward, the old papal claim to primacy of jurisdiction became translated into effective supervision over the more important affairs of all the Western churches.[203]

At the same time, this increased papal power led to not only a series of Crusades to regain territory in the Holy Land for both the kings and the popes, but the papacy's secular role in calling for and recruiting armies contributed to its increased power. In effect, the many leading kings and nobles who answered the call to go on a Crusade were working for the papacy. Moreover, by the 13th and 14th centuries, the pope was not only a spiritual leader, but a landowner and political administrator, giving the Vatican the same powers and responsibilities as a duke or lord might have.

These landholdings helped to make the papacy very rich through its various taxes, which included tithes of 10% of all profits or crops; benefices which were pieces of land given to a priest, bishop, or other member of the church by the kings and nobles; and other taxes, such as for the Crusades and additional rents. This great wealth in turn, contributed to the many struggles within the papacy to be the pope, which were finally resolved by the Council of Constance in 1409. But despite these internal divisions, the Church played a key role in politics, especially by the High Middle Ages, and it sometimes used its threat of excommunication to control the king and great lords, since this was a powerful threat at a time when religious fervor and canon law dominated society.

The Church gained this great power because by the High Middle Ages it had become the largest landowner in Western Europe, due to the king and lords giving it tracts of land as a charitable act or penance for wrongdoing. As a result, bishops and abbots sometimes became more powerful than secular lords and rulers, and they led the Church in playing an important role in politics. Also Church gained power because the people in medieval society accepted the church's central role in their lives, as the "mediator between the people and God." As a result, people looked to the church as a place to pray, attend mass, and participate in its sacraments and sacred rituals, including the seven sacraments which only a priest could perform. These marked the most important phases of everyday life from birth to death – baptism, confirmation, marriage, penance, communion, Holy Orders, and last rites. These sacraments were necessary for people to gain salvation in the next life, and anyone, including the lords and the king, could be denied the sacraments for disobeying the Church or doing evil acts. In turn, being excommunicated could mean the loss of support by others, which could be a powerful weapon in the hands of the Church, regardless of an individual's personal beliefs. As a result, many powerful lords and kings yielded to the Church when threatened with the penalty of excommunication or, even worse, an interdict, in which no one living in their territory could participate in the Church's sacraments.

Still another way in which the Church gained power was in administering most of the justice, which included the church courts trying both criminal and civil cases and making decisions about marriage, divorce, and wills, which passed on property from one individual on death to another. In turn, these decisions by the church were accepted by the English and European lords and monarchs, since they were all Christians; then public officials enforced these laws and decisions.

The power of the Church also led to the Inquisition and witchcraft trials during the High and Late Middle ages, starting around 1230. The Inquisition was a war on heresy, in which the inquisitors were responsible solely to the pope, not to the local bishops.

The increased power of the popes also contributed to a series of alliances between the current pope and the kings of England, France, and other European countries that provided political and territorial gains for both. For example, in the early 14th century, King Philip IV of France decided to go after the Knights Templars who were formed during the Crusades but had grown in power, so King Philip saw them as threat and wanted their lands in France. As a result, after accusing the Templars of blasphemous and homosexual acts and torturing them to gain confessions, the got the pope to agree to suppress the order, and in 1314 he had all of the leaders burned at the stake. Then, Philip gained most of their lands, aided by the support of the pope.

In short, during the High and Late Middle Ages, the Church, through its wealth and expanding administrative activities, played a major role in controlling everyday life and behavior, and in influencing secular politics by supporting the kings and nobles or threatening to withdraw support through excommunication or interdiction. This role of the church has many parallels with the media today, although obviously, the media, born from modern technology, didn't exist in medieval times. But what is comparable is the way the media has become like a wealthy kingdom that is pervasive in all aspects of life and plays a major role in influencing politics and bestowing its blessings on individuals who are already wealthy or gain their wealth through media support. Then, too, like the medieval Church, the modern media has the power to take it all away by denying its support or turning against a person who has fallen out of favor, much like the medieval Church might use its power of excommunication or interdiction against a king, lord, or others.

The Parallels of Today's Media with Religion's Role in the Middle Ages

Today, religion no longer plays the same role as in the Middle Ages, when there was a single wealthy Church that united believers in one Christian faith and had equal or more power to the medieval kings. In fact, the laws of separation of church and state in the United States prevent a single religious group from obtaining that kind of power; plus there are multiple religious groups which include not only different Christian denominations, but hundreds of other groups with varying numbers of adherents. Then, too, about a third of the population identifies as non-religious or non-churchgoing, and a small percentage of atheists, who deny the power of religion entirely, and agnostics, who aren't sure.

However, into this vacuum left by religion has stepped the modern media, which has accumulated its own wealth and power and not only unifies people in the U.S. but globally – and the owners and CEOs of these media companies are like the powerful religious leaders of old in running their domains. While no single leader like the pope is in charge of all these media domains, these owners and CEOs might be compared to the medieval cardinals and bishops who controlled the wealth and power in a particular territory.

The examples of the media titans today are widely known. Besides the big three networks – CBS, ABC, and NBC, plus the Fox network, there are the major cable networks, such as A&E, Bravo, CNN, HBO, Cinemax, TMC, and Stars, plus the major social media channels like Facebook, Twitter, Google, Yahoo, Pinterest, Reddit, and others. Additionally, there are video channels like YouTube, which people use to share information. And now with the pervasiveness of tablets, Smart Phones, and other mobile devices, millions of people use these as well to share the news.

Thus, while no one high authority is in charge of everything like the pope, the media as a whole plays a similar role in supporting various political leaders and movements, as well as placing its seal of approval on the celebrities, wealthy high-profile company owners and CEOS, and political leaders, who are like the medieval kings, lords and wealthy bourgeoisie of the Middle Ages. This kind of media approval is much like the blessings of the Church, and should someone say or do something that evokes a storm of criticism, the media can readily turn on that person and subject them to scorn or lead them to resign from their position.

Recent political leaders have used the media to further their aspirations and reach a new audience. President Clinton used the media to gain popular support by playing a saxophone on the Arsenio Hall show and appearing on the Jay Leno show. President Bush manipulated the media to gain support for his campaign to topple Saddam Hussein in Iraq on the grounds he had weapons of mass destruction. In 2008, Barack Obama used the power of both the mass media and social media to build support for his campaign, then swept into office as a media star. And for a time, Sarah Palin became a media star, too, after being selected by John McCain as a running mate, a choice which turned a then obscure Governor of Alaska into a media sensation. But, perhaps the most notable manipulator of the media is President Donald Trump, who used his celebrity to take the most powerful job in the world, and along the way, used Fox News, some of its talk show hosts, and the Twitter social media platform to reach out to over 80 million followers.

By the same token, the media has contributed to making some people very wealthy, so they have joined the celebrity royalty, For example, Justin Bieber initially found fame as a 15-year old teen posting music videos on YouTube and was turned by agent/manager Scooter Braun into a global phenomenon. As another example, the already wealthy Kardashian family gained superstardom with their reality show, *Keeping Up with the Kardashians,* and they turned that into a line of fashion, beauty, and other products. And most recently, many individuals have found fame by becoming celebrity influencers on Instagram with millions of followers.

For example, according a Pressboard posting in April 2020, the top influencers, primarily from the world of sports, music, film, and TV include these.[204]

1 - Cristiano Ronaldo, a superfamous soccer player with 211 million followers,

2 - Ariana Grande, a global popstar, with 179 million followers,

3 - Dwayne "The Rock" Johnson, the highest paid actor today, with 177 million followers,

4 - Selena Gomez, an actress and recording star, with 172 million followers,

5 - Kylie Jenner, the most influential and only billionaire of the Kardashian/Jenner family, with 169 followers

6 - Kim Kardashian West, the most familiar Kardashian, who is a model, actress, and entrepreneur as well as a reality star, with 164 million followers,

7 - Neymar, Jr., a Brazilian soccer player with136 million followers,

8 - Justin Bieber, a popular musician since 13, with 131 million followers,

9 - Taylor Swift, a country singer turned popstar, with 129 million followers

10 -Kendall Jenner, a supermodel and the third member of the Kardshian/Jenner family on the top 100 instagram influencerslist with 126 million followers.

A few other very well-known personalities with huge followings include these entertainment celebrities:

11 -Jennifer Lopez, an actress, singer, dancer,fashion designer, producer, and business woman with 118 million followers

12 -Nicki Minaj, a female rapper with 112 million folowers

13 -Khloe Kardashian, a star on *Keeping Up with the Kardashians* until the end with 107 million followers

14 -Miley Cyrus, a popular singer and actress, with106 million followers

15 -Katy Perry, another very popular singer, with 93 million followers.

The many media created and supported celebrities of today are well-known, and the selection of what stories to feature by the media has helped to further the fame and wealth of those featured, while the media has also helped to destroy individuals and their careers by turning against them when displeased by their words or behaviors, much like the Church used the threat and act of excommunication and interdiction to undermine the power of kings and nobles. One example is the Trayvon Martin-George Zimmerman case, where the media, fueled by the anger of numerous black and liberal groups, turned what might have been a routine fight that led to a killing, possibly in self-defense, into a racial profiling murder case and trial that turned Zimmerman into a demonized monster. In another case, newscaster Martin Bashir lost his job as a result of the backlash over his comments about how Sarah Palin should be subjected to the same treatment as a slave once was by a harsh master because of her own comments about slavery. And celebrity food guru Paula Deen found her empire in shambles and lost over $17 million dollars, when a racial remark she made over 30 years was included in the transcript of a trial over sexual harassment and racist attitudes at one of her restaurants, Uncle Bubba's Seafood and Oyster House. The statement got leaked to the media, triggering a storm of controversy, though after two years of public humiliation and apologies, she is on the comeback trail and trying to begin again.

At the same time, those already wealthy and famous have used the media to further build up their fame and thereby increase their wealth, such as Miley Cyrus, whose wild performance at the 2013 VMA awards, where she dressed provocatively in a tightfitting skin-colored outfit and used hip-thrusting twerking, led to not only a massive outpouring of outrage and massive media attention that made her an even bigger star. And many more examples can be shown to illustrate the way the modern media can make or break careers and be used by the superwealthy to support their own power, much like Church ceremonies could sanctify the rule of the medieval kings.

Additionally, like the medieval church, the modern media flaunts the wealthy lifestyle, though the source of income is different – from landholding and taxes for the medieval church versus investments and earnings from programming today. And on the top of the earnings pyramid, comparable to the pope, bishops, and abbots, are the media company owners, CEOs, and celebrity hosts, like Ellen Degeneres and Jimmy Kimmel. At the same time, the programs that have glorified the wealthy life-style, like *Real Housewives* and *Keeping Up with the Kardashians*, might be compared to the big events in which the kings, nobles, and Church officials of old put on pageants to entertain the peasants.

Another parallel is that those with wealth and power in Hollywood influence the type of pictures that get made, many now big action adventure films, where the U.S. government and military are portrayed as the good guys confronting some bad guys who try to take over but eventually meet an untimely demise. Some of the biggest budget films glamorize war and larger than life heroes, much like the knights returning from fighting the war for the king. By contrast, most indie films have trouble getting financing and distribution.

Also, much as the kings worked closely with the Church to attack threats to their rule through the Inquisition, today the government has used the fear of terrorism to gain support for expanding national security surveillance and crack-downs, such as gaining support for the Patriot Act, signed into law by George W. Bush in 2001, which has permitted expanded surveillance through roving wiretaps, searching business records, and conducting surveillance of individuals suspected of terrorist-linked activities — an act still on the book as of November 2020.

In 2013 the extent of this surveillance was revealed by Edward Snowden, who was then a CIA employee and subcontractor, who leaked NSA classified data, because he felt the public should know about this mine of information kept about them as an invasion of privacy. Then, facing the arrest and a long imprisonment for his actions, he fled to Russia to avoid protection from extradition to the U.S. to face numerous charges of undermining national security, where he remains as of November 2020. In turn, the mainstream media contributed to making him seem like a dangerous traitor, although now opinions are mixed, since he gained support from more libertarian individuals and some independent media which hailed him as a hero for revealing the extent of U.S. surveillance that has undermined personal privacy.

In many cases, the media has helped to support the prosecution by publishing statements and evidence released by the prosecutors which has suggested those arrested are already guilty, resulting in trial by press, that can sometimes be like the witchcraft trials in the Middle Ages, turning an individual into public enemy number one. For instance, this kind of public roasting occurred in the case of George Zimmerman and Casey Anthony, who have had to live their life after the media trial in hiding and in fear of death threats and potential assassins drawn by their demonization by the media, both before the case and after being acquitted by a jury.

Another good example of the way the media, wealth, and religion have melded today is the Kardashian 2013 Christmas card. The image looks like something of a medieval tapestry, with the Kardashian family members standing around, against columns and images of the Virgin mother and child, reminiscent of Church inspired artwork of the Middle Ages. At the same time, images of luxury are all around, from a descending staircase to a flowing carpet, and most blatantly, the gold dollar sign by the stair and carpet.

Then, too, much like the king and nobles had control over the messages of the day, though they used couriers on horseback to spread the word, so do the rich and famous today, with the money they can spend on advertising and publicity. So much like the kings might have used the rituals and ceremonies of the Church to sanctify their accession to the throne and key actions, such as the call to go to war or go on a Crusade, so the wealthy can turn to the media to get out their message – from gaining access to popular talk shows to creating news events that are featured on the news channels and Internet. And if they don't like what is being said, they have the power to turn to the media to build up public opposition to the spokesperson, much like the Church had the power to excommunicate or invoke an interdiction against a perceived enemy of the state or Church, such as when the Dominican and Francisco friars traveled around Europe in the 1230s seeking out heretics with the aid of torture, secret testimonies, and denial of legal counsel.

Style of Life: From Home to Education, Arts, and Recreation

The parallels between the style of life of the royalty, nobility and wealthy bourgeoisie compared to the peasants and lower working class then and the superrich and 99% now are fairly well-known and obvious. An underlying factor is the great disparity in wealth between the wealthy and lower income groups at both times, resulting in the great differences in purchase power. And today in America this disparity has become even more marked, as the wealthy have become even more wealthy while the middle class has been disappearing, giving rise to sharp parallels between the lifestyles of the wealthy and lower-income groups then and now.

Housing

One of the most dramatic differences is in the way the two classes live – both in their homes and neighborhoods.

In medieval times, as previously described, the king and nobles lived in huge castles surrounded by walls in the early Middle Ages. Initially, there was a wooden building and stockade, and beginning around the late 10th century castles were built from stone. Then, over the centuries, these buildings and the surrounding walls became larger and more expensive, with the costs paid by the growing territories conquered and the taxes collected from the peasants. For example, as George Holmes notes in *The Oxford Illustrated History of Medieval Europe*, Richard I built one such castle to protect the Angevin lands in France against the Capetians who were seeking to drive the English out, and the castle had to be strong to protect against the invaders. As Holmes notes in describing a stone castle on a hillside:

> The defense of the Angevin lands depended upon castles, hugely expensive to build and maintain because they had to be able to resist long sieges if help were slow in coming. This particularly strong example is Chateau Gaillard, just upstream from Rouen; it was built by Richard I at the vast cost of 44,000 pounds, following the loss of Gisors in 1195.[205]

Since these early castles were built for defense, they were often surrounded by a moat or ditch filled with rainwater or waste materials, and the entrance was only by a bridge that was raised or lowered to let people in or keep them out. Then, the castles became larger and larger, so they could only house the lord and his household, along with a central courtyard for the king or lord to hold court in good weather. In addition, these castles contained the workshops and kitchen to supply the occupants of the castle. Plus, there were stables, storehouses for food and weapons, and even a jail for any prisoners, and in an emergency, peasants who lived near the castle could move inside, such as in the event of an attack.

In time, as life settled down, these castles evolved into huge manor houses, surrounded by a large track of land with peasant families to work it. While a small manor might be surrounded by about 300 acres of land, a larger manor might be surrounded by several thousand acres and be worked by over 50 peasant families. Then, over the centuries, these manors evolved into the huge gracious palaces characteristic of the kings and nobles of the late

Middle Ages. An example is the royal palace of Emperor Charles IV of the Holy Roman Empire that later became Germany that was built between 1348 and 1357 in Karlestejn. The palace towers over a rocky hillside, and besides the main keep it has three other large buildings on three levels, which include the imperial apartments, church tower, and keep.[206]

As the towns developed, nobles and wealthy bourgeoisie built huge town houses, such as town house at Bruges built by Jean IV and Louis de Bruges between 1425 and 1470. It is an imposing structure with four stories and projecting turrets and towers, looking much like a building that houses government offices or a school. As Holmes describes it, the house "represents the great wealth of this family and their importance in the municipal politics of the city, as well as Louis de Bruges' position as courtier, diplomat, and soldier in the service of the Valois dukes of Burgundy."[207]

By contrast, throughout the Middle Ages, the accommodations of the peasants were very spare. Commonly, they lived in small wooden or stone huts, with the size and furnishings of the house depending upon the wealth acquired by different peasants, much like homes in lower income neighborhoods might differ in size and appearance today. But then as now, these were only slight differences. As Barbara Hanawalt describes in *The Ties that Bound: Peasant Families in Medieval England*, the peasant houses were initially built of wood, but when wood became scarce by the 14th century, wood was only used for the frame, and the walls were filled with turf, a mixture of mud and straw, or wattle and daub, through most of England. While the smaller cottages had only one bay, the larger houses had two or three bays, and commonly the floors were of clay, though sometimes they were made of stone, cobbles, or stone flags, and commonly the floors were covered with straw. Typically, the windows were small and covered with shutters.[208]

Likewise, the disparity in the homes and neighborhoods of the very wealthy and the lower income classes today is very great. For example, the superwealthy often live in wealthy enclaves, widely known for their high-income residents and high-priced homes. Many of these are well-known names like Beverly Hills, Atherton, and Hillsborough in California; Aspen in Colorado; Scarsdale, Chappaqua, and the Hamptons in New York. Some of these are even included on a list of "America's Most Expensive Neighborhoods," featured on the WallSt.com blog. In these luxury zip codes, the median price as of September 2012 was at least $2.8 million to $6.7 million, and the median household income in some of these areas was $30,000 to $50,000 higher than the U.S. median income of $51.914. According to this list, the 10 most expensive neighborhoods are these:

1. Alpine, New Jersey, located 15 miles from Manhattan, where residents commonly have iron-gated entrances. The median list price is $6.76 million, and many of the residents are celebrities, such as Stevie Wonder, Eddie Murphy, and Chris Rock.

2. Ross, California, where the median is $5.30 million and the residents are largely, older retired residents.

3. New York, New York, where the median is $5.10 million in the 10013 zip code.

4. Woody Creek, Colorado, located near Aspen, where the median list price is $4.93 million. Many of its residents include rock stars, which have helped to keep up property values.

5. Atherton, California, where the median is $4.3 million, fueled by Silicon Valley public offerings.

6. Beverly Hills, California, where the median is $3.75 million in a town best known for its high-end shopping and restaurants on Rodeo Drive.

7. Rancho Santa Fe, California, where the median is $3.29 million in the unincorporated part of San Diego County, which includes many famous residents, such as singer Janet Jackson and actress Gina Davis.

8. Santa Barbara, California, where the media list price is $3.19 million. It's another destination for the older wealthy who are retiring in the area.
9. Greenwich, Connecticut, where the median list price is $2.90 million.
10. Bel Air, California, where the median list price is $2.82 million, and like Beverly Hills, it is another community that draws high income members of the film industry.[209]

Yet, given the wide fluctuations in the real estate market, eight years later, with one exception, a new line-up of places were considered the 10 most expensive neighborhoods, according to the November 2018 Robb Report.[210] But again, properties in California were high in the list, and now Florida had become another top spot for expensive homes. Plus now these neighborhoods were more expensive than ever, reflecting the rise in the real estate market generally. These top ten places are the following:

1. Port Royal (Naples), Florida, where the median list price is $8.20 million.
2. Silicon Valley, California, where the median list price is $5.71 million.
3. Shady Canyon (Orange County), California, where the median list price is $5.70 million.
4. Sea Cliff, Presidio Heights, and Pacific Heights (San Francisco), California, where the median list price is $5.17 million,
5. Beacon Hill (Boston), Massachusetts, where the median list price is $5.14 million
6. Malibu Beach and Point Dume, California, where the median list price is $4.99 million.
7. Aspen, Colorado, where the median list price is $4.87 million
8. Palm Island (Miami Beach), Florida, where the median list price is $4.80 million.

9. Lacy Estates (San Marino), California, where the median list price is $4.70 million
10. Lido Island (Miami Beach), Florida, where the median list price is $4.60 million,

While these median list prices provide an overall guide to the most expensive neighborhoods, wealthy enclaves in other cities also draw the superrich, such as Nantucket, Rhode Island and Martha's Vineyard in Massachusetts, associated with the Kennedy's, and the Presidio Heights and Sea Cliff Neighborhoods in San Francisco, the home of many wealthy members of San Francisco society.

Some of the homes of the wealthy valued at $5 million and much more are truly palatial, and many wealthy owners own more than one home in different parts of the U.S. and abroad. For example, Bill Gates, considered the 2nd wealthiest man in the world, with a wealth estimated at $67 billion spent $8.7 million for an additional estate in Wellington, Florida, a community where equestrian sports are popular and his daughter Jennifer spent several seasons training to be a show jumper. As described in a Huff Post article, the home contains over 7000 square feet of living space, including four bedrooms, five baths, custom English cabinetry, a poolside built-in grill, a surrounding pasture of 4.8 acres, and a 20 stall barn. But even that mansion was considered "fairly modest" given the large mansions of Palm Beach County. For instance, an estate belonging to John Kluge, at one time considered the wealthiest person in the United States, was put on the market for $59 million, and another nearby estate was listed for $79 million.[211]

But even that ultra-expensive Florida mansion is only a small house compared to Bill Gates custom-built $120 million home in Medina, Washington. It's a 66,000 square foot residence, with about 20% of the house devoted to living space, which includes 7 bedrooms, 24 bathrooms, and 6 kitchens. The rest includes a reception hall, offices, conference facilities, a computer room, and other places for people to gather. There is even a trampoline room with a 20 foot ceiling, and miles of mostly fiber-optic communications run through the house.[212] It truly is like a medieval castle with its keep for the royal family and household, and the rest of the house devoted to working and meeting spaces for the many people involved in supporting or visiting the occupants and others within the castle walls.

As for the Kardashians, as reported on the celebrity gossip site TMZ, Kim Kardashian and Kanye West have an $11 million mansion in one of the wealthiest California communities – Bel Air, and now they are looking for an even larger lot to build "an enormous, super-private mansion" in a secluded section of Calabasas. [213]

In short, much like the nobles and bourgeoisie in the Middle Ages, the modern day superwealthy use their wealth to buy extremely large and luxurious mansions.

By contrast, lower and middle income individuals live in much more modest homes that vary from the small under 1400 square foot homes in the inner cities to the larger homes of about 1500-2500 square feet in middle income communities, much like the peasants and later workers in the towns varied in the size of their homes based on their own level of wealth. In contrast to the million dollar and multi-million dollar mansions of the superwealthy, the average median price of a single family home was about $203,000 as of the second quarter of 2013,[214] About 17% of these properties were distressed homes sold through foreclosure or short sales, because of the many people losing their homes after losing their jobs or businesses due to the Great Recession and aftermath from 2008 to the present. Since then, the median home prices has gone much higher. As of March 2019 they were up to $309,000 — and $320,000 in March 2020, with the highest prices in the west at $410,100; the lowest in the South and Midwest — $208,000 and $203,700 respectively. And in the high tech mecca around San Jose, California, the median prices are $1.2 million.[215]

Just drive through the lower and middle income neighborhoods in any city, and you can see examples of these homes in different neighborhoods from the poorest neighborhoods in the inner city to the lower income and working class homes in other parts of the city and in the suburbs.

Food

Given the vast differences in wealth, the food of the royalty, nobles, and wealthy bourgeoisie also differed substantially from that of the peasants, much like the food selections varies greatly between the superwealthy and lower income classes now.

For example, the diet of the nobles included plenty of protein in the form of fish, birds, and wild game, along with bread, wine, and ale. By contrast, the peasants' menu consisted mainly of vegetables, plus bread and beer since they normally didn't eat meat. For them meat was an expensive luxury item, and they normally weren't permitted to hunt for game, or they would be arrested for the crime of poaching. By contrast, the nobles could easily obtain meat through hunting on their own lands.[216]

The same kind of differences can be observed in the diet of the superrich and lower-income groups today. While the wealthy commonly can buy whatever they want in the supermarket, and may go to more expensive supermarkets, such as Andronico's, they can afford to dine in expensive restaurants with a variety of dishes prepared by well-reputed chefs. They may also get the most expensive wines or even collect special vintages, and they have access to rare, highly priced foods, such as caviar and truffles. They also have diets which include high – priced cuts of meat, from steaks to duck and quail, except for those who are vegetarians, and plenty of fruits and vegetables.

By contrast, low-income individuals are more likely to have high-starch, high-sugar diets purchased in supermarkets like Safeway, Piggly Wiggly, and Lucky's, that carry large selections of high calorie foods with less nutritional value, or they buy from small corner grocery stores and local street vendors. Thus, they may be more likely to include chips, salsa, rice, beans, potatoes, and soda in their diets, and go to fast-food restaurants, like McDonald's, Taco Bell, and Burger King, where most of the menu includes high-starch, high-calorie items. In turn, such a diet has contributed to the obesity epidemic in the U.S. that affects about 50% of the population, and is mostly a problem for low-income individuals, including teens, who are coming down with diseases like diabetes tied to obesity due to a poor high-calorie, high-sugar diet.

A report of research studies by the Food Research and Action Center (FRAC) on their website shows this general pattern. As noted on their website:

- "Wages were inversely related to BMI (an indicator of excess body fat) and obesity in a nationally representative sample of more than 6000 adults – meaning, those with low wages had increased BMI as well as an increased chance of being obese (Kim & Leigh 2010).
- "Rates of severe obesity were approximately 1.7 times higher among poor children and adolescents in a nationally representative sample of more than 12,000 children aged 2 to 19 years. (Skelton et al., 2009)[217]

Though the Food Research and Action Center cites recent studies that suggest that the gap between the rich and poor is closing, since those with higher incomes are becoming more obese, presumably by eating more of better food, the general pattern still prevails. As in the Middle Ages, the wealthy today can eat better because they have the money to do so, while those with a lower income tend to eat less healthy high-starch, high-sugar diets.

Art

Both in the Middle Ages and today, there is a big distinction between art produced for and supported by the upper classes and the everyday art created as a form of expression and recreation by the lower and middle classes. While the art produced and the form of production and support differ, the parallels are in the distinction between what is sometimes called "high" art and "folk" art.

For example, in the Middle Ages, the art that has come down through the history books and art classes taught in the schools and universities features the art sponsored and paid for by the kings and churches. As Holmes describes it in writing about the early Middle Ages of the 5th and 6th centuries:

> The spread of Christianity encouraged the production of elaborate vestments and vessels for liturgical use and the building of lavish churches. In an increasingly hierarchical society, the individual realism of classical antiquity gave way to stereotyped full-face depictions with an idealized emphasis on the figure's dignity and rank.[218]

Over the next centuries, the Church became a major patron of the arts. For example, under the Carolingian kings of the 7th and 8th centuries, the great monasteries stimulated the patronage of art, and in the 9th century, the popes continued the tradition of commissioning artists.

This continued patronage of the arts by the Church continued through the centuries, while the wealthy kings and nobles became patrons, as well. While much of the art continued to show scenes depicting Biblical narratives, others reflected the power of the king and nobility. For instance, some paintings from the rule of Otto III, who ruled from 980 to 1002 as the last emperor to claim universal authority under the Holy Roman Empire, a scene from the Gospels shows Otto III receiving homage from four parts of the world from robed nobles with crowns bringing him gifts. To receive them, he sits on a throne wearing a crown and carrying a scepter, while surrounded by members of the Church and knights in his court. Later, as a class of wealthy merchants developed in the towns, they became the patrons and subjects of paintings too, as reflected in an early to mid-14th century work which shows Venetian merchants exchanging cloth for oriental produce at a time when the Venetian empire was expanding through a network of depots and colonies where the local merchants would bring their wares.

While some art depicts peasants at work, such as a drawing of a man sowing grains from a basket, while a crow raids a seed bag and a dog drives away another crow, and a drawing of a woman reaping while a man binds wheat, these images are from church manuscripts, reflecting the role of the church as a patron of the arts.[219] In this case, both images come from the Luttrell Psalter, in the keeping of the British Library.

Obviously, it is impossible to describe the vast differences in art periods and styles during a period of over 1000 years, which art historians have classified into a half-dozen different categories, including Early Christian art, Migration Period art, Byzantine Art, Insular art, Pre-Romanesque and Romanesque art, and Gothic art, as well as many other periods within these main styles. Then, too, each region, during a time of becoming distinct cultures, had its own distinctive art style, and medieval art was created in many different media, including sculpture, illuminated manuscripts, stained glass, metalwork, and mosaics, as well as fresco wall paints and textiles, including tapestries. However, regardless of period or style, the creation of much art was primarily due to the patronage of the Church or kings, nobles, and wealthy bourgeoisie. The peasants may have created their own art, such as sculptures and weavings, but largely this has been unknown in history, since historians and art historians have focused on the high arts of the period that was the province of the upper classes and the Church.

A similar pattern continues today in the form of an art market fueled by wealthy collectors who pay sometimes stratospheric funds for art work, both to hang on their walls and as an investment, while there has been an explosion of popular art in all sorts of media by artists and craftsmen. While much of this popular art is mass produced through printing and sharing photos and images on the Internet, some works are one of a kind pieces that might be sold on the streets, at fairs, through galleries, and direct by the artist or given to friends and family or kept by the artist. But in general, except for those few artists recognized by the wealthy, so the value of their art skyrockets, most artists get little money for their art work, have trouble supporting themselves on their art alone, and survive through other jobs that support their ability to create art.

An article "How the Art Market Thrives on Inequality" by Adam Davidson illustrates how the art market has become a preserve of the very wealthy. In fact, as the growing divide between rich and poor has increased, as the middle class has declined and poverty has become more widespread, the prices paid for artwork has increased more than ever. Perhaps a reason as Davidson suggests is so the very wealthy can flaunt their wealth in a way they can't by only accumulating more and more wealth. At the time he was writing, Edvard Munch's well-known painting "The Scream" sold for about $120 million and was the most expensive artwork ever sold, while the fine-art market grew even more, even though the rest of the global economy collapsed during the great recession, since 11 of the 20 highest prices paid at an art auction occurred after 2008. Since then, still other paintings have sold for even more.

Why should the art market keep climbing despite the bad economic times? Because of the "show-off my wealth" value. As Davidson suggests:

> Many economists say that art...is not much of an investment in the first place. Unlike stocks, an artwork's price reflects numerous nonfinancial intangibles, like the pleasure of owning a painting or, perhaps more important, its ability to signal the owner's vast wealth and erudition. While stocks can provide an ongoing payment stream (via dividends) and are traded in public markets, art collectors must pay to protect their investments. It's also much harder for collectors to resell expensive art. Not only is the market opaque, but few artists have real long-term value... (and) no painting bought for $30 million or more has ever been resold at a profit...Artwork itself may be a lousy investment, but...it does a more powerful and subtle job of signaling wealth than virtually any other luxury good. High prices are, quite literally, central to the signal – you don't spend $120 million to show that you're a savvy investor hoping to flip a Munch for $130 million. You're spending $120 million,

in part, to show that you can blow $120 million on some-thing that can't possibly be worth that much in any mar-ketplace ... Art is often valuable precisely because it isn't a sensible way to make money. And perhaps as a result, it has become even more valuable of late ... Fine art ... is part of the economy of a small subset of the super-superrich, whom some economists call Ultra High Net Worth Individuals.[220]

A Huffington Post blog made a similar observation about how the art market has been profiting while social inequality has been growing, and the market likes it that way, according to Federal Reserve Bank economist Benjamin Mandel, because:

> ...the art market thrives not only when the poor are getting poorer; it must also be the richest get even richer ... Extremely expensive paintings are among the few seen as a safe investment ... It could be a matter of purchas-ing perceived quality, ensuring a good investment or simply being a showoff, but art consumption at this level has a lot to do with economic safety and little to do with that naïve notion of loving art.[221]

Then, in November 2013, the sale of the most expensive paint-ing ever sold at that time occurred at Christie's in New York – a $142.4 million triptych painted by Francis Bacon, who previously sold a 1976 triptych at Sotheby's to the Russian oligarch Roman Abramovich for $86.2 million. To others outside the rarified art world of the superrich, it might be hard to see why the Bacon trip-tych sold for so much, since it is a rather simple, stark work which shows Lucian Freud, Bacon's friend and rival, seated on a wooden chair from various angles against a yellow and brown background within a geometric frame. Yet the reputation of Bacon and the hype of Christie in promoting the sale of a number of paintings and sculptures valued at over $20 million drew nearly 10,000 visitors to the auction, which brought in $691.5 million, making this the most

THE NEW AMERICAN MIDDLE AGES

expensive auction ever, and 10 world record prices were included for the big name artists, which included Christopher Wood, Ad Reinhardt, Donald Judd, and Willem de Kooning. At the same time, a few celebrity artists made their highest sales every, such as Jeff Koons, who sold "Balloon Dog (Orange)" for $58.4 million, while Andy Warhol, who sold "Coca Cola (30)," one of only four paintings of a single coke bottle made in 1961 and 1962, for $57.2 million.[222]

However, since the Bacon sale, the market for high-priced art has become even more pricy. As described on the Invaluable website, which features the world's premier auctions and galleries, there have been four sales since 2018 that have topped the Bacon sale price. In May 2018, a painting by Amedeo Modigliani, "Nu couché," sold at Sotheby's for $157.2 million, and a second Modigliani, "Nue couché, 1917-18, solid at Christie's for $170.4 mlllion. In May 2015, a painting by Pablo Picasso "Les Femes d'Alger ("Version O") sold at Christie's for $179.4 million. But the most expensive of all was the November 2017 sale of Leonardo da Vinci's painting "Salvator Mundi, circa 1490-1500 that was sold by Christie's for $450.3 million. Why did it sell so well? According to the Invaluable site, "the sale underscored market demand for the artist's rare auction appearances, and the competition among collectors to own a work of such caliber and distinction."[223]

In turn, this high-priced art market is fueled by the super-rich billionaire collectors, such as Edye and Eli Broad, Norman and Irma Braman, and Doris Fisher[224], who most people in the general public haven't heard about, because they are part of the rarified rich who have gained their money through family money and investments, not like the celebrity super-rich who make the news.

Some real estate developers have also tapped into this super-rich art market by offering expensive art pieces to be owned by residents of a development. An example of this is the development of two Florida projects designed to lure wealthy Latin Americans – the Faena District project by developer Alan Faena and the Oceana Bal Harbor development by Eduardo Constantini, both from Argentina. They each bought two Jeff Koons' sculptures for $14 million to be featured prominently at the apartment complex,[225] much like kings and nobles might place beautiful sculptures and paintings in their own mansions.

The irony, of course, is that most artists, with a few rare exceptions, like Jasper Johns and Andy Warhol, are among the very poor, living hand-to-mouth to support their art, unless they have other jobs to support themselves. At the same time, middle and lower art markets are suffering, along with the decline of the middle class. As Kyle Chayka notes in "Why Is the Middle of the Art Market Vanishing?," while the high end of the art market is booming, the lower and middle sectors are suffering, resulting in a decline in the less widely known artists and smaller galleries. As he notes:

> The giant blue-chip galleries, among them Gagosian, Hasuer & Wirth, David Zwirner, and others ... are in all the headlines; their contemporary artists are making auction records, opening museum shows, and starring at fairs everywhere you look. This comes at the expense of less widely heralded artists and smaller galleries.[226]

A key reason for this development is the growing power of the superrich, in that the big dealers and the very rich collecting families like the Mugrabis and Nahmads "have almost complete control over the markets of contemporary art's most expensive artists," and they and the aggressive dealers have kept the prices moving up and up. Then, too, as executive editor Ben Davis of ARTINFO suggests, buying art is a "gamble by the already superrich that their own wealth will continue to grow....and buying art may also provide a genteel, culture-friendly image for the wealthy that they use to draw attention away from the source of their money."[227]

In sum, by any measure, the superrich today, as in medieval times, are the main patrons for the arts, while the more popular arts that are featured in the mass media, on the Internet, and in small galleries might be compared to the folk arts of the peasants in the Middle Ages.

Education

There are also parallels between the different levels of education of the royalty, nobility, and wealthy bourgeoisie versus the peasants and artisans of the Middle Ages and the wealthy and middle and lower classes of today.

A major difference between the two classes throughout the Middle Ages is that the children of the noble and wealthy bourgeoisie classes got an education, while most other children were not educated and were illiterate. In the early Middle Ages, education was generally provided by the Church, in part to prepare young noble boys to become monks or priests, or to provide an education for other noble boys in succession to become kings or the head of a noble's estate. In addition, some nobles' sons were trained to become pages or squires on the way to becoming knights. The daughters of the nobility were typically educated by nuns, so they could become ladies of the manor by learning how to read, write, keep accounts, do needlework, and provide first aid.

Initially, in the early Middle Ages, the teachings of the cathedral and monastery schools focused on studying the Bible and the writings of the Church fathers and counsels. But during the High Middle Ages, the schools expanded their curriculum to offer classes in the liberal arts, which included Latin grammar, rhetoric, arithmetic, geometry, astronomy, and music, all taught in Latin, which had been the language of the Church, although many sons of the nobility attended these schools to learn to read, write, and apply their knowledge to pursuits other than entering the clergy. Meanwhile, a scholastic movement gradually developed in which scholars like Peter Abelard, Peter Lombard, and Thomas Aquinas in the 11th through 13th centuries began to apply logic and reason to Christian principles. Later, with the rise of universities in the 12th century, scholars began to draw on the scientific work of Islam thinkers, who drew much of their own learning from the ancient Greeks, contributing to an even broader education for those who attended these universities. Then, too, many children of the king and nobility learned from private tutors. While a son of a peasant might enter a school, much like a student from a poor family might get a scholarship to a college or university, this was rare. [228]

Thus, while the actual subject matter might be quite different from the teachings of the schools today, what is comparable is the teaching of a special curriculum through private schools or tutors was primarily confined to the wealthy classes – the kings, nobles, and wealthy bourgeoisie of the towns, with only rare exceptions, whereas the main type of education for the children of peasants was how to farm and work on the manor, while the children of artisans and tradesmen served as an apprenticeship, so they could learn a trade. Today, education is widely available through public education, with support from different levels of government, including state contributions based on attendance and federal scholarship programs. However, a big difference is in the type of education available to the members of the wealthy and upper middle classes, since in many cities there are private schools primarily attended by the children of wealthy families, such as the Dalton School.

Among the most exclusive of these schools, which attract the children of wealthy families from all over the world, are several in the United States. According to Daniel He in 2013's "13 Private Schools for the Extremely Rich," these include the following with tuition costs per year:

- the Lawrenceville School, in Lawrenceville, New Jersey, $44,885;
- the Lawrence Academy in Groton, Massachusetts, $42,130;
- the Middlesex School, in Concord Massachusetts, $41,800;
- the Foxcroft School in Middleburg Virginia, $41,580;
- the Trinity School, in New York, New York, $41,370;
- the Hotchkiss School in Lakeville, Connecticut, $40,750.[229]

Since then the costs have only increased. According to a Business Insider article on "The 50 Most Expensive Top Private High Schools in America," these are the top 10 schools, which don't include any of the schools on the 2013 lists, though the Hotchkiss

School, ranked at #17 charges even more for tuition – $49,550 a year. The other schools, ranked from the most to the less expensive include these[230]:

- St. Paul's School, Concord, New Hampshire, $62,000;
- Episcopal High School, Alexandria, Virginia, $60,900;
- Avenues: The World School, New York, New York, $56,400;
- St. Andrew's School, Middletown, Delaware, $55,500;
- Collegiate School, New York, New York, $53,900;
- Horace Mann School, Bronx, New York, $53,200;
- Marymount School of New York, New York, $51,750;
- Milton Academy, Milton, Massachusetts, $51,460;
- Concord Academy, Concord, Massachusetts, $51,455;
- The Lawrenceville School, Lawrenceville, New Jersey, $51,440.

But these high costs haven't discouraged enrollments. In fact, both applications and enrollments are up in spite or perhaps because of the pandemic due to people fleeing the city, as well as public school parents turning to private schools, since the public schools haven't opened up.[231]

At the university level, the high cost of tuition and the assistance of family members in securing a place in a school, where the family makes a substantial contribution, help to make these schools more exclusive with a larger percentage of children from wealthy families than attending the state supported network of universities. For example, schools like Princeton, Harvard, Yale, Columbia University, and Stanford, ranked as the top five schools in the United States, tend to draw a much higher percentage of wealthy students, drawn by the prestige of these schools and able to afford the high tuition, averaging about $40,000-$50,000 a year. [232] By contrast, lower and middle income students are more widely represented at schools like San Francisco State and Cal State East Bay, which are part of the California State network of universities, where tuitions average about $15,000 a year[233], and a large percentage of students commute from homes in the nearby communities, rather than boarding in dorms.

Lower income students are also much more likely to drop out and not get a degree, in part because they can't afford to stay in school and have to find work. A comparison of the graduation rates at private and public schools reflects this difference. As described by Lynn O'Shaughnessy in a *Moneywatch* article, 52.4% of students attending private institutions graduate in four years, versus only 31.3 percent at public universities. Whereas some schools like the University of California in Berkeley and Los Angeles have a graduation rate of around 90%, some state universities have a rate of 12 to 25%, [234] and at the top universities like Harvard and Princeton, the rate is about 90%.[235]

In sum, because of their great wealth, modern day high income families are able to pay for the best in education for their kids, much like the families of the kings, nobility, and wealth bourgeoisie could afford the best in medieval times, whereas those in the lower classes tend to go to public schools which offer lower tuitions and have much higher drop-out rates.

Recreation and Entertainment

Finally, there are parallels with the recreation and entertainment of the royals, nobles, and wealthy bourgeoisie on the one hand and peasants and artisans on the other when compared with the super-wealthy and everyone else today. Again, a key reason for this difference is the disparity of wealth between the two groups, enabling the wealthy to buy much more and create exclusive enclaves to mix and meet with one another, thereby increasing their opportunity to socialize with and marry among other very wealthy families. By contrast, those with lower and middle incomes tend to create their own community, neighborhood, and special interest-based social groups. Certainly, today there are many overlapping areas of entertainment, given today's mass culture, so there are commonalties in seeing many of the same films, listening to the most popular recording artists, going to the same sport events, and the like. But even within these popular entertainments, there are distinctions in that those with higher incomes can pay the extra cost of much more desirable, closer in seats or special boxes at events, so the superwealthy and masses are kept apart.

These differences span all types of recreation and entertainment. So let the comparisons begin!

Take sports. Back in medieval times, the kings and nobles enjoyed the sport of hunting, and they would typically go out to hunt with their retinues of servants and often their dogs, such as foxhounds in England. One reason that hunting was such a popular pastime is that it helped train young men to go to battle. These hunts of the kings and nobles were very well organized, and as the men road on horseback, they sent out their hounds or trained hawks and falcons to help them find game – most commonly deer, wild boar, wolves, foxes, and sometimes bears and badgers. Afterwards, the results of a successful hunt commonly ended up on the dinner table or as part of the huge feasts in the courts of the kings and nobles that were a popular form of entertainment, too.

By contrast, these hunting preserves were commonly off limits to the peasants, and if one was caught on the land hunting, that was considered poaching, a serious crime, and whenever peasants did go hunting, it was not for recreation – rather it was to find animals to eat, although most peasants ate little meat, since they were restricted in their ability to hunt. As Norman Cantor notes in *The Civilization of the Middle Ages,* "As the forests shrank in the late Middle Ages, game became more scarce and restrictions on forest hunting were widely imposed on the peasantry. Large tracks of woodland became game preserves for the upper classes (even in the eleventh century, William the Conqueror had set aside more than a million acres for his hunting."[236]

Today, hunting itself has become democratized, so anyone can go hunting, and the image of the redneck hunter in the backwoods is a popular one in modern films and TV shows, such as in *Duck Dynasty,* featuring a family with heavily bearded men, pickup trucks, and guns. However, the big distinction is between the way the superwealthy go hunting in style with other superwealthy individuals, such as the well-known incident when Dick Cheney went hunting for quail on a private 50,000 acre ranch owned by the Armstrong family in Kenedy County, Texas, and shot Henry Whittington, a 78-year Texas attorney in February 2006. Then, too, the wealthy can mount foreign hunts, such as going on a hunting safari for lions in Kenya. But typically, lower and middle-income hunters go hunting locally or on short trips to woods and parks with no or low fees.

Another very popular pastime during the High Middle Ages was jousting, in which two knights on horseback raced towards each other to throw each other off their horses using long lances to attack and shields to defend themselves. The first recorded joust occurred in France in 1066, and over the next 200 years it spread throughout Europe and England. In the tournaments, two teams of knights would race at each other. One reason for the popularity of jousting and tournaments is these provided training for the constant warfare between the kings and nobles seeking more territory while defending their lands against outside invaders. Also, these events provided an opportunity for the knights to show off their skills and win favors for their success, much like modern day celebrities. At the same time, these combats were very dangerous, resulting in many deaths, while the kings and nobles who watched these jousts and tournaments commonly gambled on the outcome, which could result in gaining or losing fortunes.

Perhaps a good modern day equivalent would be the sports of boxing and wrestling, where two men, and sometimes women, go at it, with the goal of achieving a knock-out or at least getting in the most blows in a boxing match or of pinning the opponent to the mat in wrestling the most times. While regular boxing uses gloves, in a newer form of boxing called "extreme boxing" the fighters use bare hands, and face even more danger of being injured, much like in a brawl on the streets. In wrestling, the fight is actually staged as entertainment, with the fighters engaging in a performance, where the spectators can cheer their hero and jeer the villain, but the potential dangers of getting hurt are still real. And in both sports there are ringside seats or special sections for the wealthy, and the amount bet by the spectators generally reflects the relative wealth of the individuals betting.

In contrast to the wealthy spectators in the top tiered seats, typically, the fighters come from the lower classes, though the winners can be catapulted into the ranks of the very wealthy by become celebrities for their success in the ring, such as Mike Tyson in boxing and Dwayne (the Rock) Johnson who parlayed success in the wrestling ring into movie star fame. Mike Tyson even had a movie about his life and some cameo roles in films, like the first of the popular *Hangover* films, where three groomsmen wake up after a night of heavy drinking, and at one point see Mike Tyson running through their room. Similarly, in the Middle Ages, the sons of the lesser nobility and peasants with a knack for fighting might gain status because of success in these jousts.

Another example of the distinctive recreations for the two classes then and now is the form of the big celebrations. In the castles and manors of the kings and lords, these celebrations commonly occurred in the courts, where the lords and ladies would dress up in their finery and enjoy feasts, courtly dancing, and entertainments provided by minstrels and troupes of performers, such as "Bernard the Fool and his 54 Nude Dancers" who entertained King Edward II in 1313. But then, as now, the actors and musicians commonly came from the lower classes, although some of the more popular ones could earn a substantial amount, much more than most people, from tips, such as from Edward II, who paid his minstrels up to a pound for a performance, which was as much as a skilled worker might make in several months. Other entertainers included jugglers and jesters, who dressed up in wild costumes and performed for the king or lord of the manor, and commonly were rewarded with food and a place to stay for the night. Moreover, by the 15th century, the nobility and wealth merchants began to hire fancy chefs to prepare elaborate feasts with highly spiced dishes, with spices from the Far East.[237]

In contrast to these courtly entertainments of the kings and nobles, the peasants and artisans would do their celebrating in their homes, fields, and streets. They also had special feast days, when they would gather in the town or church yard, and sometimes they enjoyed plays by traveling troupes of performers. As Frances and Joseph Gies describe these events in *Life in a Medieval Village:*

Every season was brightened by holiday intervals that punctuated the Christian calendar. Many of these were ancient pagan celebrations, appropriated by the Church, often with little alteration of their character. Each of the seasons of the long working year, from harvest to harvest, offered at least one holiday when work was suspended, games were played, and meat, cakes, and ale were served ... Many of the games enjoyed by the villagers were played alike by children, adolescents, and adults, and endured into modern times: blind man's bluff ... bowling. Young and old played checkers, chess, backgammon, and most popular of all, dice. Sports included football, wrestling, swimming, fishing, archery, and a form of tennis played with hand coverings instead of rackets....Bull-baiting and cockfighting were popular spectator sports ... Yet the favorite adult recreation of the villagers was undoubtedly drinking. Both men and women gathered in the 'tavern,' usually meaning the house of a neighbor who had recently brewed a batch of ale ... There they passed the evening like modern villagers visiting the local pub.[238]

These distinctions in celebrations, entertainment, and games can be seen in differences between the wealthy and others today. For example, some of the celebrations of the superrich are truly on a grand scale, such as the lavish wedding ceremony of media baron Sean Parker and singer-songwriter Alexandra Lenas in Big Sur, which ironically had a medieval theme. As described in an article with exclusive photos in *Vanity Fair*, a magazine which specializes in articles on the rich and famous and features ads of luxury brands, the couple solemnized their vows amidst towering redwoods, included A-list celebrities and superrich attendees on their guest list, and featured medieval costumes in the spirit of Tolkien's *Lord of the Rings*. Parker spent $4.5 million for the site alone and millions more for other amenities[239], and later he contributed another $4 million for an environmental clean-up of the site. And Kim Kardashian and Kayne West similarly had a grand super-size wedding when they married in a lavish ceremony at the Forte di Belvedere in Florence, Italy, and before the wedding itself, one article in *Eonline* gushed about them as their upcoming nuptials as if they were America's royal couple.

America doesn't *officially* have a royal couple, but Kim Kardashian and Kanye West come pretty close...One thing's for sure though: Wherever and whenever Kimye do make it official, it's going to be a wedding to remember! 'It's going to be huge,' says a source. 'It's going to be the size of the capital...There won't be anything small about it.[240]

Still other examples include different venues for listening to music. For example, while anyone can buy tickets today to go to an opera or symphony concert, these tend to be settings for big society galas, with special front row seats and boxes for the wealthy, and special high society balls at opening events. By contrast, rock, grunge, and hip-hop concerts tend to appeal to the young and often lower – and middle-income music fans. Country music similarly has a broad appeal to the less sophisticated masses, especially in the South, Southwest, and West.

As for sports, apart from the comparisons to jousting of boxing and wrestling previously noted, other sport comparisons might be to polo, which tends to draw a well-heeled crowed of equine fanciers, compared to NASCAR racing, which tends to draw a much more diverse group, including red neck fans and drivers, and street racing, which commonly draws an inner city following, as typified by the action film series: *Fast and Furious.*

Consider the differences in restaurants, too – very expensive gourmet restaurants, many with celebrity chefs, attract the wealthy whereas fast-food and low-cost delis, sandwich shops, and Asian restaurants have their widest appeal to the masses. As an example of these gourmet restaurants for the very wealthy, *Business Insider.com* did a 2012 feature on "The 20 Most Expensive Restaurants in the U.S. Most of these are in New York, California, and Nevada.

Among them, the most expensive restaurant in the U.S. is Masa in New York City, where a meal featuring sushi costs $585 a person. The second most expensive restaurant, also featuring sushi, is Urasawa in Beverly Hills, where the cost is $488 a person. Other exclusive and expensive restaurants include Per Se in New York ($325 per person), the French Laundry in Yountville, California ($297 a person), the Brooklyn Fare Kitchen in Brooklyn ($241 a person), Joel Rubuchon in Las Vegas ($230 a person), the Herbfarm in Seattle ($215 a person), Alinea in Chicago ($199 a person), the Guy Savoy in Las Vegas ($190 a meal), and the Kitchen in Sacramento, California ($163 a person), to round out the top ten. [241]

Most of these restaurants are still in the top ten most expensive restaurants as of November 2019, though a little more expensive, according to this listing from Fox Business:[242]

- Benu, San Francisco – $325 per person for a tasting menu
- Chef's Table, Brooklyn, New York – $362 per person for a tasting menu
- The French Laundry, Yountville, California – $325-350 per person for a nine-course tasting menu
- Guy Savoy, Las Vegas – $385 per person for a tasting menu, $555 with wine pairings
- Joel Robochon, Las Veeeegas – $445 for an 18-course tasting menu
- Masa, New York, New York, $595 for dinner

- Per Se, New York, New York, $355 for a nine-course tasting menu.
- Saison, San Francisco, $298 per person for dinner
- Urasawa, Los Angeles, $400 for dinner
- Eleven Madison Park, New York, New York – $335 for a tasting menu.

By contrast, a meal in a fast-food or low-cost restaurant averages about $8-12 a person – about 10% of the cost of dining at the top.

Still another lifestyle difference is the debutante balls which mark the entrance of the daughters of wealthy parents into society when they are 17 or 18 versus the much simpler celebrations that lower and middle-income families throw for their daughters and sons, usually after graduation from high school, that are usually smaller gatherings in their homes or in a hotel room held for family and friends, and sometimes neighbors in close-knit communities.

In short, these vast differences in the lifestyles of the very wealthy – the 1% or even the top 1% of the 1% — and the rest of the population – the 99% in popular parlance — reflect the great divide due to the growing inequality today. Because of their great wealth, the superwealthy can live like the royalty, nobility, and wealthy merchants of the Middle Ages and enjoy luxury activities and events that are beyond the financial reach of others. Although there is some overlap in the mutual enjoyment of popular culture, particularly in sharing movies, TV, and popular music, and the ready access of everyone to the social media, in other spheres, as described, the distinctions are stark. On the one hand, the wealthy more commonly observe or participate in special sports like polo or pay more for prime seating arrangements at events. They also can turn an event that is open to all, like the opera or symphony, into a society occasion, where they can go all out dressing up, showing off, and socializing with their peers, whereas others are more likely to only attend and afterwards go for dinner or drinks at a moderately priced restaurant or club or simply go home.

Thus, the lifestyles and leisure of the wealthy compared to others in the U.S. today provide one more example of the way in which the superrich are like the modern-day equivalent of the nobility and wealthy merchants, while the rest of society are like the peasants and artisans and the slowly growing middle class in the towns in the late Middle Ages.

CHAPTER 9: THE GROWING INEQUALITY BETWEEN THE RICH AND POOR

The Role of Inequality in Creating the New American Middle Ages

I n the previous chapters, I described how American society has become much like the Middle Ages in the separation between the superrich – the king, nobles, and the wealthy merchants then and ultra-wealthy now, and the lower classes – the peasants and artisans then, the lower-income 99%ers now. These patterns can be summarized in a matrix with comparisons of the two groups then and now in the two time-periods below.

		Position in Society	
		Super-Rich	Others in Society
Time Period	Middle Ages	King, Nobles, Wealthy Merchants	Peasants and Artisans
	Present Day	Superwealthy Financial Investors, Company Owners, Entertainers, Media Moguls, Sports Super Stars	Lower to Middle Income Individuals, the 99%

The comparison for each group could similarly be turned into a series of comparisons to illustrate graphically the similarities and parallels in both periods.

The underlying reason for these differences in the two groups then and now is the vast disparity in wealth that has been increasingly separating the superrich from the rest of society, so they are able to live a luxurious lifestyle like the royalty, nobility, and wealthy merchants of the Middle Ages. At the same time, the spread of poverty and the decline of the middle class have meant that more and more people are struggling to survive because of their low income and high costs, must as was true of the peasants and artisans of medieval times.

Today, the signs of this glamorous lifestyle of the superwealthy are everywhere, as described in previous chapters, and you may recognize many other examples. They practically leap to you from the daily news or celebrity gossip columns, where the latest high-profile luxury spending is revealed, such as in lavish weddings, gala society balls, and multi-million payments for a single piece of art. In contrast, there are reports of the latest struggles of the down-and-out, such as stories of job losses, low pay, strikes to get a living wage, and low income people being evicted or becoming homeless and living on the streets.

In short, the world of today has become a world of deep contrasts between the rich and poor, the have and have nots, and this patterns is even more distinct in America, though the trend is worldwide, despite some recent attempts by governments to reverse the process. But can they? And is there popular support for doing so, at a time when Americans generally continue to hold the American dream of working hard and gaining success, even though the statistics belie that dream. Instead the grim reality is that most people remain in the class they were born into while the rich get richer and the poor poorer, and once middle class members are increasingly falling into the ranks of the poor. Why? In part because in a time of technological transformation, middle class jobs are shrinking, while the jobs for unskilled and service workers are increasing, as more and more jobs are taken over by automation or robots or are going overseas.

The Growth of Inequality Today

This growing divergence of rich and poor today has been captured in a number of recent books that discuss how this is a growing crisis that can undermine American society and contribute to a growing social turbulence.

One of the most important of these books is *Inequality in America: Facts, Trends, and International Perspectives* by Uri Dadush, Kemal Dervis, Sarah Puritz Milsom, and Bennett Stancil, which lays out the scope of the problem with extensive research reflected in dozens of charts and graphs. As the book describes, income equality has been growing since the late 1970s, and the problem has been made even worse by the financial crisis beginning in 2008, which led to even more unemployment that contributed to the mortgage meltdown and loss of many middle income homes.

More specifically, Dadush et. al. point out that this trend to inequality which increased dramatically since the late 1970s, coupled with the great economic crisis that hit in 2008 combined with persistent high unemployment have drawn greater attention to this divergence, characterized by a "marked concentration of income at the top, little or no progress for the middle, and precariousness at the bottom of the income distribution." [243] In the last decade, this trend to inequality has only increased, as the incomes of the wealthy increase, especially due to soaring stocks and tax breaks. Moreover, the pandemic has only furthered this trend, providing more opportunities for the high-tech tycoons and executives, while the lowest income groups have suffered the most from lost jobs and failing businesses.

One result of this increase in inequality is that it brings with it a "concentration of political power," which can interfere with efforts to reduce inequality and may even promote policies that further increase this concentration of power. Then, too, many economists have expressed concern that the "extreme concentration of income at the top may undermine macroeconomic and financial stability by making it harder to sustainably maintain strong aggregate demand or by encouraging excessive borrowing."[244] In other words, as people make less they may consume less, which can trigger a vicious cycle whereby companies have reduced sales, causing them to reduce production. Or people may borrow more and incur more debt to pay for their purchases, and in time, these high debts and the interest on them can lead borrowers into serious financial difficulties, such as defaulting on their mortgages or failing to pay their rent.

Although Dadush and his associates note that it is difficult to attribute this rise of inequality to any one specific cause, they point out that the growing gap in the United States is part of a global trend, although the disparity is greater here. Among the contributing factors they note are "technological change, international trade, changes in labor-market participation, the increasing role of the financial sector in the economy, the increased size of markets, and a decrease in the degree of progressivity of taxes." Also contributing are "the political environment, the loss of power of organized labor, and apparent changes in social norms affecting compensation at the top."[245] In other words, new technologies have disrupted the market, resulting in a loss of jobs and less power for organized labor. At the same time, individuals working in finance have made so much more, tax laws and company policies have increasingly favored the big corporations and wealthy investors, while the lower and middle classes have paid proportionately more, and the huge salaries and bonuses of the CEOs and company owners have become more widely accepted.

One of the measures they use to illustrate this growing disparity is the Gini index or coefficient (also known as the Gini concentration ratio), which derives from the name of an Italian statistician, Corrado Gini, who lived from 1884 to 1965, not a measure of inequality I can claim for myself, though this book is all about inequality in America. The scores, which range from 1 representing perfect inequality to 0 representing perfect equality are based on comparing the share of income to the percent of the population, though in practice the values range from about 0.25 to .65. Also, they use a comparison of the median income to the nation's average or mean household income; and the share of income at the top of the distribution compared to the rest of the distribution. Additionally, they consider social mobility as a reflection of one's opportunity to move up or down in the income distribution, so that low social mobility can be a sign of inequality of opportunity.

Some of the major findings they report that illustrate or result from these trends are the following[246]:

- Based on Congressional Budget Office (CBO) data, the Gini index increased from .48 to .59 in 2007, and the U.S. Census Bureau data also shows an increase in that the index hovered around .40 through the 1970s but then went up to .46 in 2007 and to .47 in 2010. And as of 2019, it increased to .48.[247]This data reflects what Timothy Noah calls the "Great Divergence," which began in the 1970s, after the "Great Compression," a time when income become more equal from 1932 to 1979, due to assorted government policies and other economic and social trends after the Great Depression, which helped to equalize income. [248]

- The relationship between the nation's average and median income also shows this divergence, since the median gives a better picture of true household income, since it is the level at which half of all households earn more and half earn less, whereas average income can be distorted by high earnings at the top. While the average real household income before taxes and transfers grew by 58%, the median income only went up 19%, reflecting the growing income gap. In other words, while all the boats were raised by greater income for everyone over the years, the bigger boats got even bigger and were raised even higher than the smaller ones.

- The growing gap between the rich and poor is due primarily to much greater gains for those at the top of the income distribution and little change for those at the bottom, as reflected in a comparison of the ratios of individuals with incomes in the top quintile compared to those in the bottom quintile. Within the top quintile, representing the top 20% of the earners, the income of the top 1% zoomed up even more. For example, according to the Congressional Budget Office, the income share of the top 1% of households doubled from around 10% of the total income in the 1970s to more than 20% in 2012. At the same time, the incomes of those in the rest of the top quintile (from the 80th to the 99th percentile) actually fell.

- This growing concentration of income at the top has not occurred since the days before the Great Recession, when the top 1% was also earning about 20% of the market income share.

- While those in the top 1% have enjoyed a rapid growth of income, those at the bottom of the distribution have experienced little or negative growth.

- Since 1970, there has been almost no increase in the average incomes of the bottom 90% of earners. Between 1970 to 2007, before the Great Recession, average real incomes, excluding capital gains, only went up about 5%. Between 1970 through 2010, which includes the post-crisis recovery, the average declined by 6%.

- A comparison with other countries around the world shows that this divergence in income has been especially pronounced in the United States. When compared to other countries in the World Top Incomes Database, the U.S. has the highest income share for the top 1%, top .1%., and top .01%. The only other nations that come close to U.S. figures are South Africa and Argentina, which both have long histories of great inequality and social divisions.

As Dadush et. al. conclude from this data, "the slow growth at the bottom and rapid growth at the top have polarized the extremes of the income distribution more than in any other advanced country... the U.S. ratios of top-quintile and top-decile incomes to bottom-quintile and bottom-decline incomes are the highest in the OECD." (This is the Organization for Economic Cooperation and Development, which includes 22 countries with the highest level of development). In other words, as shown by all measures of income inequality, this inequality is increasing to the levels which existed before the Great Depression due to the very large concentration at the top of the income distribution, and the divergence in the U.S. is far greater than in any other developed country.[249]

These trends Dadush points to are very significant in that they put real numbers on the creation of a top income class that has parallels with royalty, nobility, and the wealthy merchants at the top of the social pyramid and the large peasant and artisan class that formed the vast majority of society during the Middle Ages. This excess at the top and misery at the bottom contributed to the 1929 Depression, when the stock market bubble burst, suggesting a possible run-up to a similar bubble that could occur today. Or it could trigger a rising revolution that may be in its early stages, given the beginnings of the Occupy Wall Street movement in that began on September 17, 2011 and the wave of strikes by low-income workers for higher wages in early December 2013. These protests are continuing as of this writing in July 2014. But more about that later. Here are some more findings from Dadush et. al. that show the decline of social mobility, the growth of poverty, and the causes of inequality.

Dadush et. al.'s accounts of the lack of real mobility, despite widespread beliefs that opportunity is possible, also harks back to the Middle Ages, when there was little mobility, although at that time little was expected, as reflected [250] in the medieval notion that there was a divine order of things, since God had created a perfect order, and individuals, though imperfect themselves, were part of this perfect order. As such, humans were part of the Great Chain of Being, which descends from God to the angels, demons or renegade angels, stars, moon, kings, nobles, men, wild animals, and so on, down to precious metals and other minerals. One's position in life was therefore part of this natural order, and should be accepted, as part of the Great Chain of Being.

While beliefs may have changed, the lack of mobility from class to class hasn't. As Dadush et. al. note, a 2011 Charitable Trust survey found that 68% of Americans still believed that they could control their own economic situation and that they had achieved or would achieve the American dream, while a 2011 Gallup poll found that 70% of Americans believed that the federal government should play a part in increasing equality of opportunity. Yet this optimism may be receding, too, in that in 2011, 41% of Americans felt there was not much opportunity, up from 17% in 1998. But irrespective of beliefs, the basic reality is that little mobility exists for most people and the lack of opportunity has been increasing, and it has gotten even worse in the last decade, since Dadush's 2012 book.

For example, Dadush et. al. report the following patterns and trends[251]:

- According to the 2007 Economic Mobility Project study by the Pew Charitable Trust and Brookings Institute, approximately 40% of the children born to parents in the bottom quintile of the income distribution will remain there, and the remaining 60% will not move up very far – mostly they will just move tothe lower-middle quartile (23%) or middle quintile (19%). In fact, the chances of moving from the bottom to the top is like winning at Las Vegas, in that a 2006 Center for American Progress (CAP) report estimated that children from the bottom 20% have only a 1% chance of reaching the top 5% of the family income distribution, whereas a child born into the top 5% has a 22% chance of remaining there as an adult. In short, "those at the bottom of the distribution are much more likely to stay near the bottom."
- Mobility in the U.S. is also less than in other developed OECD countries, since according to the Gini coefficient, the U.S. has a .50 earnings mobility score, whereas some

European countries have a score of as high as 80%. In other words, compared to other countries, one's parents' income is relatively more predictive of how well one will do than in other developed countries, and the data also suggests that "countries with higher inequality tend to have lower inter-generational mobility."

This reduction of mobility in the U.S. has only increased, as Marcus Lu notes in a World Economic Forum article: "Is the American Dream Over? Here's What the Data Says. As Lu points out, it has become harder and harder from Americans to achieve the dream of outearning their parents. A key reason is stagnating wage group and the decline of the middle class, while the upper class and lower-income classes have both increased their share of U.S. aggregate income.[252]

This increase in inequality is, in turn, accompanied by several other negative trends, which include the increase in poverty, increased economic instability, and the growing expenditure on what are called "positional" goods, that are designed to show off status, rather than being based on the value or worth of the goods themselves. Again, to highlight the statistics compiled by Dadush and his associates, these patterns and trends include the following[253]:

- In 2012, the U.S. poverty rate of 15.1% was at the highest level since 1993, though it declined slightly to 12.3% in 2019.[254] Since 2007, just before the beginning of the Great Recession, the rate increased by nearly 3 percentage points, resulting in 8.8 million people below the poverty line. This level of poverty increased the most between 1975 and 2010 even more for those whose income was less than 50% of the poverty line. In other words, the poorer people were, the more that group of the poor grew. And now it is likely that the poverty rate will increase substantially, because of the millions of people who have lost their jobs, incomes, and businesses due to the pandemic, and millions of renters and homeowners are likely to lose their homes.

- The poverty rate increased even more for individuals of working age from 18 to 64, reflecting the stagnation of income for low-income employees and the growth of unemployment for that group. The poverty level for that group is 13.7%, the highest since 1966, and since then has more than doubled from 11 to 26 million in poverty. The main reason for this increase in poverty has been due to unemployment, rather than a drop in relative wages.

- The poverty rate in the U.S., based on the percentage of households earning less than 50% of the median income, is the highest among other OECD countries – even greater than in several middle-income developing countries, which include Mexico and Turkey.

- Poverty affects one's life chances in numerous ways, as noted in a U.S. Government Accountability Office Report, "Poverty in America." Among other things, lower-income individuals experience higher rates of chronic illness, disease, and disabilities, and also die younger than those who have higher incomes."[255] The life expectancy of the poor is only 75% of those with higher incomes, in part due to a lack of health insurance and the high cost of health care. Then, too, poverty limits low-income individuals in their ability to develop the necessary skills, abilities, knowledge, and habits to successfully participate in the labor force.

- The high and increasing level of inequality may also contribute to increased economic instability, since they lead to a reduced political consensus and increased borrowing by those in the middle and low income groups to keep up their consumption levels when credit is available. Then, this increased borrowing can result in an increase in debt, and this growing debt can reach a tipping point, as was the case in the U.S. in 1929 and 2007. In fact, the increase in debt, as the middle and lower income groups compensated for their stagnant real incomes by borrowing when credit was easy to come by, led to the mortgage crisis, when these debts came due and the borrowers couldn't pay.

- The growing wealth at the top has increased the money spent on positional goods, which includes luxury goods such as sports cars, boats, expensive clothing, and jewelry. This growing wealth can also increase the importance of where one send one's child to school and the satisfaction of one's job, based on how well it pays compared to the pay of one's peers. The result can be a kind of "arms race" for having the most desirable positional goods, leading everyone to spend more, such as when the superrich build larger and larger mansions and the expectations for what a CEO should earn go up. This growth of wealth at the top has also increased the cost of attending a top-ranked university, so increasingly those who attend are more likely to come from wealthy families; then they have a greater advantage in getting jobs after graduation because they come from a better branded university.

In short, all these patterns and trends creating increasing inequality today, especially in the United States, have created these parallels with the lifestyles of medieval times based on huge gaps in income and limited mobility. Though the technology and resources might be different, the basic differences, born of differences in wealth, are the same.

The Causes of Increasing Inequality Today

The causes of rising inequality can be briefly noted. The main factors noted by Dadush and associates include technology, trade, immigration, demographic changes, financialization, and the related policy and political processes. They have played a role in causing the trend to greater inequality due to these factors[256]:

- Skill-based technological change (SBTC) played a major role in "hollowing out the labor force" by providing more opportunities for employment at the ends of the wage distribution, along with a decline of middle-income jobs. Highly skilled employees, and especially high-level managers and CEOs, could make much more at a time of increasingly sophisticated technology, including computers, machine tools, and robots, putting many unskilled workers out of work. Concurrently, many low-pay service jobs, such as waiters, security guards, and janitors, who are not involved in producing goods, have been protected from automation. The net result has been more income for those on the top and more low paid jobs for those on the bottom, while many middle income jobs got eliminated. As a result, with lowered incomes and high debts from mortgages, it is no wonder that many middle income people lost their homes.

- Although trade deficits have occurred for all the OECD countries with the expansion of trade with developing countries and increased imports from them, these trade imbalances have not had much effect on wage inequality in the U.S. Likewise, despite a popular belief that immigration has contributed to depressing wages and has taken jobs from U.S.-born workers, in fact, many research studies show very little impact from immigration on wages in the U.S.

- Two key demographic changes have contributed to wage inequality – the increase in single-parent households due to the declining marriage rate, and the increase of female employment, along with the increased educational achievement and rising pay for women. For example, from 1960 to 1990, women's share of the workforce rose from 33% to 45%, and from 1979 their wages rose from 62% to 80% of men's wages. But because low-income men experienced a sharp decline in marriage rates, they were less likely to be married to a working spouse, which contributed somewhat to the increase in income inequality.

- Still another major contributor to wage inequality has been the expansion of winner-take-all markets, in which small differences in performance turn into very large differences in reward, such as in sports and entertainment, where there is just one winner in a sporting competition or one actor in a lead role in most films. A similar pattern has occurred in other entertainment arenas, such as music and TV, where just a small number of musicians, singers, and TV personalities rise to the top and command huge salaries. For example, *The Hollywood Reporter* notes that A-list movie stars commonly make $15 to $20 million for lead roles in big-budget films, while secondary lead actors earn about $1.5 million to $4.5 million. But the median salary for actors in general in films, TV, and plays regardless of the size of the role is far less — about $50,529 per year.[257]

Thus, aside from these high performers, those who come in second place or lower may earn just a fraction of what those at the top earn or even nothing, as witnessed by the high percentage of unemployed or low paying actors. For example, SAG statistics show that about 98% of the members of the union earn $5000 a year or less; in 2012, the lowest 10% earned less than $13,330 compared to the highest 10% who earned more than $106,000.[258] These yearly earnings are so low, because few actors have regular work. But for those who do work, the median hourly wage is $17.49 an hour in 2020, and the lowest 10% of the actors earned less than $8.97 an hour.[259] The earnings in this winner-take-all market have, in turn, mushroomed even more due to globalization, TV, and the decline in communication costs, so that the high profile entertainment and sports stars can now reach a global audience at the same time.

- The number of winner-take-all markets has also increased. Besides sports and entertainment stars, these markets includes the CEOs of medium to large-sized companies, software developers, Silicon Valley entrepreneurs, and investors. Moreover, as Dadush points out, the winner-take-all markets trigger "feedback mechanisms that can promote even greater inequality." For example, the top-paid employees in one market generally want the products of other top-employees, such as in purchasing the best luxury car and hiring the best cosmetic surgeon, so their prices have increased, too, contributing to further income inequality.

- Financialization — the growing centralizing of the finance sector in the economy — has also contributed to inequality. This centralization has increased the significance of the financial sector relative to other sectors of the economy, and it has resulted in transferring funds from these other sectors to the financial sector. Much of this development has occurred due to reduced deregulation of capital markets beginning in the 1980s, resulting in finance firms creating increasingly complicated and hard to understand financial instruments to maximize profits. A good example is the creation of derivatives, which are securities whose price is based on or derived from one or more underlying assets, with its value determined by the fluctuation of these assets, which include stocks, bonds, commodities, currencies, interest rates, and market indexes, and most derivatives are characterized by high leverage. This emphasis on maximizing profits has, in turn, led shareholders to have an increased interest in short-term profitability, and it has led to upping the compensation of CEOs through stock options and bonuses that rewarded risk-taking. In addition, this emphasis on profits now has encouraged speculation based on highly leveraged funds and an increase in debt, which contributed to making the economy less stable, should the value of assets decline, which has put pressure on anyone holding those leveraged funds.

- Financialization also led to increased income inequality through payments to the top earners in the form of capital gains rather than income, while the earnings of those in the financial sector zoomed as well. For example, in 1979, 5.4% of all employees were in the financial sector, and they represented 7.7% of the top 1%, excluding capital gains earnings. But by 2005, 6.1% of all employees were in this sector, and they represented 13.9% of the top 1% earners.

- The pay of a CEO relative to a worker zoomed between 1980 and 2011. In 1980, the CEO earned about 42 times as much; in 1990, about 107 times as much; and in 2011, the CEO earned a whopping 325 times as much.

- Financialization additionally has contributed to the winner-take-all attitude, whereby a small group of investors reap huge rewards.

- Inequality has been affected by politics and contributes to supporting political choices that lead to even further inequality. A key reason for the influence of government, and especially the federal government, on inequality is that it has the power to tax and spend. This means that the government can help to reduce income inequality by applying higher tax rates to higher earners and supporting poor and disadvantaged groups with direct financial support, such as through programs like Food Stamps, Social Security and Medicare. But as noted by the Congressional Budget Office report for 2011, the government's role in redistributing funds through both transfers and taxes has been declining. A key reason is that since 1980, the government has reduced its funds to the poor, while giving more to the elderly, who tend to have more wealth than the average population. At the same time, since 1979, the government has reduced income taxes and increased payroll taxes, which has put more of a burden on lower-income wage workers, thereby increasing inequality.

- Still another factor contributing to inequality is the de-unionization of the workplace, reflected in a decline of the membership of salaried and wage workers from 20.1% to 11.8% in 2011, which has contributed to reductions in the wages of low-income workers. At the same time, there has been a weakening of employment protection legislation and a reduction of regulation of products in the marketplace, which are both associated with increased income inequality.

• Finally, the increase in wealth at the top has contributed to the government adopting policies that favor the wealthy, thereby reinforcing their power, while income inequality is associated with polarization in politics, reflected in the growth of voting along party lines. This inequality might also be related to the growing standoff between the parties in Congress, as the Republicans line up against the Democrats, with the Republicans largely aligned with the interests of the wealthy in promoting no new taxes and cuts in government spending, while the Democrats seek to use more spending to aid the lower income classes. In fact, Obama has asserted that income inequality is "the defining challenge of our times," arguing that there is a need to raise the minimum wage and strengthen the social safety net for millions of struggling Americans.[260]

The struggle to create more equality through political changes could, however, be a tough struggle, because as Dadush and his associates point out, "aggregate political influence can buy wealth, and has been doing so for a long time," resulting in the problem that "income concentration at the top can become self-reinforcing through capture of the political system. High income leads to more political influence, which in turn leads to higher income." Even though political campaigns can now be supported by individuals on the Internet, having money helps win political office, and most officer seekers look to private contributions rather than public sources, since they can raise more by not taking public funds which are limited by a ceiling. Moreover, the top-spending lobbies are funded by major business interests, including pharmaceuticals, electric utilities, business associations, insurance, oil and gas industries, and the U.S. Chamber of Commerce, which were the biggest spenders in 2010, despite efforts by other interests supported by other groups, such as environmental causes and civil rights.

Thus, as Dadush and his associates conclude: "Campaign finance, lobbying, and even the composition of the U.S. political class, in combination, appear to have strongly tilted outcomes towards the interests of the very wealthy." So even though many of those on the top give large amounts to charity, they still look to the political system to protect their high income earnings.[261]

The Growing Concern with Inequality Today

These indicators of inequality today, along with the factors contributing to inequality, are extremely important, because they represent a growing trend with many negative results – from growing misery for those left behind to the destabilization of the economy. Unfortunately, these trends may be hard to reverse, because of the vicious cycle create by the causes of inequality and the political clout of those who have risen to the top and want to stay there. Since they have benefited from the current system, they want to keep it that way so they and their children can continue to benefit, and they have the power to put pressure on politicians to continue to increase their wealth and power.

While some high income individuals like Warren Buffett and Bill Gates may be calling on those with wealth to give back to the less fortunate, and they have contributed their funds or created foundations to contribute to improving the health, education, and quality of life for those on the bottom, they are just a small percentage of the superwealthy. By contrast, others in the top tier of society seek to earn even more and show it off, as a sign of their power and prestige, such as through huge mansion and lavish weddings with high-profile celebrity guests. In this way, they create a public persona of glamour and luxury, leaving those on the bottom aspiring to gain access to the top. Examples like Justin Bieber's or Billie Eilish's rise to the top of the music hierarchy from humble beginnings only fuel the belief that anyone can do it, in spite of the harsh reality that in general there is less mobility from class to class in the U.S. than in any other country. In turn, the rise of property crimes, primarily committed by members of the lower and working classes are driven, in part, by the desire to get ahead, when other channels of achievement are closed to the individual.

These patterns, trends, and concerns are reflected in a series of books that have come out since 2012 calling attention to the problem and offering varying suggestions about what to do. Among these are *The Great Divergence* by Timothy Noah, *The Price of Inequality* by Joseph E. Stiglitz, *Plutocrats: The Rise of the New Global Super-Rich and the Fall of Everyone Else* by Chrystia Freeland, and *The Rich and the Rest of Us: A Poverty Manifesto* by Tavis Smiley and Cornel West. And since 2018 to 2020, even more books on inequality have come out including *The Broken Ladder: How Inequality Affect the Way We Think, Live, and Die* by Keith Payne, *Inequality: What Can Be Done?* By Anthony B. Atkinson, *Hometown Inequality* by Brian F. Schaffner, and *Supreme Inequality: The Supreme Court's Fifth-Year Battle for a More Unjust America* by Adam Cohen.

For example, in *The Great Divergence,* Timothy Noah contrasts the increasing disparity between being rich and being middle class for the last 33 years from 1979 to 2012 with the preceding five decades from the early 1930s through most of the 1970s, when the opposite occurred. During this early period, which he calls "The Great Compression," the share of the nation's income going to the wealthy shrunk or remained stable.

Ironically, according to Noah, the prevailing viewpoint among economists as late as 1979 was that "any advanced industrial democracy would inevitably become more equal or remain stable in their distribution." [262] In part, this increased equality was due to the creation of various government programs to stimulate the economy and distribute funds to the disadvantaged, as a reaction to the misery of the Great Depression. Then, furthering this trend to greater equality, many new industries and opportunities emerged due to the wartime boom of the 1940s, along with programs to help the vets gain housing in the late 1940s and 1950s, and government made extensive investments in educational programs.

But starting in 1979, the expansion or continuity of equality came to an end. As Noah, much like Dadush and his associates notes: "When the economy recovered in 1983, incomes grew even more unequal. They have continued growing more unequal to this day." And in agreement with Dadush, Noah agrees that the trend to incomes becoming more unequal is global, though the level and growth rate of this inequality is particularly extreme in the U.S. He similarly uses the Gini coefficient as the most common measure of inequality and notes that the U..S. was the "undisputed champion" in the percentage of income distribution that went to the top 1%, making the income distribution in the U.S. "more unequal than any other OECD nation."[263]

As Noah illustrates graphically, in the United States the income share for the top 1% was 24% in 1928, just before the 1929 crash, and then during the Great Compression from 1932 to 1979, it dropped to only 9% in 1970, after going through a period of decline after 1932. But since 1979, the reversal of this trend has led to the top 1%'s share becoming 24% again as of 2007. As Noah points out, when the U.S. went through two long periods of sustained economic growth from 1980 to 2005, 80% of the total increase in income went to the top 1%. Even after factoring in federal taxes, employer-sponsored health insurance, employer contributions to Social Security, Medicare, federal unemployment insurance, and other federal benefits, the top 1% still received 36% of the total increase in the U.S. By contrast, while productivity increased about 20% from 2000 to 2009, none of that increase turned into an increase in wages for the average working-age family. Rather, it was largely claimed by the top 1%. As calculated by U.S. Census Bureau date, about two thirds of the increase in incomes during the economic expansion of 2002 to 2007 went to the top 1%. While the poverty rate fell from 14.8% to 10.5% between 2014 to 2019,[264] this is expected to increase substantially again due to the pandemic resulting in job losses, business failures, and people losing their homes.

So why is this growing divergence accepted? According to Noah, the most likely reason is the "enduring belief in upward mobility." But in fact, the American dream is not only less attainable that it once was, but it was "never as attainable as many people wanted to believe."[265]

Noah also points to the power of parentage. Using data from the 2009 Pew Charitable Trusts Economic Mobility Project, he notes that only 6% of Americans born in the lowest quintile can make it to the top fifth of the economic heap. Had they had statistics back in the Middle Ages, that finding might be much like the prospects of mobility then.

During the 1932-1979 Great Compression, opportunities for mobility were greater, though the pie for everyone was smaller, and on the whole, <u>absolute</u> mobility increased for everyone, due to advances in technology and more money in the mix. But the real barometer for how one is doing is <u>relative</u> mobility, where you compare yourself to everyone else. By that measure, people in the lower and middle classes were not doing as well, while the position of the very wealthy increased, much as occurred during the Middle Ages, after the invasions were contained and the royalty, nobility, and later the wealthy merchants became richer and richer at the expense of the other classes, who were subject to ever more taxes to support the wealthy in their luxurious lifestyle.

The statistics on recent relative mobility in the U.S. are sobering. As Noah notes, the "immigrants' *relative* position in the United States is often *lower* than their parents' *relative position* in the country of origin," and citing Julia B. Isaacs of Washington's Brookings Institution, he notes that 67% of us "have more income, after inflation, than our parents had (<u>absolute</u> mobility)," but only a third of us "end up more prosperous relative to our fellow Americans than our parents were (<u>relative</u> mobility." Thus, the greatest likelihood is that an individual's relative position will be as good as or possibly worse than one's parents. While there is some intergenerational upward mobility from one generation to the next, it is not the norm.

Still other research cited by Noah shows that mobility was "lower in the 1990s and early 2000s than it was during the 1970s, and the greatest decline was in families near the bottom of the income scale. By contrast, the children of those on top of the income ladder have a much better opportunity to stay there or make even more in absolute mobility terms, though in terms of relative mobility they can't go much higher, since they are already there. A recent article on the "Heirs and Heiresses of the Wealthiest People in America" by Mandi Woodruff points this up. As she notes, on the average, American parents plan to leave $175,000 to their children after they retire, and one out of five inheritances will be worth more than $390,000. The children of billionaire fathers can expect to inherit much more, such as the children of the Koch Brothers, who were heirs to their late father's multibillion dollar fortune and are now worth about $36 billion; Zachery and Alexa Dell, the children of Michael Dell, who founded the largest PC company in the U.S. and is worth $15.9 billion; and Brett Icahn, the son of Carl Icahn, the activist investor and founder of Icahn Enterprises.[266]

The contrast between the growing income for these wealthy families and the relative stagnation or loss of income for everyone else has made it especially difficult for many middle and lower income individuals to cover the basics. While some consumer goods, such as food or clothing cost less today, other costs for transportation, health care, and higher education are more expensive. As a result, a difficulty, such as a job loss or injury, can prove an economic tragedy, leading to piling on debt, bankruptcy, or even worse. As Noah writes:

> The stagnation of middle-class incomes since the early 1970s means that middle-income people are already living pretty close to the edge…As a consequence, for middle-income families, a job loss can easily push a family into serious debt or even bankruptcy. And, in fact, consumer debt and bankruptcy rates have exploded during the Great Divergence.[267]

The irony is that American society has grown richer due to increased production gains resulting from improvements in technology. But in relative terms, those at the bottom have done worse.

While median household income grew by 33%, according to labor economist Stephen J. Rose at Georgetown University, not 15% as reported by the Census Bureau, median income grew at only one third of the rate between 1949 and 1979, and according to Rose "those at the bottom of the income ladder have benefited only minimally from the significant gains in overall production over the past three decades."[268] In other words, due to the Great Divergence, those at the top were the main beneficiaries of gains in productivity, while others, primarily those in the middle class, fell behind, much as occurred in the High and Late Middle Ages, as the kings, nobles, and later the wealthy merchants gained the greatest benefits from the increases in trade and new more efficient ways of doing things.

Noah's discussion of changes in educational patterns during the Great Divergence also show how the access to education is becoming more like in the Middle Ages when education was confined largely to the royalty, nobility, and wealthy merchants. A key change has been that education has been becoming more expensive at the better private schools, making it less accessible to those in the lower and middle income classes, while wages for college graduates have increased, and since 1990, employers have increasingly wanted a graduate degree. As Noah puts it:

> The run-up during the Great Diverge in the 'wage premium' for high school and college graduates in the United States...reflects the simple fact that America's production of high school and college graduates is no longer keeping pace with technological change...The post-1990 slowdown in the college premium's growth likely reflects the new reality that employers increasingly demand a graduate degree...Rising tuition...since the 1980s has priced many families out of the market. Tuition surged ahead of the already high inflation rate during the 1970s, and has done so ever since. By 2005 college tuition at public and private universities averaged, respectively, 10 percent and 45 percent of median family income.[269]

As the cost of education has increased, the income of the better educated workers has risen faster compared to the general population, since their limited supply has built up their salaries. Thus, they made more, while others made comparatively less. Again, a comparison is apt with the difference between the well-educated wealthy classes and the largely illiterate or poorly educated peasants and artisans of the Middle Ages. As a matter of practice, the wealthy families of the High and Late Middle Ages arranged for a good education for their sons to prepare them for positions in running the manor or merchant business or for joining the priesthood. In comparison, the peasant and artisan families generally just provided their sons with hands-on training on the farm or as an apprentice in the family trade.

The disparity for rich and poor results in "unequal government," too, in that the laws passed and services provided by the government then and now favor the wealthy. For example, in medieval times, the government was been led by primarily the kings, nobility, and some of the wealthy bourgeoisie and run for their best interest, whether to enforce payments of taxes, restrictions on hunting on manor lands, or wage wars, while Reagan and his Republican successors to the White House made the government less beneficial to those with lower incomes and more accommodating to those with higher income, through their attempts to reduce the size of government and therefore public services, especially those targeted at those with lower incomes. The support of supply-side economics, since generally discredited, similarly benefited the rich, since it is based on the notion that lowering the marginal income tax rate would increase economic growth so "the tax cut would pay for itself."[270] But that didn't happen. Instead, this approach helped to make the rich even richer.

In fact, in the Trump years, the very rich got even more tax breaks. For instance, the Tax Cuts and Jobs Act of 2017, which was the largest overhaul of the tax system in over three decades, provided tax cuts that made the top 1% even wealthier.[271] As a result of this change, "for the first time in American history, the 400 wealthiest people paid a lower tax rate than any other group," as the economists Emmanuel Saez and Gabriel Zucman at the University of California, Berkeley found in a study of tax rates.[272] Then, if this wasn't enough of a break, the rich benefited even more from the CARES Act, which was ostensibly to help families facing stay-home orders and to help businesses from going under so workers would still have jobs once they could do so safely. But the biggest tax break was designed to help only wealthy people at a cost of $135 billion to the government.[273] Basically, the tax break was provided by a provision of the bill which allowed wealthy business owners and corporations to offset losses in certain years by not paying taxes in other years. The main beneficiaries were real estate firms, hedge funds, private equity firms, law firms, and big corporations, because the new rules essentially allowed them to game the system by amending past taxes applying current losses to offset income which they earned before 2018. The result is most millionaires have saved an average of $1.6 million on their taxes, whereas other taxpayers got a onetime $1200 stimulus check.[274]

These recent benefits for the rich are simply a continuation of benefits to the wealthy over the last several decades, dating back to the 1980s. That's because not only did the rich benefit from more tax cuts, changes in what was taxed made taxes more regressive, whereby the rich paid less and the lower and middle classes more, especially due to changes in the Reagan and Bush II presidencies. Not only did their policies halve the top margin income-tax rate, but more importantly, the federal government reduced the corporate income and estate and gift taxes, at a time when the wealthy were increasingly shifting the source of their income from that derived from capital, such as dividends, interest, and rents, towards income derived from labor, such as wages and salaries, stock options, and business income from partnerships, sole proprietorships, and S-corporations. As a result, according to Noah:

> When you factor in *all* federal taxes (and also the federal payroll tax, which started out regressive and has become

even more so), the effective tax rate on the top 1% fell from 59.3% in 1979 to 34.7 percent in 2004 – a drop of nearly 25 percentage points.[275]

At the same time, the government reduced the money it was distributing downward by 17%, so by 2007, the net effect was that during the Great Divergence, the federal government reduced its direct distribution from collecting taxes and awarding benefits by about a quarter. As a result, the effect of all federal taxes and benefits was more significant than the effect of income taxes alone. In short, by taxing the middle and lower income individuals and families more and taxing the wealthy and the companies they invested in or controlled less, the government contributed to the growing spread between rich and poor, much as in medieval times, when a king rewarded the nobles or a warrior who performed well in battle with more lands, while taxing the peasants who worked the land even more.

While Noah distinguishes between the policies of Republicans and Democrats, in that under Democratic presidents, Americans were "richer and more equal," whereas under Republican presidents, Americans were "poorer and less equal," due to pretax income growth between 1948 and 2005, under both Democrat and Republican presidents, the top 5% received favorable treatment from both.

Moreover, the effect of lobbying on behalf on business interests since the late 1970s helped the rich get richer, too. Among other things, the business interests helped to defeat a proposed federal agency for consumer advocacy, as well as a labor law reform bill increasing penalties on companies which violated laws protecting labor organizers, since business viewed these consumer-oriented laws and regulations as a threat to a company's bottom line by giving individuals more ability to sue company's for financial damages. Now the lobbyists on behalf of business have even more clout. For example, as Noah writes:

More than \$3 billion annually is spent on lobby-ing…That's nearly twice what was spent a decade ago. In 2010 the groups that spent the greatest sums on lob-bying, according to the Center for Responsive Politics, a Washington-based non-profit, were the Chamber of Commerce (\$132 million), PG&E (\$45 million); General Electric (\$39 million); Federal Express (\$26 million); and the American Medical Association (\$23 million). Not a single labor union was to be found in the top twenty, and the only lobby group in the top twenty that was unaffiliated with business was the American of Retired Persons. (And in some ways, even the AARP, as it prefers to be known today, is a business lobby because it sells health insurance.[276]

As the power of the wealthy has increased, the power of orga-nized labor has declined from a peak of about 21 million in 1979 or 21% of the workforce, to about 15 million or about 12% of the work-force in 2019. In turn, the relative power of the organized workers is even worse than in the Middle Ages, since this decline is as if most of the artisans and tradesmen who formed guilds in towns in the Late Middle Ages no longer had any organizations to represent them and contribute to improving their work conditions and prices in the face of wealthy merchants who preferred to deal with indi-vidual workers who had no standard prices or work standards as promulgated by the guild.

From the Rich to the Superrich: The Different Categories of the Wealthy

Noah distinguishes between the different categories of the wealthy, from the top 10% to the top 1% of the top 1%, which is a little like creating a scale in the Middle Ages to distinguish between the king at the top, followed by the most powerful great lords, down to the lesser nobility and finally the wealthier peasants with more land and animals. In his breakdown, anyone in the top 10% should be called rich. Then, he breaks down this top decile into five categories:

- the sort of rich, making $109,000 to $153,000 – the bottom half of the top 10%;
- the basically rich, making $153,000 to $368,000 – the bottom threshold for the top 1%;
- the undeniably rich, making $368,000 to $1.7 million – the bottom threshold for the top .1%;
- the really rich, making $1.7 million to $9.1 million – the bottom threshold for the top .01%;
- the stinking rich, everyone making $9.1 million or more — which qualifies them to be in the top .01%.

As Noah describes it, the higher one's position in this hierarchy the better one did in the Great Divergence, by further increasing their share of the national income. The top 10% increased their share from 34-48%; the top 5% went from 23-37%; the top 1% more than doubled their share from 10 to 21%; the top .1% tripped their share from 3 to 10%; and the top .01% — the stinking rich, nearly quadrupled their share from 1.4-5%. In other words, though each group had less of the national income pie, as an increasingly smaller and more rarified group, that group gained proportionately more from 1979 to 2008, reflecting "the rise of the stinking rich." These five categories still exist today, although the rich are making even more money, while those in the lower 90% are making less.

Where did they get all this money? For the top .1%, the majority were executives, managers and supervisors at nonfinancial firms and financiers, followed by those in the law, medicine, and real estate. Plus chief executives at nonfinancial companies experienced a huge increase in pay. For example, at a time when the median pay to workers declined slightly, the largest payment when to Philippe Dauman, the president and CEO of Viacom, the big entertainment corporation with many holdings, including Paramount Pictures. Another group that increased its share of the top earners' group was the financiers. In 1979, the financiers represented only 11% of the top .01% consisting of the "Really and Stinking Rich." But by 2005, they represented 18%, because of their success in mergers and expansions into new businesses, so their profits grew even faster than in any other sector of the economy – from an average of 13% of all domestic corporate profits between 1978 to 1987 to a 30% average from 1998 to 2007.

In turn, the Wall Street financiers were able to do so well because of deregulation. While Washington carefully regulated what the banks could or couldn't do after the 1929 crash, such as through the 1933 Glass-Steagall Act, which prohibited commercial banks from engaging in investment banking or investment banks from engaging in commercial transactions, beginning in the 1970s Washington faced political pressure to deregulate. In part this pressure came from the growing influence of the business lobby, and more and more new financial products weren't regulated, such as hedge funds and derivatives. Then, too, the SEC eased leverage restrictions, so investors could invest more money that wasn't their own through leveraging, and eventually the Glass-Steagall Act was removed in 1999, though the financiers had already found their ways around it. Another reason for their success is that the financiers were willing to take more risks in the expectation that the government would bail them out. Thus, during the boom years of the Great Divergence, the payments to the financiers, along with the rest of the very wealthy, went up and up, and after the failures of companies like Lehman Brothers which triggered the Great Recession, the government provided a $70 billion bailout, and most of the big bankers continued to do quite well.

Finally, like Dadush and associates, Noah points to the huge run-up in earnings for the top entertainment celebrities and athletes who are part of the top .01%. Though these high-profile individuals may be only 3% of this .01%, they are a visible segment and their earnings reflect their ability to reach a growing globalized marketplace due to improvements in technology, so they can scale up the size of their audience to a much higher level than ever before possible. Plus, the audience may have a "psychological need to focus on just a few popular personalities at a time," which has led to narrowing the competition to "a few winners who dominate a vastly expanded market."[277]

In short, just as the top of socioeconomic pyramid in the Middle Ages was dominated by a small number of superwealthy and powerful kings, nobles, and leaders of a wealthy hierarchical church, so it is today. The superrich have more power and wealth than ever, and these are continuing to increase, as companies expand and consolidate, becoming ever bigger, and the wealthy become ever more powerful through their financial contributions and their use of lobbyists to pressure the government to enact policies and tax regulations that help them make even more.

The Decline of Everyone Else

The other side of the inequality equation, where the rich have gotten richer, is that everyone else is becoming poorer, with devastating consequences, especially for those who have been middle class, but have lost jobs, businesses, or homes, due to declining opportunities and incomes, especially due to the pandemic. Concurrently, those who are already poor have experienced a loss of benefits, such as reductions in food stamps, while the wealthy clamor for even more reductions, characterizing the poor as lazy freeloaders who don't deserve government handouts. But in fact the government has given most of its handouts to the rich, since it has given special incentives through taxation and reduced regulation to many corporations — which are a type of handout, though under another name. And the opportunities to climb out of difficult straits are harder than ever. As Noah explains:

Opportunities in the United States are about the same as, or fewer than, they were prior to the Great Divergence, and they are definitely fewer than in most western European countries. Unlike America's industrial revolution, which increased both inequality and opportunity, the Great Divergence has increased only inequality... Since passage of the 1996 welfare-reform bill, the welfare state has made joblessness a good deal more difficult. Welfare assistance is now time-limited and fewer than half as many people receive assistance.[278]

During this time, the middle class – or more accurately individuals and families in the former middle class – have been harmed the most. The poor have certainly been impacted, especially by the increase in the cost of shelter, so they have little left over to spend on other basics. But the middle class has been impacted most of all, since the major large ticket items such as housing, health care, high education, and automobiles are more expensive. So those in the middle class have an increasing difficulty living a middle class life style, and the loss of a job or business can be devastating, triggering a run-up in debts and an inability to pay a mortgage, resulting in a foreclosure, bankruptcy, and the loss of a house. It can only take a few set-backs, like a job loss or illness, resulting in a reduced income, to start the process, much like a single domino falling can cause the rest of the line to fall.

Meanwhile, the rich tend to show little concern or compassion for the struggles of the lower and middle classes, apart from some philanthropists like Bill Gates and Warren Buffett, who are contributing a very small percentage of their vast wealth to help. Rather, the rich tend to want more separation, such as by creating a growing number of gated communities or hiring security guards to surround their property to keep the poor out As Noah describes this process:

> As incomes become more unequal, the rich won't likely urge or even allow the government to create or expand public spheres where they must foreswear special privileges and mingle with the proles. More likely, growing income inequality will make the rich want to create or expand private spheres that help maintain *separation* from the proles, with whom they will have less and less in common.[279]

A recent example is the battle over Martin's Beach in Half Moon Bay California. While the previous owner gave people access to the beach for a fee, after Vinod Khosla, a Silicon Valley venture capitalist and co-founder of Sun Microsystems, paid $38.5 million in 2008 for the 53-acre parcel of ocean land which includes the beach and the road, he closed the gate, and he even posted armed guards, to keep the public off what he claims is private land. So now the battle is still in the courts after a ten-year battle of litigation, protests, civil disobedience, and arrests in the fight for public access versus private use by the wealthy.

Again, there is clear parallel with the separation between the rich and the poor in the Middle Ages. On the one hand, the king and nobles, and later the wealthy merchants, lived in their castles, manors, and mansions, separated from the low-income peasants and artisans, who lived in their own special sections of the property owned by the king, noble, or merchant. Only those who worked as servants were allowed in close proximity to the person they served, where rules of social interaction kept them in a clearly subservient role. And this separation continued in various activities which kept the classes kept apart, such as the balls of the wealthy and the fairs of the peasants and in war, while the nobles and knights rode on horseback, the peasants and artisans trudged along on foot.

This effect of the concentration of the wealth on the richest individuals in the US who control about 42% of the nation's wealth is starkly illustrated in *The Rich and the Rest of US: A Poverty Manifesto* by Tavis Smiley and Cornel West. They went on "The Poverty Tour: A Call to Conscience," an 18-city bus that began on August 2011, to illustrate the plight of America's poor of all races. Their goal was to put "a human face on poverty so that the persistent poor, near poor, and the new poor" would not be "ignored or rendered invisible" during the economic downturn. [280]

In their portrait of poverty, they describe in harrowing terms the expanding web of poverty that has occurred as the wealthy have gained an even larger share of the American pie. As they write in a description that rings true nearly a decade later in 2020:

Poverty in America has a new face. In 21ˢᵗ century America, the poor are no longer just the permanently unemployable, the recently incarcerated, or the mentally ill...While many whom we met fit what some define as the 'old poor' (people who were impoverished before the beginning of the 'Great Recession' in late 2007), we also gathered with shockingly large numbers of the 'new poor' – citizens who were once bona fide members of America's middle class, whose lives have been ravaged by the new economy's middle class...They once possessed relatively predictable and reasonably comfortable lives until they were inexplicably cast into a maelstrom of economic dispossession and spiritual despair. When the bottom fell out of the American Dream, the formerly lower, middle, and upper-middle classes found themselves recast in the nightmares of the downtrodden. Their possessions repossessed, gone; their lifestyles drastically altered; their dignity destroyed; and their identities radically transformed...They remain sober, indeed somber, faced with the frightening possibility of being destitute in the future and dependent on meager public assistance with no other resources.[281]

I have known many such people myself in the San Francisco Bay Area. These are people who suddenly found themselves out of work or lost their businesses, and then their homes, turning them into a class of new renters, who found it increasingly difficult to cover their rent and other costs, when rents began going up as a new class of young new rich moved to the Bay Area due to the explosion of the tech industry and tech start-ups. I also created a series of short documentaries about this problem in 2011 called *Middle Class Homeless*, featuring interviews with people talking about the prospect of losing their homes. In fact, these conditions are what inspired this book, and most recently the even more dire conditions created by the pandemic inspired a series of songs, including "What Happened to the American Dream" and "They're Losing Their Homes."

Moreover, this desperation caused by the Great Recession has contributed to a rise of suicide rates globally, according to research reported in September 2013. As described by Melissa Pandika in *an L.A. Times* article: "Global Economic Crisis Spurred 5000 Additional Suicides, Study Says," the study was conducted by researchers at the University of Hong Kong and other institutions. They examined suicide trends in 54 countries, using data on unemployment, gross domestic product, and suicide deaths, obtained from the World Health Organization, the International Monetary Fund, and the U.S. Centers for Disease Control and Prevention. Among other things, the results showed an association between unemployment and suicide rates, especially for men in countries that used to have low unemployment. For example, in 2009 alone, Pandika notes, "a 37% higher unemployment seems to have fueled a 3.3% increase in the global suicide rate for men, (which) translates into an additional 5000 deaths." Plus the suicide rate increased slightly among women from the Americas. Why the increase? Because, according to David Gunnell, a public health researcher at the University of Bristol in England who helped lead the study, the men were probably more likely to commit suicide than women, because they tend to be the breadwinners in their family and therefore "felt more pressure in the face of the worst economic collapse since the Great Depression." [282]

Smiley and West present the dire straits of "the rest of us," when they point out that the incomes of the richest 1% — those earning $380,000 or more – grew by 33% over the past 20, while the income growth for the other 90% of Americans, including the middle class, has been at a "virtual standstill." While those in the top 1% bring in an average of $1.3 million a year, the income of the average American is only $33,000. Meanwhile, the number of people living in poverty increased 2.6 million between 2009 and 2010, and while the number of Americans living in poverty was about 50 million people, according to the 2011 Census. [283]

Echoing Dadush and Noah, Smiley and West point to the key causes of increasing poverty as job loss and the loss of a home, noting that: "The biggest blows to the already shrinking middle class were record unemployment and a housing bubble that burst, resulting in the foreclosure of nearly 4 million homes." But that was just for 2011. If one adds up the number of foreclosures for every year from 2007 when the Great Recession began (though not officially recognized until 2008) through 2012, over 20 million foreclosures occurred. Plus about 5.7 million homes were repossessed.[284] Meanwhile, the number of Americans unemployed for 6 months or more was 6.3 million in 2009, the largest number since 1948, when the government first began counting the long-term unemployed, and "for the first time in decades, the percentage of working families in poverty rose to 31.2 percent, or 10.2 million people."[285] As of November 2013, the number of unemployed people was even greater — 10.9 million, with an unemployment rate of 7%.[286] And nearly a decade later, as of October 2020, the numbers are about the same — 11.1 million, with an unemployement rate of 6.9%.[287]

Such figures help to put in stark relief the other side of the run-up of fortunes. While the news media, TV, and films may play up the glamorous lifestyles of the very very rich and famous, like the Kardashians and Trumps, as a model for everyone to envy and emulate, the suffering throughout the U.S. is growing, as the Great Divergence increasingly turns the superrich into the modern royalty, nobility and wealthy merchants, while turning others into varying classes of modern-day peasants and artisans. As for the millions of foreclosures and house repossessions, they might be comparable to a medieval lord evicting a peasant from his house due to a nonpayment or insufficient payment of taxes, turning the peasant and his family into wandering cotters or homeless beggars in the countryside or in the growing towns. As Smiley and West observe:

> The American Dream is our nation's brand. It is the strategic marketing plan that has lured millions of immigrants to these shores with hopes of accomplishing wonders unimaginable in their native lands...Yet the 'dream' is not the real problem. America's denial is...If we don our

historical lens, we'll see a once-democratic vision now compromised and corrupted by materialism and greed that has morphed into an insatiable, capitalist monster that threatens our very existence.[288]

One factor causing this dream to become corrupted is that the media helped to promote symbols of success. For example, until the late 1940s, the American dream was attainable by the average family – a house, a car, and a working parent with a "decent-paying, benefits-providing job," so Americans in the late 20th century had a good chance to achieve a modest version of this dream. But with the beginnings of television in the 1950s, the dream became "a manipulative marketing tool used to spark unprecedented consumerism," and the setting of the TV family shifted from the working class lifestyle of Ralph and Alice in *The Honeymooners* to the luxurious lifestyle of J.R. in the 1970s *Dallas* TV show. And today we can see many "lavish, decadent, and over-indulgent unreality shows." Some prime examples are, of course, Donald Trump's *Celebrity Apprentice,* which ran from 2004 to 2017, and the latest doings of the Kardashian clan in *Keeping Up with the Kardashians,* which ran from 2007 to September 2019 and provided a prime example of keeping up with their opulent lifestyle. For now, as Smiley and West observe, "the 21st –century American Dream (is) defined by wealth, power and success."[289] And this display of that version of the American Dream is continued in the hit series *Succession* that premiered in 2018 and now is in its third season. In the story, the owners of Waystar RoyCo, a global media and hospitality empire, fight for control of the company as a result of the uncertainty of the health of the family's patriarch.

This dream of wealth, power, and success is one shared globally, as the superwealthy have become a global elite, as described by Chrystia Freeland in *Plutocrats: The Rise of the New Global Super-Rich and the Fall of Everyone Else.*[290] At one time writer F. Scott Fitzgerald observed in a short story "The Rich Boy" published in 1926 that the rich "are different from you and me." [291] But now the rich are even more different. As Freeland observes, in comments equally true in 2020, the rich of today are different from the rich of yesterday because of the new globally connected economy, leading them to share more with one another than with others who are not part of this elite in their own country. As she writes:

> Our light-speed, globally connected economy has led to the rise of a new super-elite that consist, to a notable degree, of first – and second-generation wealth. Its members are hardworking, highly educated, jet-setting meritocrats who feel they are the deserving winners of a tough, worldwide economic competition … They tend to believe in the institutions that permit social mobility, but are less enthusiastic about the economic redistribution – i.e., taxes – it takes to pay for those institutions. Perhaps most strikingly, they are becoming a transglobal community of peers who have more in common with one another than with their countrymen back home.[292]

Intriguingly, this transglobal connection between the super elite is also characteristic of the elite world of royalty, nobility, wealthy merchants, and pope and cardinals in the High and Late Middle Ages, though obviously they did not have the modern means of transportation and communication. Nevertheless, they became global travelers using the forms of transportation and communication of the day – namely ship, horses, and couriers to transmit letters by sea or horseback to their peers. As such they socialized together and intermarried, often for political reasons to connect high ranking families and gain advantages for even more power or wealth, mostly in the form of land, much like the global elite travels and communicates across borders today.

Freeland also compares the modern day plutocrats to the super-rich in the Gilded Age of the 1880s and turn of the century, when a superwealthy elite was created by capitalists, such as John Jacob Astor, J.P. Morgan, and Andrew Carnegie, who found opportunity in the industrial transformation of America after the Civil War. And just like the plutocrats of today and the superwealthy of the Middle Ages, they justified the great inequality of opportunity that emerged from the industrial revolution as the natural order of things. In medieval times, this split was justified as natural because it was part of the Great Chain of Being which descended from God, while the Gilded Age winners used the rationale of the science of the day to suggest this divergence of classes was simply a function of the "survival of the fittest," as Andrew Carnegie once explained the rise of the 1% in his century. As he stated: "While the law may be sometimes hard for the individual, it is best for the race, because it insures the survival of the fittest in every department." As a result, he concluded this state of affairs was "not only beneficial, but essential to the future progress of the race." [293] Today, though not stated in terms of eugenics, the justification comes from success due to best employing power of capitalism and the market or of having the advantage of being born to wealth.

However, as Freeland points out, today there are two different gilded ages unfolding at the same time, which feed off each other. One is the rise of the super elite in the industrialized West which is experiencing a second gilded age; the other is occurring in the emerging markets, which are experiencing their first gilded age. But both are contributing to the growth of each other, since as the emerging economies industrialize, they are creating new markets and supply chains for the West. For example, consider the many new products made in Asia for the titans in the West, such as the iPhones manufactured in China, and the huge conglomerates that have arisen in Asia's booming economies, such as Samsung, based in Seoul, South Korea.

Now with rapid communications, transportation, and online meeting technologies, such Zoom and GoToMeeting, it is easy for the ultra-rich to communicate, meet, socialize, and do ever more business deals with each other. The numbers are staggering. As Freeland points out, citing a 2011 annual report on the world's rich by Credit Suisse, the international investment bank, there are about 29.6 million millionaires – people with over $1 million in net assets around the world, representing about .5% of the total world population. While 37% of these millionaires are in North America and another 37% are in Europe, the Asia-Pacific area, excluding China and India, has 19.2% of the millionaires, and China alone has 3.4%. The rest are in India, Africa, or Latin America.

To zero in even further on the wealthiest around the globe, as of 2011, there were 84,700 individuals considered ultrahigh net worth individual with assets of over $50 million, 29,000 with net assets of over $100 million, and 2700 worth half a billion or more. Within this group, the U.S. is at the top, with 35,400 or 42% of the UHNWIs, followed by China (6.4%), and then German, Switzerland, and Japan, with about 4-5% each.

Nearly a decade later, there are even more millionaires who own nearly half of the world's wealth. As the 2019 Global Wealth Report from the Credit Suisse Research Institutes indicates, there are 46.8 million millionaires worldwide, who own approximately $158.3 trillion, which is about 44% of the $360 trillion total global wealth. The 2019 report also stated that the richest 10% owned 82% of the global wealth, and the top 1% owned 45% of this wealth, while the bottom half of wealth holders only owned less 1% of this wealth. And now, for the first time, China outpaced the U.S. by having more members in the top 10% globally.[294]

The world has also seen the growth of a class of billionaires — 2095 of them worth about $8 trillion as of March 2020, although the number and their wealth was slightly less than in 2019 due to the pandemic.[295] Even so, many billionaires actually have seen gains in the pandemic, resulting in a half a trillion in games for them. For example, Jeff Bezos, ranked as the richest person in the world, increased his wealth from March to June 2020 by an estimated $48 billion, while Eric Yuan, the founder of Zoom, the popular video-conferencing platform, saw his worth increase by over $2.5 billion. The former Microsoft CEO, Steve Ballmer, increased his own net worth by $15.7 billion; Elon Musk increased his worth by $17.2

billion, and the casino tycoon Sheldon Adelson experienced a $5 billion increase.[296]

Why did the billionaires as a group continue to do so well? Aside from having certain types of online and digital business that performed very well, such as Jeff Bezos' Amazon and Eric Yuan's Zoom, the billionaires generally did very well for several key reasons noted by Hiatt Woods in his *Business Insider* article: "How Billionaires Saw Their Net Worth Increase by Half a Trillion Dollars During the Pandemic." One reason is that the government disproportionately has given more aid to larger companies. A second reason is that the billionaires have benefited when the stock market bounces back, because the unequal bailouts from the government means that the wealth still have money available to invest. Therefore they can profit by investing when the market goes down, while the middle and lower classes don't have available money to invest. And thirdly, the government has passed wealth-friendly tax laws giving them tax breaks, and they are able to find loopholes in the law to reduce their taxes even more. [297]

In short, in the last few decades, in spite of the Great Recession, the global super-elite has continued growing, leaving the "rest of us," the 99%, far behind. Experts such as economist Emmanuel Saez at the University of Berkeley, who did a study with Thomas Piketty of the Paris School of Economics on changes in the U.S. income distribution over the past century, believe this trend will continue due to the underlying forces that are transforming the world today, as evidenced by the rapid emergence of the very rich from the financial crisis. As Saez discovered, during the recovery from 2009 to 2010, "93 percent of the gains were captured by the top 1 percent. (And) the plutocrats did even better than the merely affluent, (since) 37 percent of these gains went to the top .01 percent, the 15,000 Americans with average incomes of $23.8 million."[298] At the same time, the top 25 hedge fund managers averaged more than $1 billion each – even more than they had earned in 2007, the year when the Great Recession started, which was a previous record year.

In sum, then, the inequality gap is growing bigger than ever, so the rich are accumulating more and more assets at the expense of the lower and middle classes, just as the rich royals, nobles, wealthy merchants, and superwealthy high church officials did, as new technologies brought more wealth to everyone in the High and Late Middle Ages. But the flip side of this accumulation of wealth, as previously discussed, was the growing misery of the poor peasants, which led to a series of attempted revolutions in medieval times, such as the 1381 Peasant Revolt in England and the Jacquerie in 1358 in France. Potentially such a revolt could happen today, and there are already the beginnings of that in the growing protests over inequality, such as Occupy Movement that began in 2011 on Wall Street, and in the protests of the low-wage workers of in 2014 in over 100 cities seeking better wages.

So how likely is this revolution? And what should we do about the growing divide which is causing such misery and turmoil today? I'll address those questions briefly in the conclusion, and I hope this will spark a further discussion and some action about this inequality crisis which has become one of the most important issues of our times — one that can affect our very future and survival.

CHAPTER 10: WAR, REVOLUTION, FAMINE, AND PLAGUE

O ne of the most compelling ways that medieval times are like today occurred during the late Middle Ages. This was a time of continual wars, peasant rebellions, famines, and the Black Death, which decimated half of the European population. Then, this series of horrors prepared the way for the Renaissance, which was a period of a new birth after over a century of death and destruction. The parallels with today couldn't be clearer, as reported in the news every day.

Take war, such as the 100 Years War between France and England and continuing battles for more territory between nobles. The parallels to today are the growing conflicts all over the world. Besides the local battles, most notably in the Middle East and Africa, there are trade wars, especially between the U.S. and China.

Take the peasant rebellions in response to the heavy burden of taxation to fund the continuing wars of the kings and nobles. Today, there are continuing protests for all kinds of causes, most recently the #MeToo movement and fight for racial justice sparked by the Black Lives Matter Movement.

Take famines. In medieval times, there were food shortages due to a growing population combined with climate change that brought very cold and rainy weather that destroyed crops. Today, the wars in countries around the world and a growing population have led to millions of refugees and homeless families suffering from starvation, while climate change has led to unusually hot and dry conditions that have not only destroyed crops but led to raging fires, such as the California wildfires that have burned over 22 million acres in a few months.

Take the Black Death in medieval times. Today, the world is facing a pandemic that has claimed over 33 million victims, and over 1 million deaths as of this writing[299] and put countries around the world into various stages of lockdown.

Yet, in medieval times, all of this chaos and confusion that marked the late Middle Ages opened the door to the Renaissance, as society was changed forever, leading to the end of feudalism, the growth of a new economy, and a more powerful middle class based on trade, along with the explosion of new developments in arts and sciences. Thus, if we are going through such tumultuous times today, this suggests we will come out of this terrible tunnel we are in now to experience a new world of opportunities and possibilities. The shape of this potentially transformed world is still being formed, like a baby in its beginning stages in the womb. So we won't know for a awhile how things will turn out, but at least we have hope.

In this chapter, I will discuss these developments in medieval times and today in more detail, and then end with some projections about where this might all end.

A World at War

Politically, the first part of the Middle Ages was about the creation and consolidation of smaller political units into larger ones through a mixture of alliances and conquests. The result was that the smaller units that had once been independent, such as the duchies of Essex and Wessex, became united together into a larger kingdom, such as England. In this way, all over Europe and the British Isles, nation states emerged through the consolidation of central authority. But it wasn't an easy birth, since the nation states were characterized by extensive internal battles for power in the courts. Repeatedly, one faction or another sought to promote the ascension of its leader as king or support the succession to power of a particular offspring, sibling, or other relative with some claim to the throne. Commonly, marriages between the royal families were arranged to cement alliances between kingdoms, so the kings could gain support during the wars for conquering other lands or expanding their own territory. The result of all these battles and alliances during medieval times was the formation of larger and larger territories, and finally these larger territories became the nation states that developed at the beginning of the late Middle Ages from about 1250 or 1300 for the next two hundred years. At this point, the major players that emerged were Denmark, Norway and Sweden in Northern Europe; England and Scotland in Northwest Europe; France, Burgundy, and the Netherlands in Western Europe; Germany, Bohemia, Hungary, Poland, and Lithuania in Central Europe; Italy, Spain, and Portugal in Southern Europe; and a few other powers in East Europe, mainly Russia, after the fall of Constantine and the Ottoman or Byzantine Empire in 1453.

In sum, as *The Middle Ages,* a book in the Captivating History series, describes this early medieval period,: "Western Europe was in a state of nearly complete disarray. People were fighting for scraps of the empire, seeking to create their own little power structures. The Middle Ages would be a time when nations would rise out of the ashes of the Roman Empire."[300]

Meanwhile, as these new nations emerged, a number of factors contributed to the growing population and the expanding territories these new states and rulers had under their control. To briefly summarize this situation, between 950 and 1300, as the population of Europe increased up to three times, more and more lands were cleared and turned into arable fields to support this burgeoning population. Concurrently, towns expanded in size and number, while a growing class of artisans and tradesmen emerged who were making or selling goods. The use of coins became more common for exchange, too, while the nobles and royals increased their taxes to support their growing retinues of military forces.[301] In effect, this was a time of a great economic boom, as these emerging nation states consolidated their territories, and created the administrative structures to manage their control of a growing population of peasants who worked the lands.

Besides seeking to firm up their control within the territories they already owned, the kings and nobles were determined to expand their lands, leading to increased taxes to pay for their many wars to expand territories and defend those already owned. In turn, these wars and taxes triggered a growing resistance from the peasants who suffered from both these taxes and the damages to their lands from invading armies, who were seeking to win over the peasants to their side of the battle or simply destroyed their homes and villages.

This kind of process might be seen at work today throughout the world, such as in the efforts of Israel to solidify its control over the Golan Heights, originally conquered in the 1967 war, and undermine the rights of the Palestinians; in the outreach from Russia to take over the Crimea and maintain its control, despite the objections of the U.S. and other countries in Western Europe; in the efforts of the Chinese to exercise its might over Taiwan and Hong Kong; in the efforts of Turkey to subdue the Kurds; in the actions of India to take over Kashmir, despite the protestations of Pakistan. This process is also reflected in the many battles raging in Syria, Yemen, Afghanistan, and other Middle Eastern countries to fight off the soldiers representing al Queda or the Islamic State. And so it goes, back then, as well as now.

Back in the Middle Ages, the biggest ongoing conflict was the Hundred Years' War from 1337 to 1453, though it was more accurately a war that lasted almost 120 years with occasional stops and starts again, but the Hundred Years' War moniker stuck.[302] The context for this war was the close connection between France and England during this period. Not only were these two countries close geographically, but the families had intermarried, usually due to arranged marriages, between the royal families. As a result, England already owned some properties in France, and acted much like a distant landlord, who expects loyalty and continued rents from those living on its lands. One of the most notable of these marriages was between Eleanor of Aquitaine, who married Henry II before he became king, after she divorced King Louis VII of France. Since her lands were located in Southern France, Henry the II had a basis for asserting control over her lands, though her lands kept going back and forth between the two countries over the next century, as England and France battled over who would ultimately rule the people living there. [303]

The immediate cause of the ongoing war was a fight over succession when Charles IV died in 1328, at a time when many battles between the nation states erupted over who should be the next ruler, and various factions in the challengers' countries lined up to support one contender or another. A modern-day equivalent might be the battles that have erupted during elections, when one party claims to have won an election, but the opposition claims foul play, because the election results were fixed, such as occurred in Belarus, with the incumbent Alexander Lukashenko, claiming another win. But in response, crowds of angry protesters supporting his opponent sought his resignation on the grounds that he didn't really win, because the election was fixed in that Lukashenko, in power since 1994, claimed 80.1% of the vote. But the main opposition candidate, Svetlana Tikhanovskaya, now living in exile, claimed that if the votes were properly counted she got 60-70% of the vote.[304]

Another modern example is the situation in Venezuela, where two rival politicians are claiming to be the country's legitimate leader. On the one hand, President Nicholas Madura, has governed since 2013 as the heir to the late Hugo Chavez, the leader of the socialist PSUV Party. But in 2018, the opposition National Assembly leader, Juan Guaidó, ran against him and claimed Madura only won because of a rigged poll. After thatn Guaidó obtained international support from at least 50 countries to be the rightful new president. [305] Abut after several months, the fight has continued, while Madura has retained control. [306] So essentially, Venezuela, already suffering economically, has turned into a country wracked by a continuing civil war.

The Hundred Years War

Back in the Middle Ages, the 100 Years War began because Charles IV left no clear heir to the French throne. At first it seemed like Edward III, the nephew of Charles IV, whose mother was Isabella of France, might be a strong contender. But the nobles of France resisted, refusing to let Edward III, then only 15 years old, take over the rule of the country, on the grounds that no succession could be passed on through a female, a determination made back in 1316, since his mother was the daughter of Philip the Fair. By contrast, the French favored Philip of Valois, who was the next closest relative as the son of Philip the Fair's brother.[307] For a time, Philip of Valois, who became Philip VI, ruled without a challenge, since Edward III was engaged in a fight against David II, the King of Scotland for the first few years of the 14th century. However, when Philip VI supported David II, Edward III decided to assert his rightful claim to the throne in 1337, on the grounds that Philip VI was a usurper. In assembling his army, he sought the support of the enemies of Philip VI and the nobles who were unhappy with his reign.[308]

And so began what would be a continuing battle between England and France over who was entitled to be the ruler of several different territories in France.

The war went on intermittently after 1337, characterized initially by a series of English cavalry raids around France, and sometimes the French fought back, resulting in pitched battles, which the French commonly lost. In fact, the English scored a major coup in the 1356 Battle of Poitiers by capturing the French king John II. This capture led to a period of peace during which the English enjoyed control of a greatly enlarged Gascony in the south of France. But then, as Chris Wickham describes in *Medieval Europe*, "These territorial gains were then eaten away by cavalry raids, now undertaken by the French, and the English gains were mostly lost by the 1370s."[309]

The tide turned again, when Henry V of England began a new attack in 1415, leading to a new victory in Agincourt, and by 1429, the English were in control of half the country. But with the help of

Joan of Arc's visions, Charles VII of France found back, so by 1450, the English lost all the lands they conquered after 1415, and by 1453, they lost Bordeaux, too.[310] One reason that the English were able to do so well under Henry is that the French nobles were vying for power because Henry V was actually insane, resulting in two primary factions — the Orleans and the Burgundians, leading to civil war between these two factions beginning in 1407. Then, when Henry V saw an opportunity to reclaim the lands lost during the previous century, he signed a treaty with some of the French nobles, leading to a tentative peace. That's when he attacked, leading to the big Agincourt victory, after which many nobles and the leaders of other nations were willing to back him up in seeking control of over French nobles.

But after more skirmishes and the death of both Henry V and Charles VI, Charles VI's son, Charles VII, turned around the French fortunes after he decided to trust Joan of Arc's visions. With the support of the king, Joan dressed as a fighter, and she helped the French drive the English out of Orleans. After that the French had even more victories, though unfortunately, Joan of Arc was captured in 1430, and the following year, the English burned her as a witch and launched a smear campaign against her to discredit whatever she had done to help France. Still the victory she achieved in Orleans led the Burgundy nobles to pledge their allegiance to the French king, so the English were unable to claim back any lands they had gained in France. Then, over the next 20 years, England lost its control of any French lands and no longer had any claim to the French throne.[311]

Other Battles in Other Countries

Likewise, similar battles for dominance and control played out between other neighboring countries, as each country sought to expand its territory. For example, Scotland repeatedly sought to fight off the English threat, and sometimes the king and nobles fought together, while intermarrying helped to fortify their alliances.[312] On the Iberian peninsula, Portugal sought to fight off the much large Castile, while the Aragon kings sought to rule Sicily and Naples, and those two kingdoms repeatedly fought each other.[313] Meanwhile, in Germany, for a time the rulings kings came from the western German Luxemburg family, where Charles IV was not only emperor but the dominant prince of his time. But then the Hapsburg line through intermarriage inherited the main center of Burgundian wealth and power. Meanwhile, other political battles occurred between Poland and Hungary, as well as in the three Scandinavian kingdoms of Denmark, Norway, and Sweden.[314]

In short, this late Middle Ages from about 1300 on was characterized by continuing battles on the different levels of society for power and control — within the courts for access to the throne; between nobles for more and more land; and between states for dominance over other states. In turn, all of these wars led to increasing taxes on the peasants and on the growing class of merchants in the towns to support these wars. These battles also led to improvements in weapons to fight these wars, so that knights became obsolete by the end of the 15th century, and many countries now called on standing armies rather than untrained peasants to fight their battles.[315]

All of these battles between the royals of Europe were like a series of ongoing chess matches after 1350 for the next century in which the rulers engages in continuing battles for dominance and control. To this end, they spent much of their time ruling preparing for battle. Then, once they had gotten together enough money to put together an army — or at least had assembled a strong force of local peasants, they attacked to gain lands and glory. Commonly, they attacked their neighbors to expand their territories, much like a rapacious modern day property owner might seek to put together enough capital to drive out the owner of the property next door or even force a neighbor into bankruptcy and foreclosure. But sometimes a rulerwith an even loftier visions attacked distant realms for both military glory and a territorial takeover. The rulers were also eager to impress with their power, so they spent the resources they did obtain, primarily through overtaxing the nobles and peasants or confiscating property, on displays of power. Thus, they established lavish courts with subservient nobles who sought to show-off their own power, and they built grandiose buildings during the post-1350 period. But most of the money went to building an army, which was, as Chris Wickham writes in *Medieval Europe,* "the biggest — and most expensive — display of power of all, and using it to fight someone was the logical next step."[316]

The outcome for anyone keeping score was the rise of the strongest and richest states in Europe — the Ottoman Empire, followed by France, then England and Castile, and the Burgundian Low Countries. The next in power were Hungary, Naples/Sicily, Aragon, and some German cities, and after that, though much less strong and powerful, states emerged in Bohemia and Portugal, and finally Poland-Lithuania and the rest of Eastern Europe, plus Scotland, Scandinavia, and much of the German lands.[317]

The State of War Today

Today, it would seem like there is a similar kind of battle going on, sometimes through diplomacy, sometimes through outright declarations of war and years of fighting. And today, as before, advances in science and weaponry are contributing to displays of increased power and influence.

One example is the trade war between China and the U.S., as China grows increasingly strong and has asserted its reach, not only in seeking to control neighboring Taiwan and Hong Kong, but China has sought to gain the technologies from the U.S. and other countries, now that more and more power lies in controlling new technologies. That is what the battle over the apps TikTok and WhatApp to operate in the United States is all about. Another example is the conflict between different factions in many countries in Africa, such as in Gambia. Other hotspots are in Afghanistan, as the government fights with U.S. support against the Taliban; and a simmering conflict is developing between South Korea and North Korea, especially as North Korea exercises its muscles through missile building.

In fact, there is even a Global Conflict Tracker created by the Council on Foreign Relations, a U.S. nonprofit think tank founded in 1921, which specializes in U.S. foreign policy and international affairs and has headquarters in New York City, with an additional office in Washington, D.C. [318] According to the Council, which lists these conflicts based on their impact on U.S. interests, the conflicts with the most critical impact are the war in Afghanistan, the territorial disputes in the South China Sea, the tensions in the East China Sea, the North Korea crisis, and the confrontation between the U.S. and Iran. In the second tier of conflicts, there is the civil war in Syria, the political instability in Iraq, Islamist militancy in Pakistan, political instability in Lebanon, instability in Egypt, conflict in the Ukraine, the conflict between Turkey and armed Kurdish groups, and criminal violence in Mexico due to the battles between the narcotic gangs and each other and the Mexican government. Then, too, there is the Israeli-Palestinian Conflict, the battle with the Boko Haram in Nigeria, the conflict between India and Pakistan, and the conflict between the opposition and the government in Venezuela. Finally, there are still other conflicts in less powerful countries around the globe which have a limited impact on U.S. interests. These include the civil war in Libya, the war in Yemen, the violence in the Central African Republic the violence in the Democratic Republic of Congo, the Rohingya crisis in Myanmar, the civil war in South Sudan, and fighting in Somalia.[319] And fighting these different battles is a cast of politicians and generals who are vying for their own power in leading their country or heading up these military escapades. And as they fight, the major victims are the poor people who end up variously fleeing their homes, becoming impoverished, and joining the wave of over 65 million people around the world, much like the peasants were recruited to fight in the many medieval battles.

In effect, these multiple battlefields around the globe are reminiscent of the many medieval battles between the states for power, and the victims of these battles who have lost their homes or become refugees are much like the peasants of the Middle Ages who became impoverished, when their livelihoods, crops, homes, or villages were destroyed. Then, too, the battles going on between the Republicans and Democrats are like the battles between the different groups of nobles creating alliances or fighting against each other to gain more wealth and lands. And just as the increasing taxation to fund the continuing wars in the late Middle Ages fell most heavily on the peasants and contributed to the many peasant revolts during this period, so, too, in modern times, those in the lower classes are most negatively affected by laws, such as in the recent passage of laws in the United States that give tax breaks to the wealthy and little or no relief to the poor.

This state of war today is also reflected in the high tech battles over who has the biggest market share for various social media and Internet technologies. These battles are like the medieval cavalry charges and the armies charging the castles walls to break in and take over or destroy the castle. And just like the medieval armies had their spies, so spies on the Internet seek to discover passwords to break in and seek ransom payments or steal data. In response, different companies and countries have taken different steps to protect their data, much like the government officials and army leaders in medieval times plotted their strategies for attack and defense.

For example, one of the many articles about these high tech battles describes the conflict on the Internet that played out between the United States and China. Initially, Beijing acted to create a kind of fortified castle with strong walls in that it blocked major foreign websites in order to protect Chinese tech firms, while they developed alternative technologies to that of its Western rivals. Additionally, the Chinese kept a tight grip on what people said online.[320] But to fight back, President Trump issued executive orders that could lead to the U.S. banning the world's most popular Chinese-made apps, TikTok and WeChat. Additionally, the U.S. administration ordered Byte Dance, the Chinese owner of TikTok to give up its U.S. assets and any data that TikTok had gathered in the United States, unless these were bought by an American company, and as of this writing, Oracle may acquire it.

In other words, the U.S. accused TikTok of being a way for the Chinese to spy on the U.S. Additionally, the administration further clamped down on Huawei, another Chinese tech giant which made chips used in many high-tech products, by restricting its ability to buy computer chips produced abroad using American technology. Plus the administration sought to purge Chinese apps and telecom companies from U.S. networks on the grounds that they were a security threat.[321] In effect, the actions of the U.S. and China were like the medieval armies putting up shields to protect themselves from the attacks of the other side.

These protectionist moves could similarly spread to other countries, resulting in the high tech companies and countries around the globe engaging in their own protectionist maneuvers, much like the kingdoms in Europe and England prepared themselves for battle in seeking to grow and protect their territories from incursions by others. In the process, the kingdoms consolidated into larger and larger entities until they became the nation states of the late Middle Ages. It is as if the Internet battles are turning the tech companies into a network of fief like those in the Middle Ages. It is a development described Ann Swan, Paul Mozur, and Raymond Zhong in their *San Francisco Chronicle* article:

> If more countries follow Trump by basing digital controls on diplomatic allegiances, protectionist aims or new concerns about the security of their citizens, the Internet could become more of a patchwork of fiefs as varied as the visa policies that fragment world travel.[322]

As Swan, Mozur, and Zhong point out, as more and more countries come up with restrictions and bans, this is likely to trigger retaliation and contribute to the fracturing of the Internet that has been growing in recent years — a development favored by authoritarian governments.[323]

Thus, while the battles today are based on modern technologies, used as weapons of war and a source of income, the dynamics are much the same as what occurred in medieval times. Back then the battles occurred on land and sea with large armies facing each other, as the kings and their generals sought to capture or defend territory. Then, over time their weapons improved with the development of gun powder and cannons that gradually replaced the knights fighting with swords on horseback and peasants fighting on land with axes and other handheld weapons. And now, besides the battles to increase territory, many battles have been fought to conquer and defend cyberspace, while the high-tech companies are also engaged in a battle to expand their market share and cut down the competition.

The Growing Protests and Rebellions Then and Now

From about 1350 for the next hundred years, there were a series of peasant rebellions through Europe , which were mostly quashed by the armies of the kings and nobles wherever they erupted, though the peasants experienced a few modest gains. These revolts were primarily a response to heavy taxation and the peasants' growing poverty and mistreatment.

This growing tax burden occurred because of the continuing wars to expand or protect territory, so the kings and nobles continually needed to obtain funds to support their troops, and they commonly turned to the peasants to do so. So their taxes kept going up, up, and up, putting more and more pressure on the peasants to make a living. So there was a growing threat of losing their lands if they couldn't pay to their noble or king who owned their land, turning them into a kind of slave on the land. But inevitably, many peasants resisted and rebelled, resulting in a series of peasant revolts, which have many parallels to the recent protests seeking justice for a long history of racial discrimination against blacks and other minority group members.

I previously discussed some of the major protests in England and France in Chapter 8, which occurred due to working conditions in medieval times and the series of protests about low wages that occurred in 2012-2014. These were largely local protests that attracted media attention, but they lasted a short time without any major crackdown. However, now these protests have raised fundamental issues about equality and social justice.

Initially, the protests began with the women's #MeToo movement against discrimination and sexual mistreatment in the workplace. Then, beginning in 2018, the Black Lives Matter movement sparked widespread support from not only Black Americans but from a diversity of individuals and group. This movement has not only led to protests in the United States but around the world, much like the peasant revolts in the Middle Ages spread from France and England to many other countries. At the same time, as these modern protests have grown larger, they have attracted agitators who have engaged in looting and violence, while the growing size of these protests and the violence associated with them has led to a crack-down from various police and military agencies — from the local police to Federal agents, much like the kings and nobles attacked the protesters, and often burned down their fields and villages, in medieval times.

Accordingly, I want to review the nature of these medieval protests in more detail here and then compare them to the more recent social justice protests that are happening today.

The Reasons for the Protests

One of the major triggering events for the rebellions in France and England was the 100 Years War, which led to heavy taxes to support the French and English armies, as well as the ravages caused by the armies fighting in villages and sometimes burning the peasants' crops and houses. But there were other factors. For example, seven major factors listed by Frantisek Graus in the "Late Medieval Peasant Wars" in *The Journal of Peasant Studies* are these: tax resistance, social inequality, religious wars, national liberation, resistance against serfdom, redistribution of land, and external factors such as plague and famine.[324] Likewise, many of these same drivers are fueling the current wave of protests, especially the concern with social inequality and the growing divide between rich and poor

— a kind of modern-day resistance to serfdom , exacerbated by the growing problems of homelessness, hunger, and illness, exacerbated by modern forms of the plague and famine.

While most of the attention by scholars and authors is paid to the big peasant revolts in France and England — the Jacquerie in 1358 and the Peasant Revolt in England in 1381, a few earlier revolts occurred. Then, more revolts followed in other countries throughout Europe, triggered by similar conditions, though without today's social media to spread the word, since this was a time when most peasants were illiterate and most communication between cities and countries was in the form of letters under seal sent by a courier on horseback riding from one location to another.

The earlier revolts began after a period of relative quiet during the early and middle years of the Middle Ages, when the smaller feudal kingdoms were still fighting among each other for dominance and wars and power was decentralized. Then, the first peasant revolves began in Flanders, a kingdom in France, by the Flemish peasants in 1323-1328. It was suppressed after several years of fighting, as was the 1343-1345 revolt by Estonian peasants in the Teutonic Order Kingdom of Denmark. Then, in 1358, a few years after the Black Death cut down about half of the population of Europe, the Jacquerie erupted in France.

The revolt first erupted in Oise region north of Paris, and it was called the Jacquerie because the nobles derisively referred the peasants as "Jacques." [325] The revolt was triggered after the French King, John II, was captured by the English during the Battle of Poitiers in 1356. His capture led to a battle for power between John's son, the Dauphin, who later became Charles V, King Charles II of Navarre, and the nobles who formed the Estates-General. The peasants were caught in the middle of this dispute, as the French nobility, merchant elite, and clergy sought increasing taxes from the peasants. The Estates-General even passed a law that required the peasants to defend their large mansions called "chateaux," which was especially galling, since the peasants viewed these chateaux as a symbol of their oppression.[326] As a result, they directed their uprising primarily against their local lords, rather than against the royal government, since they felt their lords had failed to protect them from the ravages of the English armies or mercenaries who stormed through their land, often pillaging their crops and sometimes burning their homes. Moreover, they were enraged because their lords not only didn't protect them, but they insisted on getting paid for their rents and services. Thus, the peasants viewed their lords as being as oppressive as ever, or even more so.[327]

But while many more peasants joined in these revolts than the rulers they fought, they were poorly armed and organized, so the united action of their feudal lords soon crushed their revolts. Moreover, the kings and nobles not only suppressed the revolt, but they went after the peasants with a great vengeance because of the acts of violence they had committed.[328]

This kind of suppression followed by a crack-down on the peasants seems much like the violence against the protestors in many cities today, such as Portland , Chicago, Rochester, and a growing number of cities subjected to protests, riots, and police or military crackdown. Today, the protestors are not protesting for tax relief, but their protest to repair a long history of racial injustice also points up the economic unfairness of a system which has created a growing underclass with a disproportionate number of blacks and other minority group members. But whatever their demands, as in the Middle Ages, many protests have been brutally suppressed by the armed forces called in to end the protest. In the Middle Ages, the military commonly swept in on horseback and used their swords to attack, and in some cases, they threw flaming torches to burn down fields or homes. By contrast, the modern day military or police deploy tear gas, pellet guns, and other modern day weapons. But the overall goal of the crackdown is the same — to end the protest as quickly as possible without trying to use negotiations or diplomacy to listen to the protesters and make the desired changes that sparked the revolt in the first place.

The same kind of crackdown led to the most well-known major peasant revolt in England in 1381. When it erupted, economic discontent was already growing since the middle of the century. One major grievance was a Statute of Laborers, which was passed in 1351 to set a maximum wage after the Black Death caused a labor shortage, which led agricultural and urban workers to seek more money for their labor. Though the government tried to keep down wages with this law, it hadn't done a very good job of enforcing this maximum, since the shortage of labor gave the workers more bargaining power, and the nobles and urban employers bent to their pressure to pay more money. Then, the triggering incident was a very unpopular poll tax passed in 1381, because the government had very high expenses due to fighting a so far unsuccessful war against the French .[329]

Already the laboring classes were upset by the new laws supported by the king and nobles to force them to work for the same wages they received before the Black Death. The law was almost impossible to enforce, because there was more demand for their labor due to the high death rate due to the plague. Still, the government kept trying to enforce a series of similar laws enacted between 1351 to 1381. Then, making matters worse, because of the high expenses from fighting the unsuccessful French war, Parliament passed law to collect the poll tax, which everyone except destitute paupers had to pay, whereas before taxes had usually been levied on land, merchandise, and other types of property. Then, when the government sought to collect these new taxes which the peasants considered unjust, they rose up in revolt, especially in southeastern England. Since they already had other grievances against their feudal lords and the local clergy, the poll tax was the final straw or match that set off the conflagration.[330]

This kind of triggering event for revolt brings to mind the killing of George Floyd, a 46-year-old black American man, who was killed in Minneapolis, Minnesota, during an arrest for allegedly using a counterfeit bill. The images of the arresting white police officer, Derek Chauvin, pressing a knee on Floyd's neck for over eight minutes, while Floyd kept pleading "I can't breathe," went quickly viral on the Internet. Soon after that, the protests began, organized with the help of the social media. Many Black Americans had died at hands of the police before, and the shooting death of Michael Brown, an 18-year-old black man in Ferguson, Missouri, while he was running away from officer Darren Wilson after a car stop, triggered about a week of protests. However, the death of Floyd was like the final straw that erupted in flames. Within days, the word of his death spread, and in the following weeks, the outrage over his death trigged protests not only in the U.S. but in other countries around the world. These protests, in turn, helped fuel the growing Black Lives Matter movement, as well as the protests of other groups that called attention to the long history of exploitation and injustice to Black Americans since the days of slavery. And soon these protests called attention to the mistreatment of other minority groups, especially Native Americans, Mexicans, and other Latin Americans.

While the specific circumstances were very different, the dynamics that set off the peasant revolt in 1381 and the modern explosion of revolts after Floyd's death are similar. In both cases, the eruption came after years of unresolved grievances, like steam finally exploding from a steaming pot. And in both cases, the underlying causes was rooted in economic injustice and exploitation by a dominant, wealthy class — the king, nobles, wealthy merchants, or clergy in the Middle Ages; the corporations and wealthy elite today.

The outcome of the English peasant revolt, as in the Jacquerie, proved similar to what has happened today — a brutal crackdown to repress a particular revolt, although the conditions that contributed to these revolts led to other revolts elsewhere — both in medieval times and today.

In the case of the English revolt, the peasants initially held out great hope that their complaints would be finally addressed. A few weeks after the uprising began in Essex in May 1382, rebels from Essex and Kent marched towards London, and on June 13th, some peasants from Kent, under Wat Taylor, entered London. There they killed some Flemish merchants and razed the palace of the king's uncle, John of Gaunt, the duke of Lancaster, who was a very unpopular noble. In response, King Richard II met with Taylor and his men outside of London, where he made a series of promises: they would have "cheap land, free trade, and the abolition of serfdom and forced labor."[331] But then Taylor's men overplayed their hand, since after the king left the negotiations, the Kentish rebels invaded the Tower of London, forced its surrender, and then beheaded both the chancellor, Archbishop Simon of Sudbury, and the treasurer, Sir Robert Hales, since both of them held both responsible for the poll tax. These actions enraged the mayor of London, and when King Richard met with Tyler and his men the following day, the mayor killed Tyler. After that, King Richard persuaded the rebels to disperse by appealing to them as their sovereign and promising reforms. As a result, the rebels left London, ending the crisis there. However, after they returned to their lands, they not only didn't get what King Richard promised, but their rebellion was finally suppressed by the armies headed by the bishop of Norwich, Henry le Despenser, on or about June 25.

But while this particular rebellion was suppressed, many others spread, triggered by similar causes — heavy taxes and years of exploitation by the wealthier classes, much like rebellions have spread to countries all over the world in the last few years to oppose the long-standing economic and social injustice the poor and minority group members have experienced. And in many cases, these rebellions have been directed against the authoritarian and corrupt leadership in these countries. For example, protests have erupted in France, Belarus, Venezuela, Russia, Lebanon, England, Hong Kong, and in many countries in Africa, with the latest protests featured in the news and social media. Back in the Middle Ages, the major protests throughout Europe included these, which were all suppressed: [332]

- the French Peasants in the Harelle rebellion in 1382,
- the peasants from Transylvania in the Kindom of Hungary in 1437,
- the Norwegian rebels in the Hillvard Graatops Revolt in 1438,

- the Danish peasants in the Funen and Jutland Peasant rebellions in the Kingdom of Denmark in 1441,
- the English peasants in the Jack Cade rebellion of 1450 and in the John and William Merfold's Uprising of 1450 and 1450-51 respectively,
- Galician peasants, led by the Galician bourgeoisie and part of the local lower nobility in the Galician Irmandinos Revolt of 1467 to 1469.

Thus, just as a series of rebellions occurred in medieval times in responsive to oppressive conditions, often triggered by a single event that helped to crystallize and mobilize longstanding anger, so a series of rebellions have been occurring now. Back in 2013 to 2014, these protests commonly occurred due to poor working conditions and low pay and were directed towards the corporations that underpaid the workers. But now these protests are triggered by social and economic injustice and are directed towards the leaders of state and federal government officials.

The Response of Business to the Revolts

Sometimes, too, these revolts are directed against companies that have permitted hate speech to be spread through their platform, such as Facebook and Twitter. Though the current administration supported by most Senators, has continued to use the same kind of law and order approach to suppress the protests as occurred in the Middle Ages, some companies have expressed their support for the protesters' goal ofovercoming discrimination and seeking racial equality.

For example, Facebook has donated $10 million to groups fighting racial inequality and on May 31, CEO Mark Zukerberg wrote in a Facebook post that "We stand with the black community." Likewise, Twitter, Nike, Disney, and other firms have come out in support of the protesters' cause.[333] Perhaps the companies might be responding in the hopes of preserving corporate profits, but they did show support for the goal of social justice, at the same time that many protests were met with tear gas and law-enforcement batons, encounters that appeared even more violent, because of the way the news media and social media played up the most dramatic police-protester confrontations, fires, and vandalism. To some viewers, these images in the media might seem like scenes from a doomsday or apocalypse scenario, but many corporations sought to play a fine line between supporting the cause of racial justice, while not supporting the violence, much of that done by outside agitators seeking to discredit the protestors. In this way, they sought to maneuver along a kind of tightrope between the goals of the protesters and those seeking to shut them down. As Amanda Mull put it in an Atlantic.com article, "Behind the scenes, brand managers worked quickly to create sensitive, aesthetically pleasing response to the protests." [334]

In the process, Nike, a company more active than most in associating itself with social movements, was one of the first to show its support in a text video in which it asserted: "Don't pretend there's not a problem in America," and then identified this problem as racism. In the next few days, as Mull notes, "hundreds of companies, sports teams, and celebrities followed suit with posts of their own, including Facebook, Citibank, and Dove.[335] Then, as more and more companies stepped forward, other companies experienced a kind of peer pressure to showing support, though many did so in a more diplomatic way. In doing so, they quietly showed their support for anti-racism, while trying to distance themselves from having been perpetrators of it in the past. In other words, they sought to show support for the protests, when it seemed politically judicious to do so, though they remained, though they remained ready to respond to the political winds, should the protesters lose community and media support. In this way, they were acting a little like the Dauphins during the Jacquerie, who at one time aligned themselves with the rebels but later shifted their allegiance to the nobles and king.

In effect, many large U.S. companies are engaged in a kind of political dance sensing what the prevailing winds are at that time.

Once protests emerged all over the country supporting the aims of the Black Lives Matter movement in seeking racial justice, the companies might throw their support that way, when everyone was talking about and positively supporting the movement. Yet, at the same time, these brands sought to set themselves outside the systems, so they were not tied too closely to a particular position in order to not antagonize those holding a different point of view or be caught holding a contrary view should popular sentiments shift.[336]

In this way, the companies are, in effect, holding up a candle to the wind to see which way the wind blows, in deciding where to throw their support. A key factor has been the large scale of these demonstrations, which have spread worldwide. Whereas individual flare ups around Europe during the late Middle Ages were suppressed by local and state actions, the social media has helped to show that the long-standing racial and economic injustice is worldwide. This scale has been much larger than anything in history, although the underlying problem of income disparity and exploitation has been a major source of the protests both then and now, regardless of the difference in the triggering incident. The result has been a growing corporate support for acknowledging the long-standing injustice raised by the protesters, although it is not certain how long the corporations will maintain their support once the social and media attention shifts to the next big issue, just as alliances have shifted back and forth, based on who seems to have the most power in the Middle Ages.

However, if a particular social movement grows in power, it may overcome the initial corporate ambivalence, as noted in a BBC article by Natalie Sherman: "George Floyd: Why Are Companies Speaking Up this Time?" As she observes: "While companies remain as reluctant as ever to wade into controversy, the scale of the demonstrations — which started din Minneapolis on 26 May and have since spread internationally — has made speaking up a 'business imperative," citing Dwayne Hayley, senior vice president at Porter Novelli, a communications firm that has advised companies such as McDonald's and Pepsi. That's how many companies follow along what seems to be a culture shift, as more and more companies take a stand, which makes it more dangerous to remain. The big challenge because some corporate leaders really do sympathize with the protestors, though they may be wary of being on the wrong side of the issue and having their reputation damaged. But as a social movement gathers force, "there's more risk in not speaking out than in speaking out," as Natalie Sherman notes.[337]

The Trigger for Worldwide Protests

While the U.S. was ground zero for the protests sparked by the George Floyd killing, his death sparked a series of protests around the world that were in response to similar problems of racism and economic injustice. These were the same kind of conditions that led to the eruption of peasant revolts around Europe from about the middle of the 14th century to the end of the 15th century, though the protests today gained even more fuel by the social media and news media. For example, some of the cites and countries that experienced their own protests were London, Paris, Australia, New Zealand, and Canada, inspired by the huge protests that spread across the United States. Thus, what at one time might have been a local outrage over another killing of a black man by a white police officer, this triggering incident led to a worldwide series of protests.

Perhaps one reason Floyd's death provided this trigger is because of the video of the police officer hold his knee on Floyd's neck, forcing him to lay helpless on the ground for nearly 8 minutes, as he cried out: "I can't breathe," and in his last breath gasped "Mom." The video showed a clear example of police brutality against a black man who was not resisting, and Floyd's death served as a vivid reminder of the long history of discrimination against Blacks in America. And then the crackdown down on peaceful protesters by the police and radical right wing groups could have inspired even more supporters to back the peaceful demonstrations, due to a "new surge of support for movements against racism and police abuses in many countries."[338] In other words, as Frida Gites explains in a *Washington Post* article on the protests: "Protesters around the world are sickened by the killings of George Floyd and other African Americans, and they are appalled by Trump's response. Yet the activism of ordinary Americans is setting off a new waves of activism."[339]

In medieval times, such protests were largely suppressed by the superior forces of the government, and in many countries today these movements could suffer a similar fate, such as in the more authoritarian countries, such as Hong Kong, Taiwan, Russia, Venezuela, and in many countries in Africa. Still other countries experiencing protests include Canada, Israel, Brazil, and Chile.[340] And these countries might be the tip of the iceberg, as more and more protests spread to other countries throughout the world. That's because the conditions of inequality and injustice for minority and lower-income groups are worldwide, and these conditions are even more severe in some countries due to the millions of refugees who have poured in from across the globe in response to war, famine, and other threats that are bringing upheaval and turmoil to their destination countries.

These developments are still unfolding, so it will be several years before we can see how they resolve. However, if the response of the authorities in the Middle Ages — the king and the nobles with their armies — is any indicator, in time it is likely that these protests will be suppressed and die down, and the forces of law and order wielded by the governments around the world will prevail.

The Spread of Famine

Still another parallel with medieval times is the spread of famine that occurred for a few years in Europe due to climate change. It was one more contributing factor to the peasants rebelling, because their reduced crops meant they had less money to pay the higher taxes to support the kings and nobles' wars and had less ability to buy or grow their own food.

The reasons for the famine in medieval times were somewhat different from today, since the climate was unusually cold and wet for a few years, which caused crops to become soaked and rot in the field. By contrast, today, climate change has resulted in increasingly hot weather, and more extreme weather, such as tornadoes, more frequent and more intense hurricanes, and destructive fires due to the high temperatures. But in both cases, the changing climate led to the destruction of food sources, resulting in food shortages and famine in many areas.

In the Middle Ages, the Great Famine occurred in 1315-1317, well before most of the peasant rebellions. But it added to the peasants' misery, so it provided more fuel for the growing rage the peasants felt at being exploited by the kings and nobles. Before the famine began, the previous years had been marked by a growing agricultural success, in part due to improvements in farming techniques and equipment, so the peasants experienced increasing prosperity, and the increased food production supported a growing population. In turn, one reason for this population growth was that despite the constant wars and Crusades, the people in Europe were surviving longer and having more children and they were surviving longer, in part because the agriculture improvements resulted in better crop yields. As a result, the country could support a larger population, and people had less concern about their daily survival than during the Dark Ages right after Rome fell. Thus, given these improved farming techniques and better equipment , much of Western Europe was able to expand through the 14th century.

Yet there were signs that this period of robust growth could readily end, as if Europe had come to a tipping point. That's because, as the authors of *The Middle Ages* explain, although the population was robust by 1315, "the amount of food produced was just barely able to keep up with the booming population."[341]

Then, the tipping point tipped when the changed weather conditions reduced food production, so there was not enough food to feed the population of most areas. The big change in the weather occurred because the spring became longer and wetter than it had in previous centuries, because the spring rains lasted much longer than usual, resulting in a cooler summer and fall began earlier.

The result was an increasingly shorter growing season and a lower crop yield.

Thus, the spring of 1315 was a disaster. Since there was more rain than usual, it was too wet for the farmers and peasants to sow their seeds properly. They couldn't plow in the areas devoted to growing food because it kept raining. As a result, many seeds rotted in the ground instead of sprouting, leading to this much smaller crop yield.

Then, when people sought other sources for food, the authorities cracked on their illegal activities, much as the struggles of the poor to survive today have led them to engage in various illegal activities, from dealing drugs to burglaries and robberies, resulting in police actions to find and arrest the suspects, sometimes leading to police killings, which have triggered many of the protests and riots today. During the Middle Ages, in response to the decline of sufficient crops to get through the cold winter, many peasants traveled into the forests to seek food, which left many forests stripped of food. Making matters worse for the peasants, some of these forests were on the lands owned by the nobles, and it was illegal to poach on them. Though the danger of getting caught by the nobles dissuaded some peasants, many others were willing to take their chances by poaching anyway, despite the risk of being punished if caught, rather than starving to death.[342] Likewise, some of the poor today take the risk of engaging in illegal activities, from selling drugs to committing burglaries and robberies, to feed themselves and their families.

Unfortunately for the medieval peasants, the suffering from famine was even worse, since they were generally weakened because of being malnourished due to the lack of food over the winter. As a result, they lacked the energy to plow as much as they had the previous spring, so they couldn't make up for the reduced crop yields of the year before. Then, adding to their misery, they faced another brutally cold and rainy winter, so many starved. According to *The Middle Ages'* authors, some families even left their children in the forest to die, because they could not feed everyone in the family, while some older family members chose to starve so their younger family members could have food.[343]

Then, though the cold spell had ended, the famine continued into 1317, since the peasants had little energy to return to planting and plowing as usual, because they had been suffering for two years for little food. Additionally, they had fewer seeds to plant, because many people at their seeds to stay alive after their food ran out. Yet, much like now, the kings and nobles were less affected by the famine,[344] since they had the money to buy and store the food that was available. Also, they had the police power to go after the poachers in their forests to stop the thefts and punish them.

Still another problem caused by the Great Famine is that people were more susceptible to illnesses such as tuberculosis, pneumonia, and bronchitis, and they were more likely to die from them — much as is the case for the poor today. As a result, about 10-15% of the population died from these illnesses, though ironically, this high death rate contributed to the people of Europe recovering from the Great Famine. That's because the peasants didn't have to grow as much food, because there were fewer people to feed.[345]

Just as the changed climate contributed to the famine that lasted three years in the Middle Ages, so climate change is widely recognized as a major factor leading to famine around the world now, as the World Food Program USA states on its website seeking support for its efforts to fight hunger worldwide. As it states, "Climate change is one of the leading global causes of hunger. It means more frequent and intense extreme weather events that increase food insecurity and malnutrition by destroying land, livestock, crops, and food supplies."[346]

The numbers of those subjected to danger of famine today are daunting. Already, there are over 68 million refugees around the world, many displaced by wars, who are affected to a greater or lesser extent by hunger. They barely survive in refugee camps, and some make perilous and sometimes deadly journeys by land or sea to find refuge in other countries. And now climate change is making the problem of hunger even worse. As the World Food Hunger Program website points out, 22 million people are displaced annually due to climate-related disasters, and 24% of the world's farmlands are degraded.[347]

The reason climate change has had this devastating effect on food production is outlined in stark terms in a "Climate Change and Famine" fact sheet by the Physicians for Social Responsibility. As they point out, not only is climate change already threatening the ability of the Earth to produce food, but these effects will get even worse as climate change worsens. That's because for every 1.8°F increase in the average surface temperature of the globe, "we can expect about a 10% decline in yields of the world's major grain crops — corn, soybean, rice and wheat."[348]

More specifically, climate change can have this devastating effect because it can disrupt food production and distribution in a variety of ways, suggested by various prediction models. For example, the World Food Hunger Program website lists the following reasons:

- More droughts will lead to large-scale crop loss.
- More frequent, severe, and longer-lasting heat waves will kill crops.
- Certain plant pests and diseases will thrive and destroy crops.
- Heavy rains and storms resulting from the warming climate will flood fields; then these floods will erode soils and wash away crops.
- Rising sea levels and storm surges will also flood the fields, and they will additionally create saltier soils which will reduce crop production.
- Melting glaciers and changing river flows will result in less water available for irrigation.
- Higher ozone levels will damage plants and reduce crop yields.[349]

In sum, all of these effects of climate change will be devastating for the entire food system, and the poorer farmers are especially likely to be hard hit. That's because they will be less able to adapt to the new conditions created by climate change. By contrast, the wealthier farmers can better adapt, since they have the money to invest in new technologies and seed varieties. They can also more easily make changes in the crops they grow. Yet, even so, regardless of their wealth, farmers won't be able to completely adapt, because an increase in extreme weather events can affect the infrastructure of the whole food system throughout the world. As an article "The Challenge of Our Time" for the *World Hunger Program USA* explains, "Storms and flooding can destroy food processing, packaging and storage facilities and disrupt transportation infrastructure, such as roads, bridges, railways, airports and shipping routes." [350] Then, these breakdowns in the infrastructure will prevent available food from being transported to where it is needed.

In turn, as food becomes more costly and difficult to obtain, this food crisis is likely to contribute to rising anger and violence. This development is reminiscent of what happened in the late Middle Ages, as the peasants became increasingly angry as their conditions became even worse, on top of the anger they already felt from being exploited by the kings and nobles. That's because when less food is available due to climate changes, food prices will increase, leading some people to become angry and even violent. So just as protesters are now angry and taking to the streets in cities around the United States because of a heightened awareness of racial injustice to the killings of blacks by the police, so protesters will be likely to respond to the spread of hunger due to rising food prices, combined with the loss of income due to the loss of jobs due to the shutdown of millions of businesses due to the COVID-19 crisis.

It's a worldwide problem. Over one billion people — one in seven people around the world – go hungry each day. It's a problem that will only get worse as the world population grows to an expected 9 billion people by 2050. Then, as food hunger authorities predict, "The combination of decreasing food production in the face of increasing food demand would likely lead to widespread social unrest and hunger — even catastrophic global famine."[351]

Unfortunately, this problem is likely to be exacerbated because of the pandemic, which parallels the Black Death that decimated up to half the population of Europe, England, and the Near East, as discussed in the next section.

In sum, the famine sweeping the world today is due to multiple factors — poverty, displacements due to war, and climate change disrupting food production, and it has many parallels with the Great Famine in Europe from 1315 to 1317. The type of climate change that occurred was different in that the unusual weather was cold and wet during the Middle Ages, while global warming has led to very hot and dry conditions destroying crops through parched lands or fires. But then as now, the underlying causes of famine are similar, and so are the results, which include social dislocations, an increase in crime, and crackdowns by the police today or by the kings and nobles in medieval times to stop the thefts, as people risk committing crimes to get money or food to feed themselves and their families.

The Pandemic Then and Now

The Black Death pandemic that knocked out up to half of the population of Europe , the British Isles, and the Middle East — about 75 million to 200 million people — between 1346 and 1353[352] has eerie parallels with the COVID-19 virus that is ravaging the world today.

Even the way the Black Death began and spread has parallels to the way the coronavirus spread, beginning initially in Central Asia, though the manner of spread is different. In the case of the Black Death, there were three forms of the plague, which was caused by the *Yersinia pestis* bacterium.

The most common form of the plague is through the bite of a flea, which was spread by rodents. Supposedly, due to climate change which resulted in more heat and drought in Asia, the rodents began fleeing dry grasslands for the cities where the disease then spread to humans. And from there the disease spread beyond Asia, possibly by ships or by Mongol armies and traders plying the Silk Road.[353] Initially, after the Europeans heard about the infections in Asia, possibly from the traders who arrived to sell their goods, they thought the plague was too far away to affect them. Their reaction was much like the initial response in the U.S. for the first weeks in January and February 2020 was to treat the coronavirus as just a localized problem in a few cities China.

This first and most common form of the plague was the bubonic plague, so named for the appearance of buboes, the dark swellings found mainly under the arms and on the neck and groin. These swellings were caused by an inflammation of the lymph glands, which become filled with pus and blood.[354] Thereafter, the victims commonly experienced a series of other symptoms, including fever, chills, vomiting, diarrhea, and strong aches and pains.[355] About 40% of the victims died, within two to seven days of the initial infection.[356]

The second most common form was the pneumonic or respiratory plague, which was spread by airborne particles from someone who already had the disease. The third type was the septicemic plague, based on an infection of the blood. These two types of the disease were especially fatal, resulting in about 100% of the victims dying. Unfortunately, anyone infected by the plague often suffered from two or all three types by the time they died.[357]

Today, of course, the coronavirus is a virus, rather than a bacterium, but it is spread in much the same way as the pneumonic form of the plague — from airborne particles, as well as on particles settling on hard surfaces. Hence the need for masks and social distancing and frequent handwashing.

The big difference, of course, is the way the people sought to treat the disease in the Middle Ages and today, though in both times, the avoidance of people with the disease was a strategy which worked when used effectively. Another commonality is the struggle in both times to come up with a cure and to use inadequate treatments — in the Middle Ages because the doctors didn't know any better, and today because as of this writing in October 2020, it is too soon to know what vaccines or treatments are effective. Also, many people have promoted ineffective or actually harmful "cures," such as chlorohydroquinone, or they have shunned wearing masks or social distancing, sometimes claiming they don't need to do this for a number of reasons, from feeling they are immune, protected by God, or the disease is a hoax.

In medieval times, doctors didn't know about antibiotics and some medical practitioners used a variety of violent methods to treat the disease, which often made the symptoms worse, such as forced vomiting, sweating, and bloodletting. Typically, they used bloodletting to combat the bubonic form of the plague by opening up a vein, usually on the victim's ankle or wrist, in the early stages of the disease, when the lymph nodes were first swelling up. But if the disease continued, they commonly used sweating, and sometimes a herbal remedy, such as snakeroot, a tall member of the sunflower family with a toxin to sweat the disease out of the patient.[358] But, given the 40% mortality rate, these methods were not particularly effective.

Though a major difference today is the death rate is much less — about 3.4-5%, based on the Worldometer daily tally of the world's rate of infection and death,[359] the factors contributing to the spread and devastating effects of the virus are similar. In the Middle Ages as today, the impact of the disease on the poor and those living together in crowded conditions is similar.

For example, during the Middle Ages, in the cities which were ground zero for the disease, the poor lived together in smaller buildings, which were closer together. This provided, according to authors of *The Middle Ages* "the ideal conditions for the spread of the pneumonic plague since anyone who breathed in the air particles near someone with this form of the plague would almost certainly become ill and then die,"[360] since the mortality rate for this form of the disease was 100%. Likewise, today, the hardest hit populations suffering from the coronavirus include the lower income Black and Latinx Americans, who are living in crowded conditions in the cities. Also the hardest hit are those who are crowded together in nursing homes and assisted living facilities or who are home-less, living in tent cities. Because of living in close quarters, these groups are similarly faced with higher infection and death rates.[361] By contrast, then and now, the wealthy were less affected, since they could more easily shut themselves off in their houses or move away when the disease was ravaging the local population, though in both times, the plague didn't discriminate. Back then, it took peasants, rulers, clergy, and merchants alike if they were exposed,[362] much as occurred with COVID-19 today. Though proportionately, many more people who are lower income and crowded together are vic-tims, some wealthy and powerful people have become victims, such as Boris Johnson, Prime Minister of England, who did recover, and Herman Cain, the chief executive of a successful pizza chain, who died after attending a rally for the President in Tulsa, Oklahoma.

Still another parallel is the way the Black Death and COVID-19 spread through popular travel routes. Back in the Middle Ages, the main source of initial entry to Europe, England, and the Middle East was through the ships bringing trade goods from Asia, where the disease initially struck in China, India, Persia, Syria, and Egypt[363]. Yet, at first, much like today, the educated and elite classes of Europe weren't alarmed by the terrible stories of the disease that seemed so far away. Then, too, some of the first countries to be hit by the plague were governed by non-Christians, or heathens as the Christians called them, many Europeans thought their God would protect them,[364] much like many evangelical Christians eschew wearing masks and go to church like nothing bad will happen to them, because, as some believes have reported on the social media: "God will protect me."

But soon the plague began its relentless spread, though the educated and elite Europeans were unaware that the plague was spreading west from where it began in China,[365] ironically the point of origin of the pandemic today, presumably in a market in Wuhan where it first jumped from a bat or pangolin to a human. In medieval times, the first stop was the port cities, initially at the port of Messina in Italy, and from there it spread to other cities in Italy. Soon it spread to the port of Marseilles in France and the port of Tunis in North Africa. Then it reached Rome and Florence, two cities that were at the hub of the trade routes of many cities.[366] By the middle of 1348, the Black Death had struck Paris, Bordeaux, Lyon, and London. Along the way, it reached Dorset, England, when a sailor arrived there from the English province of Glasony, and within a year, it had spread throughout all of England.[367] A map of Europe, the British Island, and Asia for these years show the Black Death like a wave sweeping through every country, destroying everyone in its path.

A modern day map with circles for pandemic hot spots and a listing of cases shows a similar pattern of spread. As a *Washington Post* series tracing the spread of the COVID-19 virus describes, the virus first surfaced in the Chinese city of Wuhan, where it was believed to have been transmitted to human from a bat or pangolin, a scaly ant-eater.[368] Then, it began to surge in Italy and Spain, and from there it spread throughout Europe, the U.K., South America, South Asia, the Middle East, Russia, and the United States, resulting in over 36 million cases worldwide, 7.7 million in the U.S., and 6.8 million cases in India and 5 million cases in Brazil the hardest hit country to date.[369] The corresponding death count is 215,822 cases in the U.S., and 105,000 cases in India and 148,000 cases in Brazil.[370] Both then and now, the main source of movement was the travel of humans, enabling the bacterium or virus causing the disease to easily travel from one human to another, variously infecting and causing the death of the most vulnerable, despite some differences in who was most vulnerable — the poor in both times, and now the elderly and those with chronic diseases or respiratory ailments. While the mode of transportation might differ — primarily by ship or carriages on the medieval trader routes, compared to travel by plane, cars, and trains today, after that the disease spread by infected people trans-mitting it to those they interacted with on a day to day basis.

Still another parallel is the way people reacted to the disease then and now — through avoidance in some form. For example, during the Black Plague, as described the History.com editors: "In a panic, healthy people did all they could to avoid the sick. Doctors refused to see patients; priests refused to administer last rites; and shopkeepers closed their stores."[371] Also, much like many city dwellers today have left big cities like San Francisco for the suburbs, during the Middle Ages, many people fled countryside from the cities. But much like today, they still could not escape getting infected by the disease, though the particular carriers might differ. Back then, the peasants and landowners often contracted the disease from their animals, since the plague affected cows, sheep, goats, pigs and chickens, not just people,[372] while now many people get the disease from virtually anyone — from their children who get it from their playmates or at school to people they encounter at various types of events, from gatherings with friends and relatives to attending concerts and services at church. In medieval times, many people abandoned their sick and dying loved ones in a desperate attempt to save themselves, [373] while today they may isolate the sick and dying in a room in their home or they may find a nursing home, hospice, or hospital where individuals near death can be isolated in their last days.

Also, many cities took steps to quarantine travelers who were potentially infected, and they set up restrictions to keep anyone who might be infected from entering the city and mixing with the rest of the population.[374] Likewise, today, many cities, counties, and states have imposed restrictions on holding certain types of activities or on who can enter certain locations. At many institutions, from prions, jails, and nursing homes to colleges, these organizations have set up their own guidelines, sometimes incorporating guidelines from the Center for Disease Control (CDC).[375]

Ironically, much of this description of how people sought to avoid others back then could be written today. For example, many doctors have closed their practices or restricted the number of patients they can see to enforce social distancing, and many shops and restaurants have closed down, sometimes because they have been prohibited to open or can only do so with very restricted social distancing conditions, making it uneconomical to continue in business with a small smaller clientele. Then, too, many cities, counties, and countries today have similarly set up restrictions to keep out travelers from other areas with high levels of infection, though many cities, counties, and countries additionally have set up quarantine periods for anyone with symptoms or coming from an area which has been redlined for its high infection level, including ships that have turned into coronavirus breeding grounds. And institutions with a live-in population have created guidelines for how to live more safely and securely, based on using social distancing, isolation, quarantines, and other methods to reduce the chances of getting infected or spread the infection to others.

Even the notion that the plague was God's punishment has been expressed about the coronavirus now. For example, in the Middle Ages, many people viewed the Black Death as "a kind of divine punishment — retribution for sins against God such as greed, blasphemy, heresy, fornication and worldliness."[376] So, based on this premise, people who held this belief thought the only way to overcome the plague was to gain God's forgiveness. Since some people believed the way to do this was to eliminate the heretics and other troublemakers from their communities that led mobs of believers to massacre many thousands of Jews between 1348 and 1350, while thousands of Jews escaped to safety in the less populated areas of Eastern Europe. This situation is much like today, when many blame the immigrants from Mexico and Central and South America for spreading the virus, and the government has sought to contain them in the prison-like holding centers set up even before the pandemic to reduce and discourage immigration.

There are also medieval and modern parallels in viewing the pandemic as a type of punishment from God for individual or collective sings. For instance, in the Middle Ages some upper class male believers sought to find individual forgiveness by joining processions of flagellants who traveled from town to town, beating themselves with whips to publically display their penance by punishing themselves.[377] And today, some believers — generally evangelical Christians — view the coronavirus as a plague sent by God to punish society for various sins. For example, some preachers and ministers have attributed the punishment as due to homosexuals, transsexuals, and other allegedly deviant individuals.[378] Others have railed again the Jews for spreading the disease resulting in an economic decline.[379]

Finally, both back then and now, there have been major socio-economic effects that have been devastating to some, while providing opportunities to others. During the Middle Ages, one effect of the loss of population was to undermine the traditional manorial-feudal system, since there were so many fewer peasants because of the Black Death's huge death toll. As a result, the lords of these manors found it harder to find peasants to plow their fields, harvest their crops, or produce other goods and services for them. In turn, the peasants sought higher wages and better working conditions, though some laws were passed to stop them, even providing punishments for violations, such as the Statute of Laborers enacted in 1349 which provided that violators who demanded more wages than they were getting could be fined a fee and thrown into the stocks. But these laws didn't work very well, and in the end, the peasants increased their earnings and were able to buy things they couldn't obtain before, such as nicer clothes. Some were able to move away from the land owned by the nobles or kings, and some even bought their own.[380]

The high rate of death also resulted in a surplus of land and more tools, so workers were able to be more productive, and that contributed to the higher wage for workers, too.[381] At the same time, these developments undermined the power and prestige of the lords, who now had less money to maintain their exalted position. A key reason is that they had a much smaller labor pool to work the fields, as University of Richmond scholar, David Routt explains in an article on "The Economic Impact of the Black Death." Before the plague hit, the rising population resulted in lower wages, while the lords could get higher prices for their rents and produce. In turn, the peasants felt they had to remain in their secure though dependent and demeaning position, because the lacked the leverage to demand more.[382] In effect, they were caught in an unfavorable supply and demand situation, where the growing population of peasants before the plague meant they faced a great deal of competition from other peasants because there were so many of them.

But then, the arrival of the Black Death changed everything, because with the high death rate, there were fewer peasants to perform the work in the fields. So as a result "The rural worker...demanded and received higher payments in cash (nominal wages) in the plague's aftermath...while the literate elite bemoaned a disintegrating social and economic order."[383] In effect, as Routt points out "A recalcitrant peasantry, diminished dues and services, and climbing wages undermined the material foundation of the noble lifestyle."[384]

While Europe's political elite initially looked to legal coercion to counteract rising wages, reduce the peasant's mobility, and maintain the pre-plague social order, in the end these efforts didn't work. As a result, lord and lord found it unprofitable to continue to cultivate his lands as before, so the nature of agriculture changed and the centuries-old manorial system gradually fell apart. As it did, many lords turned to other types of farming which required less labor than traditional grain agriculture. For instance, they began raising sheep to manufacture woolen cloth and respond to a growing demand for meat. Also, some lords granted leases to tenants, which created a type of sharecropping, whereby the lord contributed capital in the form of land, seed, tools, and plow teams, while the tenant did the work and gave a fraction of the harvest to the lord. As a result of these changes, the traditional manorial system was now dead.[385]

It's demise, in turn, gave the peasants a chance to obtain other types of jobs that were more profitable as well as get an education.[386] Meanwhile, in the cities, while much of the population was decimated from the plague, new workers arrived from the countryside, but they often couldn't immediately replace the skilled workers who died from the plague. So there was a decline in per capita productivity by the new workers, who needed some time for training to do the work.[387]

At the same time there was a reduced demand for goods because of the reduced population, resulting in a glut of manufactured and trade goods, and for a time, their prices plummeted. As a result, those businessmen who were able to survive this short term imbalance of supply and demand had to change what they produced to fit a smaller pool of customers.[388] A parallel today is the many companies, especially in the hard hit retain businesses, that have created online shops. Plus now there were new opportunities for business owners and entrepreneurs who found ways to exploit the bad times with new business ideas, such as by creating digital products in the cloud or available as downloadable software. And many start-ups have gained venture capital funding. Thus, entrepreneurs have more opportunities to take effective risks with this support.

Such efforts to seek new opportunities provided by the pandemic parallel those which occurred in medieval times. For example, as David Routt puts it in "The Economic Impact of the Black Death, "The successful post-plague businessman observed markets closely and responded to them while exercising strict control over his concern, looking for greater efficiency, and trimming costs."[389] For example, the Flemish producers who emphasized luxury textiles or who purchased, improved and resold cheaper English cloth prospered while those merchants who stuck with the lower-quality woolens did poorly. Likewise, the Italian producers of luxury woolens did well.

Then, too, the pandemic contributed to the mix of forces stimulating the peasant rebellions. Many of these rebellions which occurred after the Black Death were likely to have occurred anyway, because the peasants already had many grievances against the nobles and lords. But due to the Black Death, the peasants who survived were even more demanding in seeking higher wages, fairer treatment, and freedom from the control of the lords.

In turn, these upheavals in society and the economy prepared the way for the Renaissance let by the new classes of rich merchants, artists, and scientists, located primarily in the cities.

A comparison with life today shows many parallels with the way the pandemic has been changing society, though specifics vary. For example, just as the lords suddenly experienced a loss of income as the peasants on their lands died or sought increased wages because of the reduced population, so many business owners today have experienced losses and many have had to close their businesses or gone through bankruptcy due to the reduced demand for their products or services. Then, too, many had to close their business for a time due to legal restrictions on certain types of business involving close personal contact, such as bars and hair salons. And many businesses did not survive the lockdowns, due to reduced product sales, less demand for their services, or the reductions on the number of customers they were allowed to serve at any one time. So they simply closed their doors, in some cases causing a great financial loss for their landlords, who lost money when they didn't pay the rent and couldn't find new tenants. According to some reports, the number of businesses permanently closing is about 60% as of September, according to a report on national closures in the *New York Post*.[390] And certain industries have been decimated because of concerns about spreading and contracting the virus, such as the travel, hospitality, meeting, and speaking industries, though even they have been trying to adapt, such as by putting on travel videos, setting up meetings online, and speaking through PowerPoints and videos, although so far, any business is way way down.

At the same time, just as business owners and entrepreneurs in medieval times were able to take advantage of new opportunities to create or expand their businesses, so have many businesses and entrepreneurs today, and they have done very well. For example, because of the need for social distancing and the cancellation of many meetings and venues based on personal contacts, other forms of communication have evolved. Most notably, Zoom has become a place for meetings on line, since a wide variety of groups and companies are using them. For example, instead of the usual after hours meetings or referral groups, Chambers of Commerce have shifted their meetings to zoom. Artists are showing their work and musicians are performing on line. Conferences and conventions are still going ahead with the programs, but now exhibitors can get a virtual booth and attendees can attend virtual workshops. I have been to dozens of such meetings myself each month, and some business people even complain about being "zoomed out," since they spend most of the day in these meetings.

Then, too, new networking organizations have sprung up to provide for virtual networking events with breakout rooms for one and one meetings or small groups of 3 to 12 participants. Typically, a moderator or facilitator is assigned to each of these rooms to facilitate the questions and answers in the allotted time before returning back to the main room. Commonly, they have three or four questions for participants to respond to. Sometimes they begin with a more personal breakout question, such as what did you do over the weekend or how has life changed for you as a result of the pandemic. Then, participants typically have a chance to give a 30-90 second pitch for one's business, followed by a description of one's preferred referral.

In the last few months, I have participated in many of these online meetings — from a small group of songwriters and performers who record their songs on another online platform — Marco Polo and discuss their songs on Zoom – to many of the business networking groups to gain new business. With groups that have been meeting for some time before the pandemic, there are often longer presentations by a rotation to feature one or two speakers each week. And many entrepreneurs are now putting on webinars or creating online courses. Often they offer the first one for free, and then provide an opportunity to sign up for a continuing program.

At the same time, companies which already have an online presence, such as Facebook, LinkedIn, Instagram, and Twitter, have become even more central to everyone's life, while film and TV series platforms like Netflix, Amazon Prime, and HBO have seen a growth of participation.

In short, just as the Black Plague in the Middle Ages resulted in many social and economic changes because of the reduced population and fears of contagion through personal contact, so the modern landscape has been transformed through the pandemic. While some groups have experienced devastating financial losses, such as the lords in medieval times and many industries involving personal contact and travel today, others have experienced a rise in their fortunes. These beneficiaries include the peasants who could command more money and gain more freedom from the manorial system in the Middle Ages and the companies involved in providing digital products and services today. Notably, too, in both periods, the changes in the economy opened the door for entrepreneurial businesses and individuals to take advantage of new opportunities and gain new possibilities for wealth.

Also, just as the social and economic transforms triggered by the Black Death helped to prepare the way for the Renaissance, so the changes now occurring due to the pandemic are likely to lead to a whole new world when it ends. It won't, as more and more experts agree, simply end and then everything returns to the way it was. Instead, some kind of new kind of social and economic system is likely to emerge, though for now, it's too soon to tell exactly what that shape will be.

Chapter 11: The Growing Crisis and Some Ways for Further Equality

The Growing Crisis

As I described in the previous chapters, American society is coming more and more to resemble the structure and lifestyles of society in the Middle Ages because of the growing divide between rich and poor and the decline of the middle class. This increasing inequality is also a pattern that has been occurring in other Western industrialized societies, where a superrich elite has emerged in the last few decades, while the legions of poor are growing. In the United States, there is even more inequality, so that President Obama made dealing with the problem of inequality a top priority and has sought to help the disadvantaged who were hardly hit by the Recession. Now, as of this writing, President-Elect Joe Biden has made a priority of dealing with the pandemic and bringing unity to a divided land.

As described, this growing inequality today has largely been caused by the globalization of society due to technological changes making us more connected than ever. This globalization has provided expanded markets for the huge multinational corporations and the highly-paid entertainment and sports stars, who often are owners or investors in large companies, often with merchandise promoting their brand. Although the reasons for this inequality in the Middle Ages was different – largely due to success in war, controlling more and more land, obtaining more and more income through taxation, and later trade, with the rise of the wealthy merchants in the towns and cities in the Late Middle Ages, the results of this increasingly unequal society was the same. The wealthy upper classes – the kings, nobles, high church officials, and wealthy merchants then; the upper 1%, .1% or .01% now, have come to live a largely separate life of luxury made possible by their wealth, compared to the peasants and artisans then and "the rest of us" or the "99%" now.

In previous chapters I discussed how these differences between the groups at either end of the economic scale compare both then and now in terms of politics, economics, social structure, and lifestyle. I also discussed how the increasing misery of the peasants, much of this due to increased taxes because of the wars of the kings and nobles, led to a number of peasant revolts, most notably the 1381 peasant revolt in England and the 1351 Jacquerie uprising in France, in response to the pressures on the peasantry due to the Hundred Year's War. These attempts to change an unfair system involved the peasants in numerous communities getting together under the leadership of a few inspirational leaders, though these revolts were soon crushed by the armies of the kings and nobles and the leaders were executed.

Though they didn't ultimately succeed, these peasant revolts in response to inequality, unfairness, and misery in the Middle Ages are instructive for today, in that the same kind of revolt seems to be gathering force in the United States, as well as in uprisings and protests around the world. Two of the most notable of these groups in the last decade were the Occupy Movement and the low pay protests by fast-food and Walmart workers. And today, the Black Lives Matter movement has grown to seek equal justice and equal opportunity for disadvantage groups generally.

The Occupy Movement first got widespread attention in the U.S. when it occupied Zuccotti Park in Wall Street in New York City on September 17, 2011. Then, it spread to other cities in the U.S. and in other countries, so by October 9th, its protests had occurred in over 600 communities in the U.S. and 951 cities in 82 countries. One of the most hard-hit communities was Oakland, California, where I was living at the time. The protesters set up an encampment in the park across from City Hall, and for a time, Oakland became the center of the Occupy movement in the U.S., though after some uncertainty by the Mayor and City Council about whether the group should stay or go, along with pressure from the Oakland Chamber of Commerce and local merchant groups, the police finally cracked down in mid-November and cleared the group from the park. Around this time, the Occupy Oakland protesters also participated in a demonstration to shut down the port of Oakland on November 2, while protesters in New York, Boston, and Philadelphia marched to show support for the Oakland event to protest foreclosures, seek fair lending capital, and make capital available to low-income communities. Some protesters additionally blocked entrances to the branches of Chase and Wells Fargo, holding signs with statements like: "Banks got bailed out. We got sold out." [391] As a result, by the end of 2011, the authorities had cleared most of the camps, and finally evicted a group that held on in Washington, D.C. by February 2012.

Since then, many claiming to be part of or affiliated with the Occupy movement have appeared at other events, often with organizations with a similar vision, such as at several Causa Justa rallies in Oakland and San Francisco to protest various government and bank policies to stop foreclosures and allow families to move into foreclosed and vacant houses.[392] As another example, members of the Occupy movement combined with a number of groups, including Causa Justice and ACCE, the Alliance of Californians for Community Empowerment, for a protest of about 500 people at a Wells Fargo shareholder meeting in San Francisco in April 24, 2012. The protesters gathered on California Street in front of the Merchant Exchange Building and waved signs like: "Foreclose Banks, Not Homes" and "The Wall Street Banker: They Get Rich While We Lose Homes, Jobs, Services." I was there and even was interviewed for a video some filmmakers produced of the protest, which can be seen on YouTube. Since at the time, I had to sell my own home as a result of facing foreclosure due to several banks suddenly reducing or cancelling my credit line, despite nearly 20 years of regular payments, because of a tightening of bank lending policies, so now my loan to value was too high. At this protest, there were 24 arrests, including 15 for disrupting the meeting.[393] Though the protest didn't have much impact on changing bank policies, it did draw awareness to the issue through the many articles that appeared in newspapers and in online reports of the protest.

Since then, the protests have continued by the Occupy movement and other groups, sometimes separately and sometimes together in a joint protest. For example, about 100 Occupy San Francisco Protesters staged a demonstration and marched through San Francisco to mark the movement's one year anniversary, with signs and chants like: "The system has got to die, happy birthday Occupy."[394]

Subsequently, for its second anniversary, the Movement had even more rallies, such as one in which 100 Occupiers returned to the Zuccotti Park near the New York Stock Exchange in Wall Street.[395] Yet, while the movement has splintered into a number of groups promoting different causes under the Occupy banner, the basic message of the movement lives on. For example, in November 2013, the group promoted a Rolling Jubilee operation by its "Strike Debt" working group to buy up and eliminate the personal debts of debtors suffering from crushing medical debts, and there are plans to help individuals suffering from student debts, credit card burdens, and city debts.[396] The organization even has its own website at www.strikedebt.org. Then, too, there are websites for Occupy organizations in different cities, such as Occupy Wall Street in New York (www.occupywallst.org), Occupy San Francisco (occupysf.org), Occupy Oakland (occupyoakland.org), and Occupy Together (www.occupytogether.org) to link together the Occupy groups in different areas in order to help rally people to the groups' actions, meetings, and assemblies in different areas of the country.

Thus, the protest movement sparked by the original September 2011 protest in Wall Street spread to groups around the country ready to call on thousands of prospective protesters for rallies, protests, and other activities to support the interests of the 99%. This was followed by protests by the low-paid fast food and retail workers. This movement began in November 2012 when workers at fast food chains in New York began a protest, and in August, a strike occurred in over 50 cities. Then, in November 2013, marking the anniversary of the original strike, the protest against fast food chains like McDonald's, Wendy's, and Burger King spread to 100 cities across the United States. The goal was to get a wage of $15 an hour and the right to form a union without the fear of retaliation, since the average fast food worker earned only $9 an hour, and some earn only the federal minimum of $7.25. [397] The strikes – the first of many — were designed to increase awareness of the power that workers have and build up the momentum for future actions. The point of the one-day strike was to show the power that workers have when they walk off their jobs and embolden more workers within the store. [398] Then, in 2013, other low-wage income workers mobilized by striking against Walmart, the largest U.S. employer, with 1500 protests in cities around the country on Black Friday, the day after Thanksgiving, considered the largest shopping day of the year. [399]

A decade later, the Black Lives Matter movement and other protests calling for an end to racism and a fairer distribution of the wealth contributed to the outpouring of voters to oust President Trump, leading to Joe Biden's win. Many of the women inspired by the #MeToo movement have joined this call to end inequality, too.

In sum, several streams of protests by low-income workers and others who are unemployed, underemployed, or face or have experienced the loss of their homes have been growing throughout the country. They have been targeting the top 1% by protests against banks, Wall Street firms, and big retail giants, especially fast food companies and retail stores, seeking improved conditions, much like the peasants organized protests in the Middle Ages against the nobility. Much like the protests of the medieval peasants were fairly quickly contained by the large armies of the king and nobles who executed the key leaders and dispersed the rest, some modern-day protests have been shut down by the local police. But others have survived for the day or two of the planned action. And whether they were shut down or continued, the protesters got their message out through the news media and Internet posts. Thus, it seems likely that they will continue to grow, as more and more people find themselves in desperate straits due to the increasing concentration of wealth among the rich and the growth of poverty around the country. At the same time, the growth of the same technologies and the globalization that have helped the wealthy increase their wealth and power has also provided a forum for those in the 99% to organize their mass protests using the social and mainstream media. So the next series of strikes and protests is only a media blast away.

One bright ray of hope is that the Middle Ages ended with the Renaissance, which was a time of new learning and enlightenment, marked by the growth of towns and cities, new centers of education in the universities, the expansion of trade, the discovery of new lands, and a growing middle class.

Likewise, one might hope for a new Renaissance that could come from the birth of new start-ups and new ways of doing business in the years ahead.

But that is only a possibility. Meanwhile, the potential for increasing protests appears to be spreading unless something is done to deal with the growing inequality at the heart of the crisis.

What to Do Next as a Society

Thus, there is a need to do something. In *The Price of Inequality: How Today's Divided Society Endangers Our Future,* Joseph E. Stiglitz, a winner of the Nobel Prize in Economics, examines this crisis based on the growing concentration of wealth at the top. And like other writers on the crisis, he discusses how the money given to the top not only doesn't go into job creation and innovation but contributes to "distorting our politics," resulting in the use of wealth to gain further political advantages, thereby "perpetuating inequalities through the political process." He also agrees with Cornel West, co-author of *The Rich and the Rest of Us*, that the "real solution to the inequality crisis lies in focusing on *community* rather than simply on self-interest," since the "way to achieve sustained prosperity to have shared prosperity." As he observes: "If a country doesn't give a large proportion of the population the education that they need to earn a decent living, if employers don't pay workers a decent wage, if a society provides so little opportunity that many people become alienated and demotivated, then that society and its economy won't work well."[400]

In other words, there is a need to share the wealth more, which is the message of the growing protest movement by the unemployed, underemployed, low-wage workers, and those who are in danger of losing or have lost their homes.

But how to do this, in a society where deregulation has led to the "excessive financialization of the economy," where over 40% of corporate profits go to the financial sector, and the "richest 1% of all Americans pay an income tax rate in the low twenties, which is lower than the rate of Americans with more moderate incomes."[401] And how can one achieve this end, when the wealthy have a powerful control over the political process, have the benefit of low taxes, and enjoy the perks and privileges that come with having a very high income? That is the big question – how! Stiglitz offers some suggestions on what to do at the end of his book describing the problem, and then I want to share some of my thoughts on what we have to do as a society. And it is critical that we take steps now to reverse the growing inequality to create a more equal society, because otherwise the threat of destabilization of society by those with less and less to lose is very real.

What Stiglitz proposes is an economic reform agenda to simultaneously increase "economic efficiency, fairness, and opportunity," which I agree is much needed. In particular, he recommends the following fixes[402]:

- Curb excesses at the top in a number of ways. One way is to limit the financial sector by curbing excessive risk taking and the financial institutions which are too big to fail and are too interconnected. He suggests making the banks more transparent, especially in their handling of "over-the-counter derivatives", which should be more closely restricted and not underwritten by government-insured financial institutions. The banks and credit card companies should be more competitive, too. He further recommends making it more difficult for banks to engage in "predatory lending and abusive credit card practices," with which I certainly concur, as one of the victims of an out-of-the blue credit card crackdown by three banks which undermined my credit line and led me to have to sell my home. Additionally, he recommends cutting down the bonuses which encourage financial executives to take excessive risks and look for shortsighted short – term bonuses. And the government should close down the off-shore banking centers that have gotten around regulations and are used to evade or avoid taxes.
- Create stronger competition laws and enforce them more effectively, since monopolies and imperfect markets for competition result in companies charging more.
- Improve the governance of corporations, including limiting the ability of CEOs to take a company's resources for their own benefit. One way this might be done is by giving shareholders more influence over the CEOs' pay, along with accounting rules so they can better learn what the company is paying executives through wages, stock options, and bonuses.
- Reform bankruptcy laws so they are more debtor-friendly, which would encourage banks to be more careful in lending money, since poor bankruptcy laws have contributed to "a bloated financial sector, to economic instability, to exploitation of the poor and less financially sophisticated, and to economic inequality."

- End government giveaways to corporations, such as giving them public assets for too little money or by overpaying in buying their products or services. Some examples of this include the cost-plus defense contracts paid to Halliburton, the inadequate auctions for oil, the below-market royalty rates for minerals, and the giveaways of the broadcast spectrum to TV and radio.
- End the "welfare" to corporations, which include subsidies that are often hidden, such as by being buried in the tax cope through loopholes, exceptions, exemptions, and preferences, which make the tax system more regressive and prop up corporations which can't make it on their own. If they can't, they should simply come to an end. They shouldn't be kept alive by government handouts.

Another area of reform is in taxes, and here Stiglitz makes two recommendations to create a more progressive system to place more taxes on the corporations and wealthy individuals. In particular he suggests that the government should.[403]

- Create a more progressive income and corporate tax system that has fewer loopholes."
- Create a more effective and better enforced estate tax system to prevent the creation of a new oligarchy.

Finally, Stiglitz makes a series of recommendations for helping the rest of America. Among these are the following which are also primarily government driven[404]:

- Improve access to education, since education more than anything else (apart from having rich parents to begin with) shapes opportunity.
- Help ordinary Americans save money, such as by providing matching grants or expanding first-time programs, so they

have more security and opportunity, which would lead to a fairer society over time.

- Provide health care for all, since the most critical source of economic distress are the loss of a job or an illness, which often leads to bankruptcy. Though health care has traditionally been provided to employees by employers, it is an inefficient, antiquated system, which has led the U.S. to have the "most inefficient and poorest overall health care system among the advanced countries." The bottom line is that rather than spending, Americans don't get value for what they spend, and a great many people don't have access to health care. The Affordable Care Act, dubbed Obamacare, was launched in 2010 to correct the problem, although the system was plagued by many technical glitches when the health care website was first launched and complaints about the cancellations of about 50 million policies by providers of health care who didn't meet the new government standards. Additionally, the Act faced the anger of higher income people who discovered they had to pay more to help provide access to those who have less. Even so, as of 2019, about 20 million signed up and nearly about 10 million have employer coverage, so the Act has gained widespread support.[405] Yet even though the system seems to have gained a growing acceptance, the Republican party with the support of the Senate and President Trump has engaged in a campaign for four years to shut it down without success, apart from getting rid of a mandate with any penalties for not signing up. But now that Joe Biden is expected to become the next President in January 2121, he expects to save the Act.
- Strengthen other social programs, such as by providing unemployment insurance for a longer period of time to help the unemployed ride out the economic crisis, as a result of the structural changes in the economic system.

- Better balance the effects of globalization, which is disadvantaging many workers through jobs going overseas and wages and social protections being reduced in the face of global competition. In response, the U.S. should play a role on the global stage by fighting for "better worker rights and conditions, better financial regulations, better environmental conditions." Otherwise, if the effects of globalization are not better managed, the risk is that countries globally will retreat into protectionism."
- Create a fiscal policy to "maintain full employment – with equality." Increasing employment would also provide a benefit through lowering debts and deficits, encouraging faster growth in the economy, and improving the distribution of income.
- Correct trade imbalances, since the U.S. now imports much more than it exports, which contributes to reduced employment, since exports create jobs, while imports destroy them, as well as lead to financial deficits. However, make these corrections through negotiations, and end the trade wars started by President Trump against China and other countries.
- Play a more active role in the labor market and provide increased social protections for workers. For example, the government should assist workers in moving to new jobs created by the global and technological transformation after they have lost jobs due to this transformation.

Additionally, Stiglitz argues for a new social compact to improve the position of ordinary workers and citizens, given the workers' reduced bargaining power relative to the wealthy owners of capital. In particular, he recommends that the government do the following:[406]

- Support the collective action of workers and citizens, such as by helping them in standing up against special interests and strengthening the unions, which can help in countering the special interests and defending the basic social protections that are necessary if the workers accept change and are willing to adjust to the changing economic environment.

- Take affirmative action to eliminate the results of discrimination, primarily due to race or gender. Besides having strong laws to prohibit discrimination, the government should provide affirmative action programs, especially in education, to provide more opportunity, which can help reduce inequality, too.

Lastly, Stiglitz urges policies to restore "sustainable and equitable growth," through two key government approaches:[407]

- Create a growth agenda, based on encouraging public investment, which will help provide the resources to resolve some of society's most difficult problems, including those resulting from poverty. For example, the government can invest in infrastructure, education, and technology, which can all encourage more growth in the years ahead.
- Redirect investment and innovation to preserve and create jobs and protect the environment, rather than the trend to invest to save labor costs, which leads to more unemployment. The government should also not only use its funds to encourage basic and applied research, but require the firms to pay for the full environmental damage they cause, which will encourage them to save on resources, rather than replacing workers.

What Else We Can Do Now

These recommendations by Stiglitz are all valuable, important goals for government and society to seek to achieve. Yet the big question is whether and to what extent the government can make these changes, particularly given the power of the wealthy individuals and huge corporations to push for their own agenda with the help of their money, lobbyists, and the interests of politicians, particularly Republicans, who have to answer to their own constituents. These wealthy individuals and corporations have the money to influence local and state elections, as well as legislation once the elected Congressmen and Senators, along with state governors and other state officials, get into office and seek to stay there. Thus, while many noble objectives might be envisioned, a big question is whether there is the will of the government and the voting public to make those changes and recognize them as in their best interest. However, now, with Biden elected and the increased influence of the progressives in the Democratic party, more of these changes may occur.

Yet, even though Stiglitz had a New York Times bestseller, and all of these books gained powerful endorsers, including Arianne Huffington for *The Great Divergence*, Lawrence Summers, former U.S. Treasury Secretary for *Plutocrats*, and Thomas B. Edsall of the *New York Times Book Review*, not much seemed to change, apart from Obama's health care act finally passing after a three years' struggle and remaining in force, despite the efforts of the Republican Senate and President Trump to terminate the act. Instead, over the last decade, there have been continuing strikes and protests from the Occupy movement and its spin-offs, low-wage workers in the fast-food and retail industries, and most recently protests from the Black Lives Movement and other protests seeking an end or racism and inequality. Even so, the top of the 1% earns even more.

Thus, apart from a call for government action in various areas, much more needs to be done to increase wide public awareness and support for change, as well as show the growing class of oligarchs that it is in their best interest to make changes. Additionally, the public consciousness needs to be changed, so that the luxurious extravagances of the elite, especially the superrich celebrity entertainers and athletes, are no longer celebrated or set up as a role model for others to aspire to. Rather a new consciousness needs to emerge, whereby individuals and corporations, not necessarily due to government pressure, realize that they need to not only live well, but need to recognize it is in their best interest to seek a more balanced, equal society, lest they contribute to undermining economic stability and reduce their own markets for sales and success.

Much can also be done outside of any government programs, and that can happen more quickly, since government by its nature tends to be slow moving, and it can take many months if not years for the negotiation process involving multiple committee meetings, hearings, discussions, compromises, appeals to constituents, and still more hearings, before anything gets passed. And even then further appeals and other legislation may occur to stop it. A good example of this is the three year process it took to pass Obamacare as a result of repeated objections and appeals, including a two week government shutdown, by the right wing of the Republican party to Obamacare.

Likewise, a series of recommendations to end the inequality crisis through legislation to reduce or restrict the incomes of the superwealthy, such as by raising taxes or eliminating loopholes, or government programs to support the underclasses with various types of assistance, could easily run into many hurdles to get passed, so nothing gets done or is long delayed. Thus, beyond any proposals to make changes in government policies and regulations, other measures are needed outside of the government's purview to change ways of thinking and create private initiatives to promote equality. A key to the success of these measures is redirecting the income of the super-wealthy in ways that will help the economy and society as a whole, along with involving the superwealthy and others with high incomes to help the rest of us.

To this end, I make the following recommendations for changes that are needed to change the public consciousness and create a more equal society:

- A massive publicity campaign should be created to increase public awareness of the inequality problem and show why this is a crisis that needs immediate attention. People with high incomes need to realize how they are contributing to the problem and how the crisis can negatively affect them, too, by destabilizing the economy, threatening to reduce their markets and therefore their incomes, and lead to increased pressure and violence from below. The lower 99% are already well aware of the problem, since they are the victims of it, so they don't need a campaign directed to them; they just need to be aware that the campaign is being directed to the top 1%, so that they can show their support for this campaign. In turn, both the campaign and widespread support for it may help to influence the upper 1% to change their ways, while getting the political support required to pass legislation, though the campaign should be directed at getting private support and action for change which can occur immediately.

- This publicity campaign to change attitudes and actions should use all of the media, including the traditional print and broadcast media, as well as the Internet and social media. There should be press releases and press conferences to reach the traditional media, along with postings on Facebook, Instagram, LinkedIn, Twitter, and other social media platforms, including Pinterest, Reddit, Digg and Tumblr. Also, the many thousands of bloggers should be contacted to gain their support and encourage them to write articles about the campaign.

- A series of national workshops and seminars should be conducted to increase awareness of the problem, as well as encourage interaction between the 1% who want to learn more about what they can do and interested members of the 99% who can voice their concerns about the help they need.

- A network of small support groups should be organized which include both members of the 1% and the 99%, so they can share their concerns and look for ways to deal with the problem. These activities can be organized through online meetings and small local gatherings with social distancing while the pandemic rages.

- A letter-writing campaign should be organized to target members of the 1%, and especially the top .1% and top .01%, to encourage them to contribute their funds to help the disadvantaged, either individually or by joining or setting up foundations for this purpose. This campaign should not only send letters to ultra-high net worth individuals but to the CEOs and boards of the largest corporations.

- A Give Back Charitable Foundation should be created to invite ultra-high net worth individuals who don't have their own Charitable Foundation to donate funds that will be given to the cause.

- A series of Give Back Balls and other society events should be created for ultra-high net worth individuals and corporate chiefs to attend to raise funds for programs designed to give funds to the poor or provide them with scholarships for training in trade schools and universities.

- The ultra-high net worth individuals and corporations that contribute substantial funds (say $1 million or more) to these foundations or at these Give Back Balls should be honored and celebrated. Doing so will not only give them the prestige and glory of giving, but will serve as an example to other high net worth individuals and corporations to contribute, too.

- Employers who provide training or jobs for formerly unemployed or underemployed individuals should be recognized for their assistance, and they might be celebrated by the local media for their contribution.

- An outreach campaign to the superstar celebrities in the entertainment industry and sports should be organized to gain their contributions and public support to help the 99%. The press should be contacted to publicize the participation of high profile contributors, as well as reduce or end the coverage given to the lavish displays of a star's wealth, such as through huge homes, expensive clothing and jewelry, plastic surgeries, and expensive travel, since these are all reflections of a lifestyle that sets them apart from everyone else. Instead, high wealth individuals should be encouraged to give generously to help the less fortunate, as well as demonstrate the ways they are like other ordinary individuals, such as by running on the beach with their dog or exercising at a local gym. These high wealth individuals can also use the photo ops that result from these campaigns as a platform in which they invite others who are more fortunate to similarly contribute.

- The religious leaders at denominations with high-income members should be invited to participate in this campaign, such as by making public statements to their congregations and the media about their support. They might also set up charities for church or temple members to contribute, such as by donating 10% of their income, which will be given to the poor by the church.

- TV and radio hosts should be invited to join the effort by inviting celebrity guests, writers, economists, and others supporting this movement to talk about the need for change and the financial contributions they are making themselves, so their influence can help to change public opinion.

- A series of TV specials and documentary films might be created to show how this Give Back movement is spreading to create more equality.

- A series of short videos should be created to show the need for change and to advocate making particular changes. These videos might be put up on the campaign's websites and offered to anyone else who wants to use them. Not only might campaign organizers create these videos, but people around the U.S. and even the world might be encouraged to create their own videos supporting the need for more equality, and they can post them on the many sites for sharing videos, as well as on the campaign websites, their own website, and social media pages.

- The campaign to educate the public might also show high net worth individuals and corporations how they can use these contributions to reduce their tax bills, providing them a further incentive to contribute to the 99%.
- Universities might be encouraged to create courses to show the development of inequality throughout history, including during the Middle Ages and today, as well as teach about possible solutions.
- A series of campaigns by individuals might be developed to selectively get behind certain changes in legislation, such as those proposed by Stiglitz, to show public support and get members of Congress, the President, and state officials to back these changes.
- Others may have still more ideas for how to get out the message and gain the commitment of high net worth individuals to contribute to the 99% and publicly show their support.

In sum, besides anything the government might do, private individuals and corporations can do a great deal to change the consciousness and build up the momentum needed to reverse the concentration of income at the top. For many ultra-rich individuals the accumulation of capital is not something they need; rather it has become like a game to show how much one can accumulate in order to win, rather than putting those funds into productive use in creating new products and jobs. Thus, the idea of a high-profile campaign to "Give Back" is in the spirit of the "Givers Gain" approach of Business Network International (BNI) and other business referral organizations, and the goal is to change the game, so it becomes advantageous for the very rich to contribute to others.

It is not necessary to wait for new government legislation to make changes, which can take years to occur and generally requires much contentious wrangling by different political factions to get it done, though any favorable legislation will certainly help. But such legislation is not needed, because the proposed changes can begin by individuals, community groups, and companies right now. Anyone can help spread the message; and any high net worth individuals or company can start the process by contributing now and encouraging others to do the same. These changes are vital to the health of our economy and society – and they can and should begin now. In fact, they can contribute to the New American Renaissance, as described in the next chapter.

Chapter 12: What an American Resaissance Might Look Like

J ust like the social and economic upheavals of the Middle Ages after the Black Plague led to a restructuring of society, new types of work and job opportunities, and the emergence of an expanded middle class, so the upheavals of today due to the pandemic could result in a transformed society. Assuming the social order isn't destroyed by the raging divisions in society, protests, counter protests, riots, wildfires, floods, and other disasters that have befallen 2020, there could well be a new Renaissance that emerges from the tumult.

What might it be like? Here I'll simply speculate on the possibilities, based on the kinds of changes that occurred, as the late Middle Ages gave way to a blossoming Renaissance.

1) Just as the period after the Black Death, unleashed new artists and writers, so the period after Covid-19 ends may lead to an explosion of art and writing, both dealing with the events of the past period of turmoil and using new forms of presentation. At the end of the Middle Ages, this new Renaissance, especially in Italy, featured artists, such as Leonardo da Vinci, Michelangelo, Raphael, and Botticelli. It also marked the emergence of the two famous writers, Giovanni Boccaccio, who wrote the *Decameron* in 1353, featuring stories of love and lust, and Francesco Petrarch, most famous for *Il Canzoniere*, a collection of over 350 love poems

about a woman named Laura, completed over 40 years until 1368. [408] Likewise, today there will probably be an outpouring of writing to make sense of what happened and recount the stories of those who survived or perished during these years. Similarly, artists will draw on this imagery. At the same time, given the explosion of new technologies, from new software to Zoom calls, writers and artists are likely to seek new formats to express their work, say by creating books to be produced through writing and audio on Zoom, just as the printing press created a new way to share information after it was developed in 1440 by Johannes Gutenberg in Germany.

2) Another development might be new formats for holding meetings. The Zoom call and other webinar technologies, like GotoWebinar and GotoMeeting, gained popularity because people were confined to their homes to shelter in place during the lockdown, and most organizations cancelled in-person meetings to use these technologies. However, this online meeting approach might well outlast the lockdown. Certainly, regular meetings might start up again, but these online meetings have become increasingly sophisticated and convenient. For example, trained facilitators now set up and run break-out rooms with two up to about a dozen participants, and they use various questions to guide discussions. Also, many meetings now span the globe or attract thousands of participants in a given industry, so they become a way to readily meet people without the expense and inconvenience of having to travel. Such online meetings also result in savings in gas at a time when there are efforts to cut down on carbon emissions, so these online meetings contribute to sustainability. And with more and more employees working at home, perhaps permanently, such meetings may make more and more sense for companies and organizations with a worldwide reach. Additionally, these meetings cut

down on spending for conference facilities as well as work environments.

3) We can expect a growing digital economy. Many business based on in-person contacts have already been forced to shut down, reduce the number of customers in their facilities at a time, or otherwise scale back their business. Many companies, especially in the hospitality, restaurant, and travel industries, have already gone out of business, and many may not be able to come back after the lockdowns end, since many customers will be gone permanently, and it can take years to build back their business to the way things were if ever. On the other hand, those businesses that have been able to develop a digital footprint or are already working with customers online may continue to do very well. For example, some retailers have set up online platforms for selling their merchandise, and some, like Stitch Fix, a $1.6 billion company, which sends customers clothing they may like based on information gathered about them and lets customers return what they don't want, have already built up a solid and expanding customer based. Then, too, online workers, such as writers, publishers, and print-on-demand companies, like KDP and IngramSpark, have continued to do well, since they don't need personal contact to write, publish, and provide digital products and services online. And if these companies need to talk to customers, they can always use email, online chat, call centers, phone calls, and Zoom rooms.

4) Another predictions is that there will be a kind of "New Deal" to shore up the disadvantaged and contribute to the welfare of all, since America's long history of racial injustice and inequality has come to the fore, leading to growing protests around the land. These protests have also drawn attention to the growing inequality in America that affects minority

GINI GRAHAM SCOTT, PhD

group members even harder. This new awareness has all combined into a very volatile mix, reflected in the huge protests
that have roiled the land, accompanied by counter protests,
and agitators promoting violence, looters taking advantage of the situation, leading to various police and military
responses in cities around America. At the same time, some
wealthy families, such as the Gates, are trying to ameliorate
the situation by funding programs to alleviate hunger, while
Mike Bloomberg has contributed $1 billion to help recently
released prisoners pay off their debts so they can vote.

Thus, much like the ravages of the Black Death helped
to redistribute the wealth by causing many landowners to
lose their lands, while former peasants found new work and
became part of a growing middle class in the cities, there
could well be a redistribution of wealth, today. This redistribution might result from contributions by some wealthy and
from the realization of government officials that they need
to pass legislation to help the economically disadvantaged in
order to tamp down the protests sparked by inequality and
injustice. Then, too, given the changing job market with new
digital jobs, some of these funds might be used to finance
new types of education, perhaps offered digitally, to train
the unemployed or underemployed workers in new skills
needed for the growing digital economy.

5) I think we will see a period of reconciliation to heal the many
divisions in society, just like the plague in the Middle Ages
led to a period of greater harmony in Europe and England,
along with a burst of new ideas. Today, some of this reconciliation may occur because of the growing realization that these
vast divisions in wealth are unsustainable, since the loss of
so many businesses and jobs has led to a growing recession.
In response, those with great wealth and power may come
to recognize that it is in their interest to contribute more to
promoting economic gains for individuals struggling with

320

poverty and for the disappearing middle class, so they will have more to spend, which will help jump start the economy. In turn, this distribute the wealth approach will help to reduce the rage of those feeling left behind, which is contributing to the divisions in society. Perhaps this reconciliation and redistribution might accompany a New Deal, and it might include promoting more equality and racial justice for all, most notably for women and minority groups, since their anger has been a major fuel for the divisions in society. This new approach may also lead to a growing political peace, based on groups with different views seeking common ground and putting country over party.

6) Just like the last few years have seen hundreds of books come out about what is wrong with society, including what is wrong with the White House, I think the New American Renaissance will give rise to a series of books and other media focused on community healing and change. In the last few years, all kinds of self-help books have been published dealing with overcoming anxiety, fear, depression, and other negative emotions unleashed by this grim dark period of life in America, capped by over six months of different strategies for social distancing, leading people to feel very isolated and alone. I think once this period ends, there will be new books, videos, and ideas promoting what people can do to come together again, not just physically but emotionally, mentally, and spiritually. In medieval times, the period after the pandemic was followed by a rebirth of ideas in music, literature, and the arts, and the printing press invented in 1440 and the Reformation beginning in 1517 was part of this, since the printing press provided a way to spread new ideas, while the Reformation sparked a religious revolution. I believe a similar explosion of new ideas will occur now, spread by the social media and new forms of communication technology.

7) As these new ideas spread along with greater economic equality, another prediction is a reduction in violence — both on the streets, in sports, and in relationships. With more economic equality, there will be less incentive for committing robberies, thefts, and burglaries, which are often due to criminals not having a source of legitimate income. That increased economic equality could also contribute to reducing the market for illegal drugs, since there will less need for drugs to escape the despair of everyday life. At the same time, the effort to have safer sports will get a boost from the reduction in violence in society — a development that is already occurring given research findings that show the long lasting damage of injuries, such as concussions in football and other sports.

8) There will be a renewed period of peace, because COVID-19 has led people and governments to focus on what they can do to save people in their communities and country, so they will put aside ideas of expansion. Instead, they will look to other countries to partner up, realizing if they don't work together, that can result in mutual destruction for all.

9) There will be an increased interest in and acceptance of the knowledge of medicine, science, and health, since the pandemic has focused on the need for this information so society can be ready for any dangerous pathogens in the future. This growing interest will also lead to more students wanting to study in these fields, because scientists, medical workers, and health practitioners have been viewed as heroes because of their work on the front lines in the pandemic. Religious leaders will similarly embrace science and teach how it is compatible with having faith in God.

10) There will be a new acceptance of diversity, much as happened in the Renaissance when there was a celebration of

new ideas. In this case, much of this acceptance will grow out of the contributions made by low-income people of different ethnic groups on the medical frontlines and in the role of first responders and firefights to conflict and natural disasters, from hurricanes and floods to fires.

11) There will be a growth of training opportunities for the many new jobs due to new technologies, along with higher wages for needed workers, much as occurred in the Middle Ages after the loss of lives from the Black Death led to increased wages for the peasants and new occupations in the towns. This training will include learning how to use the new types of equipment that will be developed.

12) There will be an increased interest in healthy living and nutrition in reaction to the devastation wrought by the pandemic and the hunger experienced by many lower income people. The result will be a growing number of companies offering healthy products, and many people will become entrepreneurs promoting and selling these products, much like the Renaissance led to many new products and services in the growing urban areas.

13) There will be a growing recognition of climate change, as a result of the growing problems resulting from an increasingly hot climate, such as more fires, stronger hurricanes, a rising ocean, and other hard to deny results. This recognition will result from the growing acceptance of science and increasing scientific discoveries, much as occurred in the Renaissance.

14) There will be a new spiritual renaissance as people of different backgrounds seek spiritual solace after going through difficult times. But they will seek more personalized forms

of spiritual expression, so traditional religious institutions will need to adapt and be more flexible in ministering to their members, while individuals will seek out new religious doctrines and organizations that foster this more personal relationship with God, much as they did when the Protestant Reformation occurred beginning in 1517 during the Renaissance.

15) There will be criminal justice reforms based on increasing community-based rehabilitation, resulting in more prisoners released and other sentencing approaches. These reforms will be accompanied by the recognition that many sources of crime occur due to poverty and lack of jobs, leading to drug addiction to escape dire conditions, drug dealing to make money, and increased burglary, robbery, and theft to obtain money to survive the difficult times. Likewise, the harsh conditions for treating prisoners eased up somewhat during the Renaissance.

16) The economy will be increasingly transformed and expanded by the growing digital world that will connect everyone all over the world, much like the Renaissance brought new connections that stimulated trade and increased the power of the central governments. Due to new digital technologies, the modern world will be increasingly interconnected through databases, surveillance information on individuals, and global communication between criminal justice agencies as crime goes digital, too.

17) Increasingly, online courses and workshops will be used to teach new ideas and skills, while teachers will gain increased power and influence as a result of these courses that are beamed to millions throughout the world.

18) Increasingly, the media will have a new interest in what everyday people are doing, as a result of new roles, new technologies, and the new spirit of democracy and helping others. This will lead to the rise of new celebrities and influencers who reflect this new spirit of the times, showing a commitment to help others and support their community, rather than show them as celebrities who glory in the display of their wealth and glamorous lifestyles.

19) There will be a growing interest in a new category of "help-others" books rather than "self-help" books focused around helping oneself, as part of this new emphasis on supporting the community and others. This outward focus will also be reflected in books celebrating the accomplishments of teams at work and in the community. Likewise, this changed attitude will lead to films and TV shows celebrating the accomplishments of individuals working together, along with the leader or leaders of these groups.

20) This renewed interest in science will lead to new theories, such as post-materialistic science in which subjective experiences and one of a kind non-measureable phenomena are incorporated into scientific analysis. This includes the acceptance of ESP, telepathy, synchronicity, serendipity, near-death experiences, and other forms of information leading to the discovery of alternative energy sources and technologies which will simplify and improve all aspects of life. This new approach to science will bring science and spirituality closer together and show the interconnectedness of all life. As this theory gains more acceptance, this new way of thinking can lead to more ecologically sustainable and more generous behavior based on understanding that we are all interconnected, leading to less confrontation and greater cooperation between diverse populations and

cultures, assuming the support of government leaders and the multi-national corporations which control our present world economy, and are likely to continue to hold power in the coming decades.

21) You may think of other changes as a result of this new modern Renaissance. List them here, and then watch over the next few years what changes start to happen.

REFERENCES

Following is a list of the best-selling books about medieval and modern times which were used in analyzing the parallels between the Middle Ages and today. The references also include articles and websites cited in the book.

Books about the Middle Ages

Bauer, Susan Wise, *The History of the Medieval World: From the Conversion of Constantine to the First Crusade.* W. W. Norton & Company, 2010

Batchelor, Stephen. *Medieval History for Dummies.* For Dummies, 2010.

Bishop, Morris. *The Middle Ages.* Mariner Books, 2001.

Harawalt, Barbara A. *The Middle Ages: An Illustrated History.* Harawalt, Oxford University Press, 1999

Mills, Dorothy. *The Middle Ages.* Memoria Press, 2012.

Monod, Gabriel and Bemont, Charles. *Medieval Europe, 395-1270,* Amazon Digital Services, 2012.

Mortimer, Ian. *The Time Traveler's Guide to Medieval England.* Touchstone, 2011.

Tierney, Brian. *The Middle Ages, Volume I, Sources of Medieval History.* McGraw – Hill, 1998.

Books About Inequality and the Rich and Poor in Modern Times

Dadush, Uri, et. al. *Inequality in America: Facts, Trends, and International Perspectives.*, Brookings Institution Press, 2012.

Freeland, Chrystia. *Plutocrats: The Rise of the New Global Super-Rich and the Fall of Everyone Else.* Penguin Press, 2012.

Noah, Timothy. *The Great Divergence: America's Growing Inequality Crisis and What We Can Do About It.* Bloomsbury Press, 2013.

Pinketty, Thomas. *Capital in the Twenty-First Century.* Belknap Press, 2014.

Rycroft, Robert S. *The Economics of Inequality, Poverty, and Discrimination in the 21st Century.* Praeger, 2013.

Smiley, Tavis. *The Rich and the Rest of Us: A Poverty Manifesto.* Smiley Books, 2012.

Stiglitz, Joseph. *The Price of Inequality: How Today's Divided Society Endangers Our Future.* W. W. Norton & Company, 2012.

Books Comparing Contemporary Society to the Dark or Middle Ages

Berman, Morris. *Dark Ages America – The Final Phase of Empire.* W.W. Norton, 2007.

Shlapentokh, Vladimir and Woods, Joshua. *Feudal America: Elements of the Middle Ages in Contemporary Society.* Penn State Press, 2011.

ABOUT THE AUTHOR

G INI GRAHAM SCOTT, Ph.D., J.D., is a nationally known writer, consultant, speaker, and seminar leader, specializing in business and work relationships, professional and personal development, social trends, and popular culture. She has published over 50 books with major publishers. She has worked with dozens of clients on memoirs, self-help, popular business books, and film scripts. Writing samples are at www.ginigrahamscott.com and www.changemakerspublishingandwriting.com.

She is the founder of Changemakers Publishing, featuring books on work, business, psychology, social trends, and self-help. It has published over 150 print, e-books, and audiobooks. She has licensed several dozen books for foreign sales, including the UK, Russia, Korea, Spain, and Japan.

She has received national media exposure for her books, including appearances on *Good Morning America, Oprah,* and *CNN.* She has been the producer and host of a talk show series, *Changemakers,* featuring interviews on social trends.

Her books on social issues include:

The Science of Living Longer: Developments in Life Extension Technology (Praeger)

Lies and Liars: How and Why Sociopaths Lie (Skyhorse Publishing)

Scammed: Learn from the Biggest Consumer and Money Frauds How Not to be a Victim (Allworth Press)

Scott is also active in a number of community and business groups, including the Lafayette, Pleasant Hill, and Walnut Creek Chambers of Commerce.

She received her Ph.D. from the University of California, Berkeley, and her J.D. from the University of San Francisco Law School. She has received several MAs at Cal State University, East Bay.

Other Books by the Author

Other books by the author on social issues include:

The Science of Living Longer: Developments in Life Extension Technology, published by Praeger, 2018.

Lies and Liars: How and Why Sociopaths Lie and How You Can Detect and Deal with Them, published by Skyhorse Publishing, 2016.

Transformations: How New Developments in Science, Technology, Business, and Society Are Changing Your Life, published by Changemakers Publishing, 2013.

The Very Next New Things: Comments on the Latest Developments that Will Be Changing Your Life, published by Praeger, 2011.

The Truth About Lying: Why and How We All Do It and What to Do About It, published by Changemakers Publishing, 2011.

Playing the Lying Game: Detecting and Dealing with Lies and Liars, from Occasional Fibbers to Frequent Fabricators, published by Praeger, 2010.

CHANGEMAKERS PUBLISHING
3527 Mt. Diablo Blvd., #273
Lafayette, CA 94549
changemakers@pacbell.net . (925) 385-0608
www.changemakerspublishingandwriting.com

BIBLIOGRAPHY

Articles

"America's 60 Families." *Tracking the Entire World,* http://www.nndb.com.

"America's Cup." *Wikipedia: The Free Encyclopedia,* 2014.

"America's Most Expensive Neighborhoods." *247 Editors,* November 5, 2012.

"America's Self-Made Women 2020, Profile: #33 Marissa Mayer, CEO, Yahoo," *Forbes,* https://www.forbes.com/profile/marissa-mayer/?sh=138370d74c5e

ATTOM Data Solutions "U.S. Foreclosure Activity Drops to 13-Year Low in 2018," 2019.

Bain, David. "The World's Top 750 Family Businesses Rank," *Family Capital,* March 3, 2020. https://www.famcap.com/the-worlds-750-biggest-family-businesses

Ballmer, S. Chief Executive Officer." *Microsoft News Center,* http://www.microsoft.com/en-us/news/exec/steve/default.aspx.

Barr, J. "Behind the Scenes, Apple Planned Jobs' Succession by the Book." *Business & Money,* October 7, 2011. http://business.time.com/2011/10/07/behind-the-scenes-apple-planned-jobs-succession-by-the-book/.

Barr, M. "Occupy Wall Street Plans Rallies on Second Anniversary of Movement." *Huffington Post,* September 17, 2103.

"Belarus: Thousands Protest Outside State TV Building," BBC. Com, August 15, 2020.

Benson, Craig. "Povery: 2018 and 2019," The United States Census Bureau, September 2020. https://www.census.gov/content/dam/Census/library/publications/2020/acs/acsbr20-04.pdf

Bersin, J. "The Real Succession Plan for Steve Jobs: Apple Thinks Different with Apple University." *The Business of Talent*, August 26, 2011. http://www.bersin.com/blog/post/The-Real-Succession-Plan-For-Steve-Jobs-Apple-Thinks-Different-With-Apple-University.aspx.

"Bill Gates Buys $8.7M Home in Wellington." *HuffPost Miami*, June 26, 2013

"CDC COVID Data Tracker, Center for Disease Control, October 6, 2020. https://covid.cdc.gov/covid-data-tracker/#cases_casesinlast7days.

Cerny, P. "Neomedievalism, Civil War, and the New Security Dilemma: Globalization as Durable Disorder." *Civil War*, Spring, 1998.

Chayka, K. "Why Is the Middle of the Art Market Vanishing." Hyperallergic: *Senstive to Art & It's Discontents*, January 25, 2013.

Chestang Jr., C., J. "The U.S. Army Officer Corps: Changing with the Times." ResearchGate, March 15, 2006.

Chinni, D. "Income Inequality Gap Widens Among U.S. Communities Over 30 Years." *PBS The Rundown* 2011.

Coates, D. "Poverty in America: Half-Forgotten or Totally Forgotten." *The Huffington Post*, 2013.

Collins, T. "Wells Fargo Protest in San Francisco: Dozens Arrested Outside Shareholder Meeting." *HuffPostLive*, April 24, 2012.

Conger, C. "Top 10 American Political Dynasties." *How Stuff Works*, http://www.howstuffworks.com.

"Coronavirus (COVID-19), Center for Disease Control and Prevention, https://www.cdc.gov/coronavirus/2019-nCoV/index.html

Coronavirus (COVID-19) Mortality Rate, Worldometer, May 14, 2020

Covert, B. "Dozens of Walmart Workers Walk Out on Strike in Miami." *Think Progress*, October 21, 2103.

Covert, B. "Walmart Workers in Seattle to Walk Out on Strike." *Think Progress*, November 12, 2013.

COVID-19 CORONAVIRUS PANDEMIC", Worldometer, October 7, 2020

Crook, C. "All This Inequality Talk Does Nothing for the Poor." *BloombergView*, 2013.

Cuccinello, H., C. "Top 20 Richest American Billionaires." *Forbes*, 2020.

Daniel H. "13 Private Schools for the Extremely Rich." *Epoch Times*, July 27, 2013.

Davidson, A. "How the Art Market Thrives on Inequality." *The New York Times*, May 30, 2012.

DeAgonia, M., Gralla, P., & Raphael, J. "Battle of the Media Ecosystems: Amazon, Apple, Google and Microsoft." *Computer World*, August 2, 2013.

DeParle, J. "Harder for Americans to Rise from Lower Rungs." *The New York Times*, January 4, 2012.

Domhoff, G. W. "Wealth, Income, and Power." *Who Rules America*, 2013.

Doyle, Alison. "The 25 Lowest Paying Jobs in America," The Balance Careers, May 21, 2020. https://www.thebalancecareers.com/top-worst-paid-jobs-2061699.

Duffin, Erin. "U.S. Household Income Distribution by Gini-coefficient 1990-2019, Statista. September 17, 2020. https://www.statista.com/statistics/219643/gini-coefficient-for-us-individuals-families-and-households.

"Earnings for Actors, Producers, and Directors." *Stage Agent*, 2013.

Edelson, J. "Breaking: Massive Black Friday Strike and Arrests Planned, As Workers Defy Wal-Mart." *Salon.com*, November 29, 2013.

Editors of the Encyclopedia Britannica, "Peasants Revolt," *Britannica.com*

Eichler, A., & McAuliff, M. "Income Inequality Reaches Gilded Age Levels, Congressional Report Finds." *The Huffington Post*, 2011.

Eidelson, J. "Breaking: California Wal-Mart Workers Strike Today, Following Stunning Florida Victory." *Salon*, November 6, 2013.

Eidelson, J. "Guest Workers Who Sparked June Walmart Supplier Walk-Out Hail Strike Wave's Spread." *The Nation.com*, November 30, 2012.

Eidelson, J. "Wal-Mart Workers Strike Target Workers Threaten to Join Black Friday Walkout." *Portside*, November 12, 2013.

Elias, N. "The Civilizing Process: Sociogenetic and Psychogenetic Investigations." *Blackwell Publishing*, 2000.

"Employment Situation Survey." *U.S Bureau of Labor Statistics*, December 6, 2013.

"Employment Situation Survey," *U.S. Bureau of Labor Statistics*, November 6, 2020. https://www.bls.gov/news.release/empsit. nr0.htm.

Enderle, Rob. "The Secrets of HP's Success: A New Standard Emerges," *ITBusinessEdge*, November 2, 2018. https://www. itbusinessedge.com/blogs/unfiltered-opinion/the-secrets-of-hps-success-a-new-standard-emerges.html

Eskenazi, J. "Sea Monsters: There's Only One America's Cup Winner. But There Are Many Losers." *San Francisco Weekly*, 2013.

"Exclusive Photos: Sean Parker's Lavish Big Sur Wedding." *Vanity Fair.Com*, September 2013.

"Facebook Closes in on New Milestone of 3 Billion Total Users Across Its Platforms." *Social Media Today*, April 29, 2020.

Fagan, K. "Tech Boom Forcing Longtime S.F. Family Out of Home." *SFGate*, 2013.

Fickenscher, Lisa. "Nearly 60 Percent of COVID-19 Business Closures Are Permanent: Report," *New York Post*, September 17, 2020. https://nypost.com/2020/09/17/majority-of-covid-19-business-closures-are-permanent-report

Finz, S. "Low Pay is Costing Billions, Study Say." *San Francisco Chronicle*, October 16, 2013.

Fitzgerald, F., S. *Wikipedia*, en.wikiquote.org/wiki/Talk:F._Scott_ Fitzgerald.

Fox, E., J. "Wal-Mart Warns Workers on Black Friday Strike." *CNN Money*, November 21, 2012.

Friedman, H., S. "The American Myth of Social Mobility." *HuffPost Business*, July 16, 2012.

Friedrichs, J. "The Meaning of the New Medievalism." *European journal of International Relations,* 2001.

Galante, M. "The 20 Most Expensive Restaurants in the U.S." *Business Insider,* October 25, 2011.

Gale, Jason and Lauerman, John."What You Need to Know about the Spreading Coronavirus," *The Washington Post,* February 25, 2020.

Garling, C. "Patent Trolls Are Damaging Our Economy." *San Francisco Chronicle: Business Report,* November 3, 2013.

"Geneaology (Family Trees of England's Rulers)." *TimeRef.com.* http://www.timeref.com/ftree.htm.

Ghitis, Frida. "This Could Be a Turning Point in the Fight Against Racism — in America and Abroad," *The Washington Post,* June 8, 2020

"Gini Coefficient." *Wikipedia: The Free Encyclopedia* 2014.

Gleason, M. "The Art World's Wealthiest One Percent: A Commentary on Life at the Top." *ArtBusiness.com.*

"Global Conflict Tracker," Council on Foreign Relations, August 17, 2021.https://www.cfr.org/global-conflict-tracker/?category=us

Graus, Franntisek. "The Late Medieval Peasant Wars," *The Journal of Peasant Studies,* Vol. 3, 1-9, February 5, 2008.

Greenhalgh, Hugh. "Religious Figures Blame LGBT+ People for Coronavirus," *Reuters,* March 9, 2020.

Gregory, S. "Corporate Scandals: Why HP Had to Oust Mark Hurd." *Time,* August 10, 2010, http://content.time.com/time/business/article/0,8599,2009617,00.html.

Terry Gross, "How the CARES Act Became a Tax-Break Bonanza for the Rich, Explained," NPR, April 30, 2020. https://www.npr.org/2020/04/30/848321204/how-the-cares-act-became-a-tax-break-bonanza-for-the-rich-explained.

Grove, A. "Best 4-Year Graduation Rates." *About.Com.*

History.com Editors, "Black Death," *History.com,* June 6, 2020.

Hobbs, J. "Peasants' Revolt: 14th Century Poll Tax Riots." *Britannia.*

Hoge, P. "Book's Portrait of Twitter's Earliest Days Isn't Pretty." *SF Business Times,* October 11-17 2013.

"Home Foreclosure Statistics." *Statistic Brain,* October 15, 2012.

Hopkins, M. "Median Home Price Hits 8-Year High." *Housingwire,* August 8, 2013.

Horowitz, Juliana Menasce; Igielnik, Ruth; and Kochhar, Rakesh. "Trends in Income and Wealth Inequality, Pew Research Center, January 7, 2020. https://www.pewsocialtrends.org/2020/01/09/trends-in-income-and-wealth-inequality

Hsu, T. "Hundreds of fast food workers strike over minimum wage." *LA Times,* July 29, 2013.

Huang, C., & Marr, C. "Raising Today's Low Capital Gains Tax Rates Could Promote Economic Efficiency and Fairness, While Helping Reduce Deficits." *Center on Budget and Policy Priorities,* 2012.

Hungerford, T. "Changes in Income Inequality Among U.S. Tax Filers between 1991 and 2006." *Economic Institute,* 2013.

Infoclutch, "Hewlett Packard Success Story," March 19, 2020. https://www.infoclutch.com/infographic/hewlett-packard-hp-company-history-timeline

Invaluable, "31 of the Most Expensive Paintings Ever Sold at Auction," Invaluable.com. https://www.invaluable.com/blog/most-expensive-painting.

Jackson, Eric. "Steve Ballmer Deserves His Due as a Great CEO," CNBC, January 17, 2018. https://www.cnbc.com/2018/01/17/steve-ballmer-deserves-his-due-as-a-great-ceo.html

"Jakob Fugger." *Wikipedia,* http://en.wikipedia.org/wiki/Jakob_Fugger.

Jilani, Z. "How Unequal We Are: The Top 5 Facts You Should Know About the Wealthiest One Percent of Americans." *Think Progress,* 2011.

Jones, S. "For Low-Wage Workers, the Fight For 15 Movement Has Been a Boon." *New York Magazine* 2018.

"Just Cause and Occupy Oakland Fight Fannie Mae and Banks." *Labor Press.Org,* December 8, 2011.

Kaplan, Juliana; Akhtar, Aliana; and Casada, Laura. "A World on Fire : Here Are All the Major Projects Happening Around the Globe Right Now," *The Business Insider.com*, June 4, 2020.

Kavoussi, B. "Top One Percent Captured 121 of All Income Gains During Recovery's First Years: Study." *The Huffington Post*, 2013.

Karmon, J. "Bill Gates' Custom-Built Home in Medina, Washington." *Huffington Post,* October 28, 2013.

"Key Players in Yahoo's CEO Succession." *SF Gate*, July 22, 2013. http://www.sfgate.com/news/article/Key-players-in-Yahoo-s-CEO-succession-3555871.php.

Khazan, O. "Can We Fight Poverty by Ending Extreme Wealth." *Washington Post*, 2013.

Kiersz, Andy and McDowell, Erin. "The 50 Most Expensive Top Private High Schools in America," *Business Insider,* August 29, 2019. https://www.businessinsider.com/most-expensive-top-private-high-schools-america-2018-12

Kilkenny, A. "Fast Food Strikes Hit 100 Cities Thursday." *The Nation*, December 4, 2013.

King, I., Frier, S., & Bass, D. "Ballmer Exit Leaves Microsoft Searching for Hero in Slump." *Bloomberg*, August 13, 2013, http://www.bloomberg.com/news/2013-08-23/ballmer-exit-leaves-microsoft-searching-for-hero-in-slump.html.

Kneebone, E., Nadeau, E., & Berube, A. "The Re-Emergence of Concentrated Poverty: Metropolitan Trends in the 2000s." *Brookings*, 2011.

Kovach, Steve. "Tim Cook Has Had a Stellar Run at Apple — Even Without Another Mega-Smash Like the IPhone," CNBC, January 15, 2020. https://www.cnbc.com/2020/01/15/apple-ceo-tim-cook-has-had-a-stellar-run-without-a-product-like-iphone.html

Levy, A., & Kucera, D. "Hewlett-Packard Reeling Accelerates CEO Succession Crisis." *Tech, Bloomberg,* Sept. 21, 2011, http://www.bloomberg.com/news/2011-09-22/hewlett-packard-shares-reeling-47-accelerates-ceo-succession-crisis-tech.html.

Liberto, J. "CEOs Earn 280 times in Pay More than Average Worker's." *CNNMoney*, 2010.

"List of Peasant Revolts," *Wikipedia*.

Liu, Jennifer. "Google Is the First Major Company to Formally Extend Work-From-Home Until Summer 2021 – Who's Next?" NBC Make It, July 27, 2020. https://www.cnbc.com/2020/07/27/google-is-first-major-company-to-extend-work-from-home-to-summer-2021.html

Livni, Ephrat, "Congress Is Facing Fury Over Cares ACT Tax Breaks for the Rich," *Quartz*, May 8, 2020. https://qz.com/1854006/congress-faces-fury-over-cares-act-tax-breaks-for-the-rich. "Congress Is Facing Fury Over Cares ACT Tax Breaks for the Rich," *Quartz*, May 8, 2020. https://qz.com/1854006/congress-faces-fury-over-cares-act-tax-breaks-for-the-rich.

LoveMoney, "The World's Richest Families,"

LoveMoney.com, March 20, 2020.https://www.lovemoney.com/gallerylist/49551/worlds-richest-families.

Lu, Marcus. "Is the American Dream Over? Here's What the Data Says," World Economic Forum, September 2, 2020. https://www.weforum.org/agenda/2020/09/social-mobility-upwards-decline-usa-us-america-economics.

Luckerson, V. "The One-Day Strike: The New Labor Weapon of Last Resort." *Time*, December 7, 2013.

Luckerson, V. "Fast Food Strikes Go Viral: Workers Expected to Protest Low Wages in 35 Cities Thursday." *Time*, http://business.time.com.

Macatee, R. "Kim Kardashian and Kanye West Not Planning Wedding at Palace of Versailles." *Eonline*, December 4, 2013.

Maldonado, Camilo. "Trump Tax Cuts Helped Billionaires Pay Less Taxes than the Working Class in 2018," *Forbes*, October 10, 2019. https://www.forbes.com/sites/camilomaldonado/2019/10/10/trump-tax-cuts-helped-billionaires-pay-less-taxes-than-the-working-class-in-2018

Maneker, M. "$14M Koons Sculptures to Lure Wealthy Latin Americans to Miami Condo Development." *ArtBase,* September 27, 2013.

Masschaele, J. *"A Regional Economy in Medieval England." Centre for Medieval Studies University of Toronto,* 1989.

Melin, Anders and Sam, Cedric. "Wall Street Gets the Flak, But Tech CEOs Get Paid All the Money," Bloomberg, July 10, 2020. https://www.bloomberg.com/graphics/2020-highest-paid-ceos

Mercier, G. "Life on $2 a Day: US Extreme Poverty." *Newsjunkiepost. com,* 2013.

Milanovic, B. "An Estimate of Average Income and Inequality in Byzantium Around Year 1000." *Review of Income and Wealth,* September 3 2006.

Mishel, Lawrence and Wolfe, Julia. "CEO Compensation Has Grown 940% Since 1978," Economic Policy Institute," August 14, 2020. https://www.epi.org/publication/ceo-compensation-2018

Mull, Amanda. "Brands Have Nothing Real to Say about Racism," TheAtlantic.com, June 3, 2020.

Murphy, R., M. "Making the Cut." *Town & Country,* May 2013.

Nania, Rachel. "Blacks, Hispanics Hit Hrder by the Coronavirus, Early U.S. Data Show," AARP, May 8, 2020. https://www.aarp. org/health/conditions-treatments/info-2020/minority-com- munities-covid-19.html

National Conference of State Legislatures (NCSL), "State Minimum Wages: 2020 Minimum Wage by State, August 20, 2020. https:// www.ncsl.org/research/labor-and-employment/state-mini- mum-wage-chart.aspx

Naughter, J. "Facebook legal battle: Why the Two Heads of the Winklevoss Twins Weren't Better than One." *The Observer,* Janauary 15, 2011.

Nicks, D. "Walmart Seeks Food Donations to Help Needy Employees." *Time.com,* November 18, 2013.

Nowacki, Lauren. "The Tiny House Movement: Tiny Home Ideas and Costs," Rocket Homes, January 6, 2020. https://www. rockethomes.com/blog/home-buying/tiny-house

Nudelman, Geoff. "The 10 Priciest Neighborhoods in America (And How They Got to Be That Way)," Robb Report, November 28, 2018. https://robbreport.com/feature/most-expensive-neighborhoods-america-2830894.

ObamaCareFacts.com, "American Health Coerage Continues to Rise," ObamaCareFacts.com, November 4, 2020.

"Occupy's Rolling Jubilee Keeps Rolling – and the Band Plays On." *Huffington Post*, November 13, 2013.

"Occupy SF Protesters Vow to Retake Justine Herman Plaza." *NBC Bay Area.com*, September 17, 2012.

Oh, K., C. "CEO Success Planning: Did Microsoft Get It Right." *JD Supra Law News*, September 5, 2013. http://www.jdsupra.com/legalnews/ceo-succession-planning-did-microsoft-g-65046.

"Oracle v. Google," Electronic Frontier Foundation, https://www.eff.org/cases/oracle-v-google

"Organisation for Economic Co-Operation and Development." *Wikipedia: The free encyclopedia,* 2014.

O'Shaugnessy, L. "50 State Universities with the Best, Worst Grad Rates." *Moneywatch,* October 1, 2012.

Pandika, M. "Global Economic Crisis Spurred 5000 Additional Suicides, Study Says." *Los Angeles Times*, September 18, 2013.

Parsons, C. "Obama on Income Inequality: 'I Take This Personally." *Politics Now, Los Angeles Times*, December 4, 2013.

Peters, Jay. "HP Has a New CEO," *The Verge,* August 22, 2019. https://www.theverge.com/2019/8/22/20828807/hp-new-ceo-dion-weisler-enrique-lores-meg-whitman

Peterson, H. "America's Most Powerful Dynasties Revealed: Rahm Emanuel and His Brothers Join Bush and Kennedy Clans on List of 50 Most Prominent Families." *Mail Online*, April 9, 2013.

Peterson, H. "McDonalds' Hotline Caught Urging Employee to Get Food Stamps." *Business Insider,* October 24, 2013.

Picchi, Aimee. "Almost Half of All Americans Work in Low-Wage Jobs," Moneywatch/CBS News, December 2, 2019. https://www.cbsnews.com/news/minimum-wage-2019-almost-half-of-all-americans-work-in-low-wage-jobs.

Pisani, Bob. "Wealth Gap Grows as Rising Corporate Profits Boost Stock Holdings Controlled by Richest Households," *Trader Talk*, August 27, 2020. https://www.cnbc.com/2020/08/27/wealth-gap-grows-as-rising-corporate-profits-boost-stock-holdings-con-trolled-by-richest-households.html#

Pozzebon, Stephano; Kiley, Sam; and Said-Moorhouse, Lauren, "Protestors Flood Venezuelan Streets to Call for Change," CNN. com, February 12, 2019.

Project Casting, "The Average Salary of an Actor," Project Casting, April 5, 2020. https://www.projectcasting.com/tips-and-advice/actors-salary.

Ramsey, Dave. "2020 Home Prices: What You Need to Know," DaveRamsey. com https://www.daveramsey.com/blog/housing-trends

Reich, R. "Why the Anger?" *The Huffington Post*, 2013.

"Relationship Between Poverty and Overweight or Obesity." *FRAC: Food Research and Action Center.*

Ritholtz, B. "Poverty Spikes in America...While the Government Throws Money at the Super-Elite." *The Big Picture*, 2013.

Rogers, S. "US Poverty: Where are the Super Poor." *The Guardian*, 2011.

Ross, Martha and Bateman, Nicole. "Low-Wage Work Is More Pervasive Than You Think, and There Aren't Enough 'Good Jobs' to Go Around," Brookings, November 21, 2019. https://www.brookings.edu/blog/the-avenue/2019/11/21/low-wage-work-is-more-pervasive-than-you-think-and-there-arent-enough-good-jobs-to-go-around.

Routt, David. "The Economic Impact of the Black Death," Eh.Net, Economic History Association, https://eh.net/encyclopedia/the-economic-impact-of-the-black-death

Sauter, M., Hess, E., E., M., & Frohlich, T. "24/7." *Wall Street*," November 15, 2013.

Schaeffer, Katherine. "6 Facts about Economic Inequality in the U.S." FACTTank, Pew Research Center, February 7, 2020, https://www.pewresearch.org/fact-tank/20202/02/07/6-facts-about-economic-inequality-in-the-u-s

Schilling, Owen. "The Economic Impact of the Black Plague," ArcStoryMaps, November 21, 2019.

Schmidt, Ann. "These Are the Most Expensive Restaurants in the U.S.," *Fox Business*, November 29, 2019. https://www.foxbusiness.com/money/10-most-expensive-restaurants-us

Schwartz, Felicia. "Coronavirus Sparks Rise in Anti-Semitic Sentiment, Researchers Say," *The Wall Street Journal*, April 20, 2020.

Semega, Jessica; Killar, Melissa; Shrider, EmilyA.; and Creamer, John. "Income and Poverty in the United States: 2019", *U.S. Census*, Report#P60-270, September 15, 2020. https://www.census.gov/library/publications/2020/demo/p60-270.html

Sherman, Natalie. "George Floyd: Why Are Companies Speaking Up this Time?" BBC.com, June 7, 2020.

Siegel, J. "When Steve Jobs Got Fired by Apple." *ABC News*, October 6, 2011.

Snyder, M. "21 Statistics About the Explosive Growth of Poverty in America that Everyone Should Know." *Investment Watch*, 2013.

Social Media Today, "Facebook Closes in on New Milestone of 3 Billion Total Users Across Its Platforms, April 29, 2020.

Squeo, A., M. "Microsoft's Lack of CEO Succession Plan a Lesson for Other Companies." *Forbes*, September 25, 2013. http://www.forbes.com/sites/annemariesqueo/2013/09/25/microsofts-lack-of-ceo-succession-plan-lesson-for-other-companies.

Stiglitz, J., E. "Of the 1%, by the 1%, for the 1%." *Vanity Fair*, 2011

Strebel, P. "Pitfalls in CEO Succession." *IMD*, November 2012. http://www.imd.org/research/challenges/TC080-12-ceo-succession-appointing-paul-strebel.cfm.

Sullivan, J. "Learn from HP's Errors – A checklist for Designing an Effective Succession Plan." *Ere Webinars*, August 16, 2010. http://www.ere.net/2010/08/16/learn-from-hp%E2%80%99s-errors-a-checklist-for-designing-an-effective-succession-plan.

Sullivan, Paul, "Private Schools Hold New Attention for Rich Parents," *The New York Times*, October 12, 2020. https://www.nytimes.com/2020/10/09/your-money/private-schools-wealthy-parents.html

Suneson, G. "What are the 25 lowest paying jobs in the US? Women usually hold them." *USAToday.com*, April 4, 2019.

Swanson, Ann; Mozur,Paul; and Zhong, Raymond. "Trump's Attacks Could Fracture Internet Further," *San Francisco Chronicle*, Business Report: Section C, August 18 2020. P. C1-3.

Tahmincioglu, E. "The 8 Lowest-Paying Jobs in America." *NBCNews. com*, Nov. 20, 2013.

Tam, P., Lublin, J., S., & Worthen, B. "H-P Looks Beyond Its Ranks." *Wall Street Journal Online*, August 9, 2010. http://online.wsj.com/news/articles/SB10001424052748704268004575417682006400508.

TBS Report, "10 Richest Billionaires in the World in 2020," The Business Standard, October 15, 2020. https://tbsnews.net/world/10-richest-billionaires-world-2020-145480.

Teamster Nation. "Truck Drivers Who Haul for Walmart Strike at the Port of LA." *Labor's Edge*: Views from the California Labor Movement, November 18, 2013.

Telford, T. "Income inequality in America is the highest it's been since Census Bureau started tracking it, data shows." *Washington Post,* 2019.

"The Challenge of Our Time," *World Food Hunger Program USA*. https://www.wfpusa.org/explore/wfps-work/drivers-of-hunger/climate-change

"The Military Caste System." *TOD Advisor's Notebook*, www.tourofdutyinfo.com.

The VAR Guy. "CEO Succession Planning: What HP Can Learn from IBM, Apple." *The VAR Guy*, October 25, 2011. http://thevarguy.com/information-technology-channel-partner-programs/ceo-succession-planning-what-hp-can-learn-ibm-apple.

Thompson, D. "A Giant Statistical Round-Up of the Income Inequality Crisis in 16 Charts." *The Atlantic* 2012.

Thorbecke, Catherine. "Nearly half of the world' entire wealth is in the handsofmillionaires," *ABCNews,* October 22, 2019. https://abcnews.go.com/Business/half-worlds-entire-wealth-hands-millionaires/story?id=66440320#

"Tiny Homes: Simple Shelter by Lloyd Kahn," *Tumbleweed Tiny House Company* (2014).

TMZ Taff. "Kim and Kanye: We Want Dr. Dre's Land for Our Mega Mansion." *TMZ*, November 18, 2013.

Toh, Michelle. "Black Lives Matter: Facebook, Netflix, Peloton, and Other Companies Take a Stand as Protests Sweep America," CNN.Com, June 1, 2020.

Tuttle, Brad. "Here's How Much Everyone Gets Paid on a Movie Set — From the Key Grip to the Director," *Money*, October 3, 2017. https://money.com/movie-jobs-how-much-get-paid-actors.

"Unemployment Insurance Weekly Claims," Department of Labor, November 5, 2020. https://www.dol.gov/ui/data.pdf

U.S. Census Bureau, "Income, Poverty and Health Insurance Coverage in the United States: 2019, U.S. Census Bureau, September 15, 2020. https://www.census.gov/newsroom/press-releases/2020/income-poverty.html#

Vance, A. "Steve Ballmer Reboots." *Bloomberg Businessweek,* January 12, 2012. http://www.businessweek.com/magazine/steve-ballmer-reboots-01122012.html.

"Venezuela Crisis in 300 Words," BBC.com, January 9, 2020.

Vogel, C. "At $142.4 Million, Triptych Is the Most Expensive Artwork Ever Sold at an Auction." *The New York Times*, November 12, 2013.

Walls, Justin. "The Top 100 Instagram Influencers in the World," Pressboard, April 8, 2020. https://www.pressboardmedia.com/magazine/the-top-100-instagram-influencers-in-the-world

"Wal-Mart Workers in 12 States Stage Historic Strikes, Protests Against Workplace Retaliation." *Democracy Now,* October 10, 2012. http://www.democracynow.org.

"What is the Tiny House Movement." *The Tiny Life*, 2013.

"Why the Art Market Profits When Social Inequality Is Growing." *HuffPost Arts & Culture*, September 17, 2012.

Weinmann, K., & Groth, A. "The 10 Largest Family Businesses in the U.S." *Business Insider*, November 17, 2011.

Williams, P. "From the New Middle Ages to a New Dark Age: The Decline of the State and U.S. Strategy." *Strategic Studies Institute,* June 2008.

Wise Sloth. "An Overdue Critique of the American Military Caste System." *Wisesloth,* June 4, 2011. http://wisesloth.wordpress.com.

Wollan, M. "Oakland's Port Shuts Down as Protesters March on Waterfront." *New York Times,* Nov. 2, 2011.

"Women's Earnings: The Pay Gap." *Catalyst,* March 2, 2020.

Woodruff, M. "Heirs and Heiresses of the Wealthiest People in America." *Yahoo Finance,* December 9, 2013.

Woods, Hiatt. "How Billionaires Saw Their Net Worth Increase by Half A Trillion Dollars During the Pandemic," *Business Insider,* October 30, 2020. https://www.businessinsider.com/billionaires-net-worth-increases-coronavirus-pandemic-2020-7.

"Your Money, Your Life." *The Economist,* 2013.

Worldometers, https://www.worldometers.info/coronavirus

Books

Ariely, D. *Wealth Inequality,* Dan Ariely 2010.

Batchelor, S. *Medieval History for Dummies,* Wiley, 2010.

Batou, J., & Szlajfer, H. Chapter Ten: Economic and Political Divisions in Medieval and Early Modern Europe, in *Studies in Critical Social Sciences,* 2009.

Batou, J., & Szlajfer, H. The Problem of the Inequality of Economic Development in Europe in the Later Middle Ages, in *Studies in Critical Social Sciences,* 2009.

Bekar, C., T., & Reed, C., G. Land Markets and Inequality, Evidence from Medieval England, *University of Oxford,* October 2009.

Bekar, C., T., & Reed, C. Risk, Asset Markets and Inequality: Evidence from Medieval England, *University of Oxford,* October 2009.

Bilton, N. *Hatching Twitter: A True Story of Money, Power, Friendship, and Betrayal,* Portfolio, 2013.

Bishop, M. *The Middle Ages,* A Mariner Book, Houghton Mifflin, 2001.

Cantor, N., F. *The Civilization of the Middle Ages,* Harper Perennial, 1963, 1994.

Cleough, J. *The Medici: A Tale of Fifteen Generations,* Robert Hale & Co, 1975.

Dadush, Uri; Dervis, Kemal; Milsom, Sarah Puritz; and Stancil, Bennett. *Inequality in America: Facts, Trends, and International Perspective,* Washington, DC, Brookings Institution Press, 2012.

Dommanget, Maurice. *La Jacquerie,* f. Maspero, 1971

Doehaerd, R. *The Early Middle Ages in the West: Economy and Society,* North-Holland Publishing Company, 1978, 2010.

Dyer, C. *Making a Living in the Middle Ages,* Yale University Press, 2002.

Freeland, C. Plutocrats: *The Rise of the New Global Super-Rich and the Fall of Everyone Else,* The Penguin Press, 2012.

Gies, F., & Gies, J. *Life in a Medieval Village,* Harper Perennial, 1990.

Hall, T., C. *The Middle Ages,* Alpha, 2009.

Hanawalt, B., A. *The Ties that Bound: Peasant Families in Medieval England,* Oxford University Press, 1986.

Hibber, C. *The Rise and Fall of the Medici,* Allen Lane, 1974.

Holmes, G. The Oxford Illustrated History of Medieval Europe, *Oxford University Press,* 1988, 2001.

Medieval England, Captivating History, 2020

Mills, D. *The Middle Ages,* Memoria Press, 2012.

Mollat, M., & Wolff, P. *The Popular Revolutions of the Late Middle Ages,* Allen & Unwin, 1973.

Noah, T. *The Great Divergence,* Bloomsbury Press, 2012.

O'Hayon, G., L. B. *Big Men, Godfathers, and Zealots: Challenges to the State in the New Middle Ages,* University of Pittsburgh, 2003.

Schofield, P., R. *Peasant and Community in Medieval Community 1200-1500,* Palgrave Macmillan, 2003.

Stiglitz, J., E. *The Price of Inequality: How Today's Divided Society Endangers Our Future,* W. W. Norton & Company, 2012.

The Black Death, Captivating History, 2019

The Middle Ages, Captivating History, 2019.

Thorndike, Lynn. *The History of Medieval Europe,* Houghton Mifflin Company, 2019.

Tierney, B. *Western Europe in the Middle Ages,* McGraw-Hill College, 1999.

Tuchman, Barbara. *A Distant Mirror.* Alfred A. Knopf, 1978

Wickham, Chris, *Medieval Europe,* Yale University Press, 2016

ENDNOTES

1 Dan Ariely, "Wealth Inequality," *Dan Ariely* (2010).
2 Zaid Jilani, "How Unequal We Are: The Top 5 Facts You Should Know About the Wealthiest One Percent of Americans," *Think Progress,* 2011.
3 Jennifer Liberto, "CEOs Earn 380 times in Pay More than Average Worker's," *CNNMoney* . 2012.
4 "The State of America's Children 2020: Income and Wealth Inequality," Children's Defense Fund, https://www.childrensdefense.org/policy/resources/soac-2020-income-inequality.
5 Juliana Menasce Horowitz, Ruth Igielnik, and Rakesh Kochhar, "Trends in Income and Wealth Inequality, Pew Research Center, January 7, 2020. https://www.pewsocialtrends.org/2020/01/09/trends-in-income-and-wealth-inequality
6 Ibid.
7 Katherine Schaeffer, "6 Facts about Economic Inequality in the U.S." FACTTank, Pew Research Center, February 7, 2020, https://www.pewresearch.org/fact-tank/20202/02/07/6-facts-about-economic-inequality-in-the-u-s
8 Phil Williams, "From the New Middle Ages to a New Dark Age: The Decline of the State and U.S. Strategy, Strategic Studies Institute, Published by the U.S. Government, June 2008, p. ix.
9 Ibid., p. 3.
10 Gregory Laurent Baudin O'Hayon, *Big Men, Godfathers, and Zealots: Challenges to the State in the New Middle Ages,* University of Pittsburgh: Dissertations and Theses, 2003.
11 Jorg Friedrichs, "The Meaning of the New Medievalism," *European Journal of International Relations,*Vol 7, No. 4, 20901.
12 Philip Cerny, "Neomedievalism, Civil War, and the New Security Dilemma: Globalization as Durable Disorder," *Civil Wars,* Vol. 1, No. 1, Spring 1998, pp. 34-64.
13 Williams, pp. 3, 9.

14 Ibid., p. 19.

15 Ibid., p. 34.

16 Renee Doehaerd, *The Early Middle Ages in the West: Economy and Society,* New York: North-Holland Publishing Company, 1978, p. xv.

17 Ibid., p. 1

18 Ibid., p. 6.

19 Ibid., pp. 7-8.

20 Ibid., p. 28.

21 Ibid., p. 29.

22 Ibid., pp. 57-58.

23 Ibid., p. 151.

24 Ibid., p. 162.

25 Ibid., p. 193.

26 Branko Milanovic, "An Estimate of Average Income and Inequality in Byzantium Around Year 1000," *Review of Income and Wealth,* Series 52, Number 3, September 2006, p. 449-470.

27 The Gini coefficient is based on the theory of an Italian statistician and sociologist, Corrado Gini, first presented in a 1912 paper. It has nothing to do with my name, though it seems an appropriate name for an inequality index, since I'm writing about this.

28 Cliff T. Bekar and Clyde G. Reed, "Land Markets and Inequality: Evidence from Medieval England," Sept. 13, 2011, working draft.

29 Ibid., p. 3.

30 Phillip R. Schofield, *Peasant and Community in Medieval Community 1200-1500.* New York: Palgrave Macmillan, 2003, p. 76.

31 Christopher Dyer, *Making a Living in the Middle Ages: The People of Britain: 850-1520,* New Haven, Yale University Press, 2002, p. 183.

32 Cliff T. Bekar and Clyde Reed, "Risk, Asset Markets and Inequality: Evidence from Medieval England," *University of Oxford: Discussion Papers in Economic and Social History,* Number 79, October 2009, p. 16.

33 James Masschaele, "A Regional Economy in Medieval England," Centre for Medieval Studies; a Thesis for the Ph.D. Degree at the University of Toronto, 1989.

34 Ibid., pp. 274-275.

35 Ibid., p. 275.

36 Jean Batou and Henryk Szlajfer, Editors, "Chapter Ten: Economic and Political Divisions in Medieval and Early Modern Europe," in *Studies in Critical Social Sciences, Vol .16: Western Europe, Eastern Europe and World Development 13th-18th Centuries: Collection of Essays of Marian Malowist.* Boston: Brill Academic Publishers, 2009, p 231.

37 Batou and Szlajfer, Chapter Seven: "The Problem of the Inequality of Economic Development in Europe in the Later Middle Ages," pp. 162-162.

38 Ibid., p. 166.

39 Michel Mollat and Philippe Wolff, *The Popular Revolutions of the Late Middle Ages:* New York: Allen & Unwin, 1973.

40 Norbert Elias, *The Civilizing Process: Sociogenetic and Psychogenetic Investigations,* Blackwell Publishing, 2000.

41 "Popular Revolt in the Late-Medieval Europe," *Wikipedia,* 2014.

42 Jeff Hobbs, "Peasants' Revolt: 14th Century Poll Tax Riots," *Britannia.*

43 Ibid.

44 "Popular Revolt in Late-Medieval Europe," Wikipedia.

45 Sarah Jones, "For Low-Wage Workers, the Fight for 15 Movement Has Been a Boon," *New York Magazine,* 2018.

46 Joe Nocera, "House of Cards," *The New York Times,* June 21, 2012

47 ATTOM Data Solutions "U.S. Foreclosure Activity Drops to 13-Year Low in 2018," 2019.

48 Kevin Fagan, "Tech Boom Forcing Longtime S.F. Family Out of Home," *SFGate,* 2013.

49 "Tiny Homes: Simple Shelter by Lloyd Kahn," *Tumbleweed Tiny House Company,* 2014.

50 Lauren Nowacki, "The Tiny House Movement: Tiny Home Ideas and Costs," Rocket Homes, January 6, 2020. https://www.rockethomes.com/blog/home-buying/tiny-house

51 "What is the Tiny House Movement?" *The Tiny Life.* 2013.

52 "1. In the Beginning," *America's Cup,* 2014.

53 "America's Cup," *Wikipedia: The Free Encyclopedia,* 2014.

54 Joe Eskenazi, "Sea Monsters: There's Only One America's Cup Winner. But There Are Many Losers," *San Francisco Weekly,* 2013.

55 Ibid., p. 15.

56 Taylor Telford, "Income inequality in America is the highest it's been since Census Bureau started tracking it, data shows." *Washington Post,* September 26, 2019.

57 Wikipedia Contributors, "Gini Coefficient," *Wikipedia: The Free Encylcopedia.* 2014.

58 Wikipedia Contributors, "Organisation for Economic Co-Operation and Development," 2014.

59 Alexander Eichler and Michael McAuliff, "Income Inequality Reaches Gilded Age Levels, Congressional Report Finds," *The Huffington Post.* 2011.

60 Bob Pisani, "Wealth Gap Grows as Rising Corporate Profits Boost Stock Holdings Controlled by Richest Households," *Trader Talk,* August 27, 2020. https://www.cnbc.com/2020/08/27/wealth-gap-grows-as-rising-corporate-profits-boost-stock-holdings-controlled-by-richest-households.html#

61 Ibid.

62 Dante Chinni, "Income Inequality Gap Widens Among U.S. Communities Over 30 Years," *PBS The Rundown,* 2011.

63 Derek Thompson, "A Giant Statistical Round-Up of the Income Inequality Crisis in 16 Charts," *The Atlantic,* 2012.

64 S. M., "Your Money, Your Life," *The Economist,* 2013.

65 Olga Khazan, "Can We Fight Poverty by Ending Extreme Wealth?" *Washington Post.,* 2013.

66 Clive Crook, "All This Inequality Talk Does Nothing for the Poor," *BloombergView.* 2013.

67 Salvatore Babones, "More than 46 Million Americans Still in Poverty," *Inequality.org,* 2012.

68 Gilbert Mercier, "Life on $2 a Day: US Extreme Poverty," *Newsjunkiepost. com,* 2013.

69 Elizabeth Kneebone, Carey Nadeau, and Alan Berube, "The Re-Emergence of Concentrated Poverty: Metropolitan Trends in the 2000s," *Brookings,* 2011.

70 Simon Rogers, "US Poverty: Where are the Super Poor?" *The Guardian,* 2011.

71 Jessica Semega, Melissa Killar, Emily A. Shrider, and John Creamer, "Income and Poverty in the United States: 2019", U.S. Census, Report#P60-270, September 15, 2020. https://www.census.gov/library/publications/2020/demo/p60-270.html

72 "Unemployment Insurance Weekly Claims," Department of Labor, November 5, 2020. https://www.dol.gov/ui/data.pdf

73 David Coates, "Poverty in America: Half-Forgotten or Totally Forgotten?" *The Huffington Post,* 2013.

74 Bonnie Kavoussi, "Top One Percent Captured 121 of All Income Gains During Recovery's First Years: Study," *The Huffington Post,* 2013.

75 Barry Ritholtz, "Poverty Spikes in America…While the Government Throws Money at the Super-Elite," *The Big Picture,* 2013.

76 Michael Snyder, "21 Statistics About the Explosive Growth of Poverty in America that Everyone Should Know," *Investment Watch,* 2013.

77 Ritholtz.

78 Joseph E. Stiglitz, "Of the 1%, by the 1%, for the 1%," *Vanity Fair,* 2011.

79 Pisani.

80 G. William Domhoff, "Wealth, Income, and Power," *Who Rules America: Wealth, Income, and Power,* 2013.

81 Thomas Hungerford, "Changes in Income Inequality Among U.S. Tax Filers between 1991 and 2006," *Economic Institute,* 2013.

82 Chye-Ching Huang and Chuck Marr, "Raising Today's Low Capital Gains Tax Rates Could Promote Economic Efficiency and Fairness, While Helping Reduce Deficits," *Center on Budget and Policy Priorities,* 2012.

83 Lawrence Mishel and Julia Wolfe, "CEO Compensation Has Grown 940% Since 1978," Economic Policy Institute," August 14, 2020. https://www.epi.org/publication/ceo-compensation-2018

84 Robert Reich, "Why the Anger?" *The Huffington Post,* 2013.

85 Brian Tierney, *Western Europe in the Middle Ages: 300-1475, 6*ᵗʰ *Edition,* New York: McGraw-Hill College, 1999, p. 17.

86 Timothy C. Hall, *The Middle Ages,* Alpha, 2009.

87 Tierney, p. 58.

88 Stephen Batchelor, *Medieval History for Dummies,* West Sussex, England, Wiley, 2010, pp. 25-26.

89 Tierney, p. 71.

90 Ibid., p. 104.

91 Batchelor, p. 49.

92 Nick Bilton, *Hatching Twitter: A True Story of Money, Power, Friendship, and Betrayal,* New York: Portfolio Hardcover, 2013.

93 Patrick Hoge, "Book's Portrait of Twitter's Earliest Days Isn't Pretty," *SF Business Times,* October 11-17, 2013, p. 3.

94 John Naughter, "Facebook legal battle: Why the Two Heads of the Winklevoss Twins Weren't Better than One," *The Observer,* Janauary 15, 2011.

95 Social Media Today, "Facebook Closes in on New Milestone of 3 Billion Total Users Across Its Platforms, April 29, 2020.

96 Joel Siegel, "When Steve Jobs Got Fired by Apple," ABC News, October 6, 2011.

97 Michael deAgonia, Preston Gralla, and JR Raphael, "Battle of the Media Ecosystems: Amazon, Apple, Google and Microsoft," Computer World, August 2, 2013.

98 Hall, pp. 72-73.

99 Caleb Garling, "Patent Trolls Are Damaging Our Economy," *San Francisco Chronicle: Business Report,* November 2, 2013, Section D, p. 1.

100 "Oracle v. Google," Electronic Frontier Foundation, https://www.eff.org/cases/oracle-v-google

101 Jennifer Liu, "Google Is the First Major Company to Formally Extend Work-From-Home Until Summer 2021 – Who's Next?" NBC Make It, July 27, 2020. https://www.cnbc.com/2020/07/27/google-is-first-major-company-to-extend-work-from-home-to-summer-2021.html

102 Hall, p. 83.

103 Ibid., p. 86.

104 Jonathan Barr, ""Behind the Scenes, Apple Planned Jobs' Succession by the Book," *Business & Money,* October 7, 2011. http://business.time.com/2011/10/07/behind-the-scenes-apple-planned-jobs-succession-by-the-book/

105 Josh Bersin: "The Real Succession Plan for Steve Jobs: Apple Thinks Different with Apple University," The Business of Talent, Bersin by Deloitte, August 26, 2011, http://www.bersin.com/blog/post/The-Real-Succession-Plan-For-Steve-Jobs-Apple-Thinks-Different-With-Apple-University.aspx

106 Steve Kovach, "Tim Cook Has Had a Stellar Run at Apple — Even Without Another Mega-Smash Like the IPhone," CNBC, January 15, 2020. https://www.cnbc.com/2020/01/15/apple-ceo-tim-cook-has-had-a-stellar-run-without-a-product-like-iphone.html

107 Steve Ballmer, Chief Executive Officer, Microsoft News Center, http://www.microsoft.com/en-us/news/exec/steve/default.aspx

108 Ashley Vance, "Steve Ballmer Reboots" *Bloomberg Businessweek,* January 12, 2012. http://www.businessweek.com/magazine/steve-ballmer-reboots-01122012.html

109 Ibid.

110 Ian King, Sarah Frier & Dina Bass, "Ballmer Exit Leaves Microsoft Searching for Hero in Slump," Bloomberg, August 13, 2013, http://www.bloomberg.com/news/2013-08-23/ballmer-exit-leaves-microsoft-searching-for-hero-in-slump.html

111 Kenneth C. Oh, "CEO Success Planning: Did Microsoft Get It Right?" JD Supra Law News, September 5, 2013. http://www.jdsupra.com/legalnews/ceo-succession-planning-did-microsoft-g-65046/

112 Anne Marie Squeo, "Microsoft's Lack of CEO Succession Plan a Lesson for Other Companies, *Forbes,*" September 25, 2013, http://www.forbes.com/sites/annemariesqueo/2013/09/25/microsofts-lack-of-ceo-succession-plan-lesson-for-other-companies

113 Eric Jackson, "Steve Ballmer Deserves His Due as a Great CEO," CNBC, January 17, 2018. https://www.cnbc.com/2018/01/17/steve-ballmer-deserves-his-due-as-a-great-ceo.html

114 Sean Gregory, "Corporate Scandals: Why HP Had to Oust Mark Hurd," Time, August 10, 2010, http://content.time.com/time/business/article/0,8599,2009617,00.html

115 The VAR Guy, "CEO Succession Planning: What HP Can Learn from IBM, Apple," The VAR Guy, October 25, 2011. http://thevarguy.com/information-technology-channel-partner-programs/ceo-succession-planning-what-hp-can-learn-ibm-apple.

116 Dr. John Sullivan, "Learn from HP's Errors – A checklist for Designing an Effective Succession Plan," Ere Webinars, August 16, 2010. http://www.ere.net/2010/08/16/learn-from-hp's-errors-a-checklist-for-designing-an-effective-succession-plan

117 Pui-Wing Tam, Joann S. Lublin, and Ben Worthen, "H-P Looks Beyond Its Ranks," Wall street Journal Online, August 9, 2010, http://online.wsj.com/news/articles/SB10001424052748704268004575417682006400508

118 Art Levy and Danielle Kucera, "Hewlett-Packard Reeling Accelerates CEO Succession Crisis: Tech, Bloomberg, Sept. 21, 2011, http://www.bloomberg.com/news/2011-09-22/hewlett-packard-shares-reeling-47-accelerates-ceo-succession-crisis-tech.html

119 Rob Enderle, "The Secrets of HP's Success: A New Standard Emerges," ITBusinessEdge, November 2, 2018. https://www.itbusinessedge.com/blogs/unfiltered-opinion/the-secrets-of-hps-success-a-new-standard-emerges.html

120 Jay Peters, "HP Has a New CEO," The Verge, August 22, 2019. https://www.theverge.com/2019/8/22/20828807/hp-new-ceo-dion-weisler-enrique-lores-meg-whitman

121 Infoclutch, "Hewlett Packard Success Story," March 19, 2020. https://www.infoclutch.com/infographic/hewlett-packard-hp-company-history-timeline

122 Professor Paul Strebel, "Pitfalls in CEO Succession," IMD, November 2012, http://www.imd.org/research/challenges/TC080-12-ceo-succession-appointing-paul-strebel.cfm

123 "Key Players in Yahoo's CEO Succession," SF Gate, July 22, 2013, http://www.sfgate.com/news/article/Key-players-in-Yahoo-s-CEO-succession-3555871.php

124 "America's Self-Made Women 2020, Profile: #33 Marissa Mayer, CEO, Yahoo," Forbes, https://www.forbes.com/profile/marissa-mayer/?sh=138370d74c5e

125 Dorothy Mills, *The Middle Ages"* (citing Joan Evans, *Mediaeval France*, New York, Oxford University Press), New York: Memoria Press, 2012, p. 168.

126 Ibid., p. 168.

127 Ibid., p. 196.

128 Ibid., p. 197.

129 http://en.wikipedia.org/wiki/Piers_Plowman

130 Mills, citing *The Vision of Piers Plowman*, pp. 197-198.

131 Mills, citing *The Second Shepherd's Play*, pp. 199-200.

132 Frances and Joseoph Gies, *Life in a Medieval Village*, New York: HarperPerennial, 1991, initial hardcover published in 1990, pp. 133.

133 Morris Bishop, *The Middle Ages*, A Mariner Book, Houghton Mifflin, 2001, p. 215.

134 Gies, pp. 141-142.

135 Eve Tahmincioglu, "The 8 Lowest-Paying Jobs in America," NBCNews. com, Accessed Nov. 20, 2013.

136 Aimee Picchi, "Almost Half of All Americans Work in Low-Wage Jobs," Moneywatch/CBS News, December 2, 2019. https://www. cbsnews.com/news/minimum-wage-2019-almost-half-of-all-ameri-cans-work-in-low-wage-jobs.

137 Martha Ross and Nicole Bateman, "Low-Wage Work Is More Pervasive Than You Think, and There Aren't Enough 'Good Jobs' to Go Around," Brookings, November 21, 2019. https://www. brookings.edu/blog/the-avenue/2019/11/21/low-wage-work-is-more-pervasive-than-you-think-and-there-arent-enough-good-jobs-to-go-around.

138 Ibid.

139 Alison Doyle, "The 25 Lowest Paying Jobs in America," The Balance Careers, May 21, 2020. https://www.thebalancecareers.com/top-worst-paid-jobs-2061699.

140 Mark Sauter, Alexander E.M. Hess, and Thomas Frohlich, 24/7 Wall Street, November 15, 2013,

141 Anders Melin and Cedric Sam, "Wall Street Gets the Flak, But Tech CEOs Get Paid All the Money," Bloomberg, July 10, 2020. https:// www.bloomberg.com/graphics/2020-highest-paid-ceos

142 Ibid.

143 Mark Sauter.

144 Stacy Finz, "Low Pay is Costing Billions, Study Says," Business Report, The Chronicle with Bloomberg, San Francisco Chronicle, October 16, 2013, p. C1.

145 Denver Nicks, "Walmart Seeks Food Donations to Help Needy Employees," Business & Money, Time.com, November 18, 2013.

146 Tiffany Hsu, "Hundreds of fast food workers strike over minimum wage," Business, LA Times, July 29, 2013.

147 Tiffany Hsu, "Hundreds of fast food workers strike over minimum wage," Business, LA Times, July 29, 2013.

148 Victor Luckerson, "Fast Food Strikes Go Viral: Workers Expected to Protest Low Wages in 35 Cities Thursday," Business & Money, *Time*, http://business.time.com.

149 "Wal-Mart Workers in 12 States Stage Historic Strikes, Protests Against Workplace Retaliation," *Democracy Now*, October 10, 2012. http://www.democracynow.org

150 Emily Jane Fox, "Wal-Mart Warns Workers on Black Friday Strike," CNN Money, November 21, 2012.

151 Josh Eidelson, "Guest Workers Who Sparked June Walmart Supplier Walk-Out Hail Strike Wave's Spread," *The Nation.com*, November 30, 2012.

152 Bryce Covert, "Dozens of Walmart Workers Walk Out on Strike in Miami," *Think Progress*, October 21, 2103.

153 Josh Eidelson, "Breaking: California Wal-Mart Workers Strike Today, Following Stunning Florida Victory," *Salon*, November 6, 2013.

154 Bruce Covert, "Walmart Workers in Seattle to Walk Out on Strike," *Think Progress*, November 12, 2013.

155 Teamster Nation, "Truck Drivers Who Haul for Walmart Strike at the Port of LA," *Labor's Edge*: Views from the California Labor Movement, November 18, 2013.

156 Josh Eidelson, "Wal-Mart Workers Strike Target Workers Threaten to Join Black Friday Walkout," *Portside*, November 12, 2013.

157 Hayley Peterson, "McDonalds' Hotline Caught Urging Employee to Get Food Stamps, *Business Insider*, October 24, 2013.

158 National Conference of State Legislatures (NCSL), "State Minimum Wages: 2020 Minimum Wage by State, August 20, 2020. https://www.ncsl.org/research/labor-and-employment/state-minimum-wage-chart.aspx

159 Grant Suneson, "What are the 25 lowest paying jobs in the US? Women usually hold them," USAToday.com, April 4, 2019.

160 Hayley C. Cuccinello, "Top 20 Richest American Billionaires, *Forbes*, 2020.

161 Mills, p. 229.

162 Bishop, p. 178,

163 Ibid.

164 Tierney, p. 279.

165 Mills, p. 237.

166 Tierney, p. 280.

167 "Women's Earnings: The Pay Gap," Knowledge Center, *Catalyst*, March 2, 2020.

168 Bishop, pp. 77-78.

169 Ibid., p. 78.

170 Wise Sloth, "An Overdue Critique of the American Military Caste System," June 4, 2011. http://wisesloth.wordpress.com.

171 Lieutenant Colonel Carlen J. Chestang, Jr., "The U.S. Army Officer Corps: Changing with the Times," March 15, 2006,

172 Wise Sloth.

173 "The Military Caste System," TOD Advisor's Notebook, www.tou-rofdutyinfo.com.

174 Barbara A. Hanawalt, *The Ties that Bound: Peasant Families in Medieval England*, New York: Oxford University Press, 1986; paperback, 1988.

175 Ibid., pp. 3-4.

176 Ibid., p. 24.

177 Ibid., p. 68.

178 Ibid., pp. 82-83.

179 Ibid., p. 111.

180 Ibid., p. 121.

181 Karlee Weinmann and Aimee Groth, "The 10 Largest Family Businesses in the U.S.," Business Insider, November 17, 2011.

182 David Bain, "The World's Top 750 Family Businesses Rank," *Family Capital*, March 3, 2020. https://www.famcap.com/the-worlds-750-biggest-family-businesses

183 Ibid.

184 Jason DeParle, "Harder for Americans to Rise from Lower Rungs," *The New York Times*, January 4, 2012.

185 Howard Steven Friedman, "The American Myth of Social Mobility," *HuffPost Business*, July 16, 2012.

186 "Geneaology (Family Trees of England's Rulers), TimeRef.com, http://www.timeref.com/ftree.htm

187 Hall, p. 106.

188 "The Medici Family," citing the work of James Cleough, *The Medici: A Tale of Fifteen Generations*, London: Robert Hale & Co, 1975, and Christopher Hibber, *The Rise and Fall of the Medici*, London: Allen Lane, 1974.

189 "Jakob Fugger," Wikipedia, http://en.wikipedia.org/wiki/Jakob_Fugger

190 "America's 60 Families," NNDB: Tracking the Entire World, http://www.nndb.com.

191 Hayley Peterson, "America's Most Powerful Dynasties Revealed: Rahm Emanuel and His Brothers Join Bush and Kennedy Clans on List of 50 Most Prominent Families," *Mail Online*, April 9, 2013

192 Richard McGill Murphy, "Making the Cut," *Town & Country*, May 2013.

193 Peterson.

194 Cristen Conger, "Top 10 American Political Dynasties," How Stuff Works, http://www.howstuffworks.com

195 "The Ten Most Enduring Families," http://www.townandcountry-mag.com

196 Murphy.

197 Ibid.

198 LoveMoney, "The World's Richest Families," LoveMoney.com, March 20, 2020. https://www.lovemoney.com/gallerylist/49551/worlds-richest-families.

199 Tierney, pp. 214-215.

200 Ibid., p. 216.

201 Ibid., pp. 228-229.

202 Ibid., p. 312.

203 Ibid., p. 315.

204 Justin Walls, "The Top 100 Instagram Influencers in the World," Pressboard, April 8, 2020. https://www.pressboardmedia.com/magazine/the-top-100-instagram-influencers-in-the-world

205 George Holmes, *The Oxford Illustrated History of Medieval Europe*, New York: Oxford University Press, 2001, initially published 1988, p. 170.

206 Ibid., pp. 303-304.

207 Ibid., p. 304.

208 Barbara A. Hanawalt, *The Ties That Bound: Peasant Families in Medieval England*. Oxford University Press, 1986. pp. 34-38.

209 "America's Most Expensive Neighborhoods, 247 Editors, November 5, 2-12.

210 Geoff Nudelman, "The 10 Priciest Neighborhoods in America (And How They Got to Be That Way)," Robb Report, November 28, 2018. https://robbreport.com/feature/most-expensive-neighborhoods-america-2830894.

211 "Bill Gates Buys $8.7M Home in Wellington, Florida, HuffPost Miami, June 26, 2013.

212 Jennifer Karmon, "Oct. 28: Bill Gates' Custom-Built Home in Medina, Washington," *Huffington Post,* October 28, 2013.

213 TMZ Taff, "Kim and Kanye: We Want Dr. Dre's Land for Our Mega Mansion," TMZ, November 18, 2013.

214 Megan Hopkins, "Median Home Price Hits 8-Year High," Housingwire, August 8, 2013.

215 Dave Ramsey, "2020 Home Prices: What You Need to Know," DaveRamsey.com https://www.daveramsey.com/blog/housing-trends

216 Hall, p. 90.

217 "Relationship Between Poverty and Overweight or Obesity," FRAC: Food Research and Action Center.

218 Holmes, p. 52.

219 Frances and Joseph Gies, *Life in a Medieval Village,* New York: Harper Perennial, 1990 pp. 138-139.

220 Adam Davidson, "How the Art Market Thrives on Inequality," *The New York Times,* May 30, 2012.

221 "Why the Art Market Profits When Social Inequality Is Growing," *HuffPost Arts & Culture,* September 17, 2012.

222 Carol Vogel, "At $142.4 Million, Triptych Is the Most Expensive Artwork Ever Sold at an Auction," *The New York Times,* November 12, 2013.

223 Invaluable, "31 of the Most Expensive Paintings Ever Sold at Auction," Invaluable.com. https://www.invaluable.com/blog/most-expensive-painting.

224 Mat Gleason, "The Art World's Wealthiest One Percent: A Commentary on Life at the Top," ArtBusiness.com.

225 Marion Maneker, "$14M Koons Sculptures to Lure Wealthy Latin Americans to Miami Condo Development," ArtBase, September 27, 2013.

226 Kyle Chayka, "Why Is the Middle of the Art Market Vanishing?" Hyperallergic: Senstive to Art & It's Discontents, January 25, 2013.

227 Ibid.

228 Hall, pp. 156, 160-167.

229 Daniel H, "13 Private Schools for the Extremely Rich," *Epoch Times,* July 27, 2013,

230 Andy Kiersz and Erin McDowell, "The 50 Most Expensive Top Private High Schools in America," *Business Insider,* August 29, 2019. https://www.businessinsider.com/most-expensive-top-private-high-schools-america-2018-12

231 Paul Sullivan, "Private Schools Hold New Attention for Rich Parents," *The New York Times,* October 12, 2020. https://www.nytimes. com/2020/10/09/your-money/private-schools-wealthy-parents.html

232 "National University Rankings," *U.S. News Report,* September 9, 2013, and Kelsey Sheehy, "10 Most, Least Expensive Private Colleges and Universities," *U.S. News,* September 10, 2013.

233 "2013-14 California State University Tuition and Fee Rates," http://www.calstate.edu/budget/student-fees/fee-rates/ TuitionFeesAllCampus.pdf

234 Lynn O'Shaugnessy, "50 State Universities with the Best, Worst Grad Rates," Moneywatch, October 1, 2012.

235 Allen Grove, "Best 4-Year Graduation Rates," About.Com.

236 Norman F. Cantor, *The Civilization of the Middle Ages,* New York: Harper Perennial, 1994 (originally copyright in 1963), p. 479.

237 Ibid., p. 479.

238 Frances and Joseph Gies, *Life in a Medieval Village,* pp. 101-102.

239 "Exclusive Photos: Sean Parker's Lavish Big Sur Wedding." *Vanity Fair.Com,* September 2013.

240 Rebecca Macatee, "Kim Kardashian and Kanye West Not Planning Wedding at Palace of Versailles," *Eonline,* December 4, 2013.

241 Meredith Galante, "The 20 Most Expensive Restaurants in the U.S., *Business Insider,* October 25, 2011,

242 Ann Schmidt, "These Are the Most Expensive Restaurants in the U.S.," *Fox Business,* November 29, 2019. https://www.foxbusiness. com/money/10-most-expensive-restaurants-us

243 Uri Dadush, Kemal Dervis, Sarah Puritz Milsom, and Bennett Stancil, *Inequality in America: Facts, Trends, and International Perspective,* Washington, DC, Brookings Institution Press, 2012.

244 Ibid., p. 2.

245 Ibid., pp. 2-3.

246 Ibid., pp. 6-14.

247 Erin Duffin, "U.S. Household Income Distribution by Gini-coefficient 1990-2019, Statista. September 17, 2020. https://www.statista.com/ statistics/219643/gini-coefficient-for-us-individuals-families-and-households.

248 Timothy Noah, *The Great Divergence,* New York: Bloomsbury Press, 2012, pp. 3-4.

249 Dadush, pp. 14-16.

250 "The Natural Order," Macroevoluton.net, http://www.macroevolution.net/natural-order.html#.UqTZwNLETzM

251 Dadush, pp. 21-23.

252 Marcus Lu, "Is the American Dream Over? Here's What the Data Says," World Economic Forum, September 2, 2020. https://www.weforum.org/agenda/2020/09/social-mobility-upwards-decline-usa-us-america-economics.

253 Ibid, pp. 26-35.

254 Craig Benson, "Povery: 2018 and 2019," The United States Census Bureau, September 2020. https://www.census.gov/content/dam/Census/library/publications/2020/acs/acsbr20-04.pdf

255 U.S. Government Accountability Office, 2007, p. 9.

256 Dadush, pp. 39-68.

257 Brad Tuttle, "Here's How Much Everyone Gets Paid on a Movie Set — From the Key Grip to the Director," *Money*, October 3, 2017. https://money.com/movie-jobs-how-much-get-paid-actors.

258 "Earnings for Actors, Producers, and Directors," Stage Agent, 2013.

259 Project Casting, "The Average Salary of an Actor," Project Casting, April 5, 2020. https://www.projectcasting.com/tips-and-advice/actors-salary.

260 Christy Parsons, "Obama on Income Inequality: 'I Take This Personally,'" Politics Now, *Los Angeles Times*, December 4, 2013.

261 Dadush, pp. 69-72.

262 Timothy Noah, *The Great Divergence,* New York: Bloomsbury Press, 2012, p. 1.

263 Ibid., pp. 3-4.

264 U.S. Census Bureau, "Income, Poverty and Health Insurance Coverage in the United States: 2019, U.S. Census Bureau, September 15, 2020. https://www.census.gov/newsroom/press-releases/2020/income-poverty.html#

265 Ibid. p. 27.

266 Mandi Woodruff, "Heirs and Heiresses of the Wealthiest People in America", Yahoo Finance, December 9, 2013.

267 Noah, p. 54.

268 Ibid., p. 58.

269 Ibid., p. 91-92.

270 Ibid.,, p. 108.

271 Camilo Maldonado, "Trump Tax Cuts Helped Billionaires Pay Less Taxes than the Working Class in 2018," *Forbes*, October 10, 2019. https://www.forbes.com/sites/camilomaldonado/2019/10/10/trump-tax-cuts-helped-billionaires-pay-less-taxes-than-the-working-class-in-2018

272 Ibid.

273 Terry Gross, "How the CARES Act Became a Tax-Break Bonanza for the Rich, Explained," NPR, April 30, 2020. https://www.npr. org/2020/04/30/848321204/how-the-cares-act-became-a-tax-break-bonanza-for-the-rich-explained.

274 Ephrat Livni, "Congress Is Facing Fury Over Cares ACT Tax Breaks for the Rich," *Quartz*, May 8, 2020. https://qz.com/1854006/congress-faces-fury-over-cares-act-tax-breaks-for-the-rich.

275 Ibid.,, p. 112.

276 Ibid., p. 124.

277 Ibid., pp. 162-163.

278 Ibid., p. 167.

279 Ibid., p. 172,

280 Tavis Smiley and Cornel West, *The Rich and the Rest of Us: A Poverty Manifesto*, New York: Smiley Books, 2012.

281 Ibid., p. 14.

282 Melissa Pandika, "Global Economic Crisis Spurred 5000 Additional Suicides, Study Says," Los Angeles Times, September 18, 2013.

283 Smiley and West, pp. 15-16.

284 "Home Foreclosure Statistics," *Statistic Brain*, October 15, 2012.

285 Smiley and West, p. 18.

286 "Employment Situation Survey," U.S. Bureau of Labor Statistics, December 6, 2013.

287 "Employment Situation Survey," U.S. Bureau of Labor Statistics, November 6, 2020. https://www.bls.gov/news.release/empsit.nr0.htm.

288 Smiley and West, pp. 33-34.

289 Ibid., pp. 36-37.

290 Chrystia Freeland, *Plutocrats: The Rise of the New Global Super-Rich and the Fall of Everyone Else,* New York: The Penguin Press, 2012.

291 Talk: F. Scott Fitzgerald, Wikipedia, http://en.wikiquote.org/wiki/Talk:F._Scott_Fitzgerald

292 Freeland, p. 5.

293 Ibid., pp 9-10.

294 Catherine Thorbecke, "Nearly half of the world' entire wealth is in the hands of millionaires," *ABC News*, October 22, 2019. https://abcnews.go.com/Business/half-worlds-entire-wealth-hands-millionaires/story?id=66440320#

295 TBS Report, "10 Richest Billionaires in the World in 2020," The Business Standard, October 15, 2020. https://tbsnews.net/world/10-richest-billionaires-world-2020-145480.

296 Hiatt Woods, "How Billionaires Saw Their Net Worth Increase by Half A Trillion Dollars During the Pandemic," *Business Insider*, October 30, 2020. https://www.businessinsider.com/billionaires-net-worth-increases-coronavirus-pandemic-2020-7.

297 Ibid.

298 Ibid., pp. 35-36.

299 Worldometers, https://www.worldometers.info/coronavirus

300 *The Middle Ages,* Captivating History, 2019, p. 25.

301 Chris Wickham, *Medieval Europe,* Yale University Press, 2016, p.121.

302 *Medieval England,* Captivating History, 2020, p. 63.

303 *The Middle Ages,* pp. 64-64.

304 "Belarus: Thousands Protest Outside State TV Building," BBC.Com, August 15, 2020.

305 Stefano Pozzebon, Sam Kiley, and Lauren Said-Moorhouse, "Protestors Flood Venezuelan Streets to Call for Change," CNN.com, February 12, 2019.

306 "Venezuela Crisis in 300 Words," BBC.com, January 9, 2020.

307 Lynn Thorndike, *The History of Medieval Europe,* Houghton Mifflin Company, 2019, p. 393.

308 *The Middle Ages,* p. 65-66.

309 Chris Wickham, *Medieval Europe,* p. 211.

310 Ibid., pp. 211-212.

311 *The Middle Ages,* pp. 68-71.

312 Wickham, *Medieval Europe,* p. 220.

313 Ibid., pp. 221-223,

314 Ibid., p. 226-231.

315 *The Middle Ages,* p. 71.

316 Wickham, pp. 231-232.

317 Ibid., pp. 232-233.

318 "Global Conflict Tracker," Council on Foreign Relations, August 17, 2021. https://www.cfr.org/global-conflict-tracker/?category=us

319 Ibid.

320 Ann Swanson, Paul Mozur, and Raymond Zhong, "Trump's Attacks Could Fracture Internet Further," *San Francisco Chronicle,* Business Report: Section C, August 18 2020. P. C1-3.

321 Ibid., p. C-3.

322 Ibid.. C-3.

323 Ibid., C-3.

324 Franntisek Graus, "The Late Medieval Peasant Wars," *The Journal of Peasant Studies,* Vol. 3, 1-9, February 5, 2008.

325 Barbara Tuchman, *A Distant Mirror.* Alfred A. Knopf, 1978, p. 155.

326 Maurice Dommanget, *La Jacquerie,* f. Maspero, 1971.

327 Thorndike, pp. 399-400.

328 Ibid., p. 400.

329 Editors of the Encyclopedia Britannica, "Peasants Revolt," *Britannica. com.*

330 Thorndike, p. 401.

331 Editors of Encyclopedia Britannica.

332 "List of Peasant Revolts," *Wikipedia.*

333 Michelle Toh, "Black Lives Matter: Facebook, Netflix, Peloton, and Other Companies Take a Stand as Protests Sweep America," CNN. Com, June 1, 2020.

334 Amanda Mull, "Brands Have Nothing Real to Say about Racism," TheAtlantic.com, June 3, 2020.

335 Ibid.

336 Ibid.

337 Natalie Sherman, "George Floyd: Why Are Companies Speaking Up this Time?" BBC.com, June 7, 2020.

338 Frida Ghitis, "This Could Be a Turning Point in the Fight Against Racism — in America and Abroad," *The Washington Post,* June 8, 2020.

339 Ibid.

340 Juliana Kaplan, Aliana Akhtar, and Laura Casada, "A World on Fire : Here Are All the Major Projects Happening Around the Globe Right Now," *The Business Insider.com,* June 4, 2020.

341 *The Middle Ages,* pp. 72-73.

342 Ibid., pp. 73-74.

343 Ibid., p. 74.

344 Ibid., p. 74.

345 Ibid., p. 74.

346 "The Challenge of Our Time," *World Food Hunger Program USA.* https://www.wfpusa.org/explore/wfps-work/drivers-of-hunger/ climate-change

347 Ibid.

348 Ibid.

349 Ibid.

350 Ibid.

351 Ibid.

352 *Medieval England,* p. 103.

353 Ibid.

354 Ibid.

355 History.com Editors, "Black Death," *History.com,* June 6, 2020. https://www.history.com/topics/middle-ages/black-death

356 *The Middle Ages,* p. 76,

357 Ibid., p. 75.

358 *Medieval England,* p. 105.

359 Coronavirus (COVID-19) Mortality Rate, Worldometer, May 14, 2020

360 *The Middle Ages,* p. 76.

361 Rachel Nania, "Blacks, Hispanics Hit Hrder by the Coronavirus, Early U.S. Data Show," AARP, May 8, 2020. https://www.aarp.org/health/conditions-treatments/info-2020/minority-communities-covid-19.html

362 *The Middle Ages,* p. 76.

363 *The Black Death,* Captivating History, 2019. pp. 25.

364 Ibid., pp. 25-26.

365 Ibid., p. 25.

366 History.com Editors, "Black Death.".

367 *Medieval England,* p. 103.

368 Jason Gale and John Lauerman,"What You Need to Know about the Spreading Coronavirus," *The Washington Post,* February 25, 2020.

369 COVID-19 CORONAVIRUS PANDEMIC", Worldometer, October 7, 2020.

370 "CDC COVID Data Tracker, Center for Disease Control, October 6, 2020. https://covid.cdc.gov/covid-data-tracker/#cases_casesinlast7days

371 History.com Editors.

372 Ibid.

373 Ibid.

374 *The Middle Ages,* p. 76.

375 "Coronavirus (COVID-19), Center for Disease Control and Prevention, https://www.cdc.gov/coronavirus/2019-nCoV/index.html

376 History.com Editors.

377 Ibid.

378 Hugh Greenhalgh, "Religious Figures Blame LGBT+ People for Coronavirus," *Reuters,* March 9, 2020.

379 Felicia Schwartz, "Coronavirus Sparks Rise in Anti-Semitic Sentiment, Researchers Say," *The Wall Street Journal,* April 20, 2020.

380 Owen Schilling, "The Economic Impact of the Black Plague," ArcStoryMaps, November 21, 2019.

381 David Routt, "The Economic Impact of the Black Death," Eh.Net, Economic History Association, https://eh.net/encyclopedia/the-economic-impact-of-the-black-death

382 Ibid.

383 Ibid.

384 Ibid.

385 Ibid.

386 *The Black Death,* p. 82.

387 Schilling, "The Economic Impact of the Black Death,"

388 Ibid.

389 Ibid.

390 Lisa Fickenscher, "Nearly 60 Percent of COVID-19 Business Closures Are Permanent: Report," *New York Post,* September 17, 2020. https://nypost.com/2020/09/17/majority-of-covid-19-business-closures-are-permanent-report

391 Malia Wollan, "Oakland's Port Shuts Down as Protesters March on Waterfront," New York Times, Nov. 2, 2011.

392 "Just Cause and Occupy Oakland Fight Fannie Mae and Banks," December 8, 2011.

393 Terry Collins, "Wells Fargo Protest in San Francisco: Dozens Arrseted Outside Shareholder Meeting," HuffPostLive, April 24, 2012.

394 "Occupy SF Protesters Vow to Retake Justine Herman Plaza, NBC Bay Area.com, September 17, 2012.

395 Meghan Barr, "Occupy Wall Street Plans Rallies on Second Anniversary of Movement," *Huffington Post,* September 17, 2103.

396 "Occupy's Rolling Jubilee Keeps Rolling – and the Band Plays On,"*Huffington Post,* November 13, 2013.

397 Allison Kilkenny, "Fast Food Strikes Hit 100 Cities Thursday," *The Nation,* December 4, 2013.

398 Victor Luckerson, "The One-Day Strike: The New Labor Weapon of Last Resort." *Time,* December 7, 2013.

399 Josh Edelson, "Breaking: Massive Black Friday Strike and Arrests Planned, As Workers Defy Wal-Mart," *Salon.com,* November 29, 2013.

400 Joseph E. Stiglitz, *The Price of Inequality: How Today's Divided Society Endangers Our Future,* New York: W. W. Norton & Company, 2012, p. xvii-xxii..

401 Ibid., p. xxxi-xxxii.

402 Ibid., pp. 336-341.

403 Ibid., pp. 341-343..

404 Ibid., pp. 344-351.

405 ObamaCareFacts.com, "American Health Coerage Continues to Rise," ObamaCareFacts.com, November 4, 2020.

406 Ibid., pp. 352-353.

407 Ibid., pp. 353-355.

408 *The Black Death*, p. 91.

9 781951 805319